Richard Killeen is a publisher and historian. His previous books include *A Concise History of Modern Ireland*, *Historic Atlas of Dublin*, *A Timeline of Irish History* and *A Short History of Scotland*. He lives and works in Dublin.

Recent titles in the series

A Brief History of Roman Britain
Joan P. Alcock

A Brief History of the Private Life of Elizabeth II
Michael Paterson

A Brief History of France
Cecil Jenkins

A Brief History of Slavery
Jeremy Black

A Brief History of Sherlock Holmes
Nigel Cawthorne

A Brief Guide to Angels and Demons
Sarah Bartlett

A Brief History of How the Industrial Revolution Changed the World
Thomas Crump

A Brief History of King Arthur
Mike Ashley

A Brief History of the Universe
J. P. McEvoy

A Brief Guide to Secret Religions
David Barrett

His Finest Hour: A Brief Life of Winston Churchill
Christopher Catherwood

A Brief History of Witchcraft
Lois Martin

A BRIEF HISTORY OF

IRELAND

RICHARD KILLEEN

ROBINSON   RUNNING PRESS
PHILADELPHIA · LONDON

Constable & Robinson Ltd
3 The Lanchesters
162 Fulham Palace Road
London W6 9ER
www.constablerobinson.com

First published in the UK by Robinson,
an imprint of Constable & Robinson, 2012

A copy of the British Library Cataloguing in Publication
Data is available from the British Library

UK ISBN 978-1-84901-439-7

3 5 7 9 10 8 6 4 2

US Library of Congress Control Number 2009943290
US ISBN 978-0-7624-3990-4

Running Press Book Publishers
2300 Chestnut Street
Philadelphia, PA 19103-4371

Visit us on the web!
www.runningpress.com

Printed and bound in the UK

CONTENTS

INTRODUCTION

We can only know fragments of the past, dependent as we are on written sources of varying degrees of importance and reliability. For most of history, there are no newspapers, no oral testimonies, few personal diaries, none of the stuff that offers a glimpse of the dull, quotidian life. For the period from about 1000 CE, depending on where you are, there will be increasing deposits of official documents, government and legal papers and proclamations of various sorts. Reliance on these archival fragments means that most histories are perforce political and military – an examination of the pursuit of power and the rise and fall of states. This bias is well understood and, in truth, it is what interests general readers. Still, the narrative is further edited by the knowledge of where we are now; the temptation – necessity, perhaps – to choose disproportionately those events and developments that carried us here or that endorse and validate a current orthodoxy.

The history of Ireland is as prone to these temptations as that of any other place. The grand narrative, almost impossible to avoid, is the freedom song: the story of insular difference and particularism, which eventually finds its supreme expression in nationalism and independence. This book does not pretend to evade or bypass this way of framing the story of

Ireland's past, precisely because it is impossible to do so. What it hopes to do instead is to maintain an alertness to other possibilities and to mitigate the dangers of a one-dimensional perspective.

Let's start with the obvious. Ireland is an island. A mental map of the place sees it as a unity, because islands – especially small ones – seem to propose a kind of natural integrity. To divide them seems artificial. We think of Iceland, Sicily, Crete and Corsica quite correctly as undivided entities, and many islands are indeed like that. It is the exceptions that should give us pause: Cyprus, Hispaniola, New Guinea, Borneo, Timor. And, er, Great Britain. But even where islands remain undivided, national independence is no automatic corollary. Islands can be unitary and independent (Iceland) or divided politically (Hispaniola) or partitioned (Cyprus) or federated in archipelagic states (the Philippines, Indonesia, the north and south islands of New Zealand and Japan) or can have any other set of relations imaginable. There is no causal link between being an island and being – well, anything in particular, at least in terms of state formation.

This is important in the Irish case because the dominant paradigm in Irish history – the nationalist freedom narrative – takes unity and independence as moral axioms. They are something properly to be desired, their absence something to be deplored. On the other hand, a nineteenth-century Tory could just as plausibly (or perhaps that should be implausibly) argue that the archipelagic United Kingdom of Great Britain and Ireland created by the Act of Union of 1801 was the most natural order of things, given precedents elsewhere, the proximity of the two islands, their location at the northwest margin of continental Europe, their long historical entanglement with each other, their more recently acquired linguistic unity and so on. It was a view that, even then, persuaded very few people in Ireland and will persuade no more than a handful of eccentrics in the Republic today. That said, some of the arguments implicit in it have vaulted right over the UK and have found positive approval in Irish attitudes to the European Union (EU).

Interrogating Ireland's past with reference to such theories opens more doors and offers potentially richer and more nuanced answers than a relentless focus on the freedom narrative. It all might have worked out differently. Why is Ireland more Cyprus than Sicily? And crucially, what impelled it to take the course that it did – what was the critical variable in the historical equation? For the fact is that, in nationalist Ireland at least (and that encompasses about 80 per cent of the island's population), the freedom narrative is not merely taken for granted as forming the shape of the past, it is also a powerful enabling myth in sustaining the present. This is both reason to acknowledge its potency and to suspect its easy answers.

Islands are generally different in some way, great or small, relative to the mainland or metropole. The differences can express themselves in language and dialect, dress and diet, social hierarchies, patterns of political behaviour, patron–client relations and economic activity. Yet difference is not isolation. Sicily, standing in the middle of the Mediterranean astride all the major trade routes, is obviously of enormous commercial and strategic importance. Its interaction with the rest of the world has been in large part determined by geography, yet it has retained a stubborn and secretive code of differences, while remaining rather obviously Italian. Ireland, whose strategic importance is not nearly as great, has nonetheless felt the push and pull of invaders and emigrants and has always retained a sense of its own difference, while remaining rather obviously European (or, some might say, British).

Invaders. The freedom narrative imagines an ancient Arcadia that has been violated by Vikings, Normans, Cromwellians and others in successive waves. Of course, the indigenous Gaels thus disturbed had themselves been invaders in the remote prehistoric past. Their title to the island in perpetuity was no greater than anyone else's. It is the way with islands: they are both open to conquest and skilled at absorbing the invaders.

The key point here is that the freedom narrative occludes as much as it illuminates. If the story of Ireland is simply the rejection of foreign rule and control and the recovery of native autonomy, the whole set of relationships between it and the rest of the world (not just Britain) is reduced to a static tableau. Without invaders, immigrants and the influences they have brought over time, modern Ireland is literally unimaginable. To take the simplest example: I am writing this in English. Without external influences – very often hostile or aggressive in the beginning – we would have no English language, no towns or cities, no counties, no parliamentary government, a different legal system, no idea of nationalism. That last point is important. Nationalism itself, the very heartbeat of modern Irish particularism, is an import from France, and a fairly recent one at that in terms of historical time.

I am less concerned to subvert the freedom narrative, which has much merit in explaining how modern Ireland developed, as to augment it by stressing the importance of historical developments that sit uneasily with it or with which it feels uncomfortable. The intention is to give an overview that is as nuanced as possible. Not least, it helps to recall that there is more to Ireland than the nationalist tradition: there is another Irish community in the province of Ulster that holds fast to the British metropole, rejects nationalism and is entitled to have its voice heard, albeit that voice can some-times be shrill and exasperating. The unionists of Northern Ireland are the most visible example of a historical commu-nity, once settlers, now established on the island for four centuries, whose moral legitimacy is at best only grudgingly acknowledged by the nationalist majority.

Small islands are seldom ethnic frontiers, where different tribes collide and mix. In the nature of things, these ethno-cultural boundaries are more usually found at pressure points on continental land masses. The Balkans and the Caucasus are the most obvious examples in modern Europe. But as recently as 1939, the continent was a potpourri of ethnic and religious groups, with ubiquitous minorities. The old multi-ethnic and multilingual empires were far better at accommodating and reconciling these differences – in allowing diverse tribes to coexist in relative harmony – than the unitary nation states that succeeded them. Such nation states are now the norm in Europe. Only a wholesale process of ethnic cleansing and forced migration during and after the Second World War created this series of monocultural nation states, purged of their minorities. Yet ethnic frontiers remain – not just the obvious two in south-eastern Europe, but also in pockets such as the Alto Adige (a German-speaking enclave in northern Italy) or the large Russian minority in Estonia.

Ireland and Cyprus are alone in Europe in having ethnic frontiers on small islands. In both cases, the response has been the same: partition, the solution that no one wanted but everyone can somehow live with. In the Irish case, the presence of a regional minority in the north-east, dissenting from the mainstream national consensus, is a reminder of the persistence of such anomalies as well as their universality. One might almost say that Scotland ends, not at the North Channel, but along the line of the River Bann.

Ireland's story may be that of an island, but not an island that stands alone or that behaves differently to the rest of humanity. Everything that has happened there has also happened somewhere else. Ireland, like any other place, is at once unique and stereotypical.

Until the middle of the sixteenth century, there was little about Irish history that was remarkable in a comparative European context. It had remained outside the ambit of the Roman Empire but so had all of Germany and much of central Europe. In the post-Roman world, however, there was a significant departure from the European norm, or rather an absence. The great wave of Asiatic, and later Germanic, tribes that pushed ever westward from the vast continental heartland towards the Atlantic margin did not occupy Ireland. It was left in the possession of a Celtic people already in occupation for the best part of a millennium.

The Angles, Saxons and Jutes that settled Great Britain from the fifth century on never pushed west into Ireland. The only substantial linkage between the two islands in the early Middle Ages was the seaborne Gaelic kingdom of Dal Riada, with twin poles in north-east Ulster and south-west Scotland, a nice example of medieval archipelagic possibility. For the rest of the island, there was no violent intrusion of new settlers, such as marked the post-Roman world from Lithuania to Portugal. There was an immemorial cultural integrity about Ireland that made the shock of invasion, when it finally arrived, so traumatic.

That invasion was the work of the Vikings. As in England, their impact was enduring but not permanent. In both instances, the subsequent incursion by the Normans – themselves of remote Viking origins – was more decisive. But because Ireland had been spared the general European experience of invasion, colonization and settlement by nomadic tribes in the fifth and sixth centuries, these later arrivals irrupted into a space that enjoyed cultural (but not political or administrative) unity and that felt cocooned from seaborne violence.

This is not the same as saying that Gaelic Ireland was an introverted dead end. It was different, but not isolated. For in the fifth and sixth centuries – the very times when the tribal invasions of continental Europe were at their height – the island belatedly embraced a version of the now defunct Roman Empire. It converted to Christianity. This is by far the most significant thing that happened in the first millennium CE. The version of Christianity that took root in Ireland was Latin, in that it acknowledged the authority of the Pope in Rome and conducted its liturgy in that language. Given the later triumph of Latin Christianity in the world at large it is worth recalling that at the time of Ireland's evangelization, the Eastern or Greek church centred on Byzantium had a far wider reach. (Had history worked out differently, that church – the one that embraces Orthodox and Coptic Christianity – might well have achieved the pre-eminence later enjoyed by Rome.)

So Ireland became part of the Latin Christian world. Well, sort of: from the start it was semi-detached. Its early missionaries brought the Christian faith to the newly established pagan tribes on the continent, beyond question the most enduring achievement of any Irish enterprise in history. But the Irish church itself was outside the central usages of the mainstream Latin church. Its structure was monastic, not diocesan, reflecting the absence of towns in Gaelic Ireland. The diocesan system, on the other hand, had developed in the old post-Roman heartland – Italy, eastern and southern France, and in parts of the Rhineland. Here, a network of towns had been the basic building blocks of civil society for generations, so it was unsurprising that the church founded its organizational structure on this network – a stable remnant in a shattered world.

No such structure was possible in Ireland. The monasteries that developed profusely in early Christian times have sometimes been described as proto-towns, but the term is both ambiguous and fanciful. The monasteries were simply not designed to act as potential towns and never developed the sinews of urban life in terms of trade, commerce, secular settlement or civic administration. It is significant that when proper towns were finally established in Ireland by the Vikings, and later augmented by the Normans, the call for the organizational reform of the medieval Irish church focused on the need to supplant the monastic system with a diocesan one. Once the towns were in place, the essential and necessary condition for diocesan organization was present.

In sum, early medieval Ireland made a notable contribution to post-Roman Europe by helping to evangelize the successor states formed by Germanic and Asiatic tribes both inside and outside the boundaries of the old empire. It did this from a base which was in communion with the papacy but organizationally distinct from the heartland of Latin Christianity until the twelfth century. Like many other corners of Europe, it retained its own particular practices and structures.

Indeed, its ascetic monasticism mirrored that of the Eastern church, and there are teasing suggestions that Irish monastic scribes may have had contact with scriptoria as far away as the great monastery of St Catherine on Mount Sinai, the source of the largest single collection of illuminated manuscripts in the early Christian world. The Irish place name 'Dysert', as in Dysert O'Dea, Co. Clare, meant a hermitage or place of retreat, to which holy men repaired to pray atonement for the sins of the secular world and to deepen their own spirituality. 'Dysert' is cognate with the Latin *desertus* or English 'desert'. Early Irish Christianity diverged from the norms then developing in the Latin heartland, but it may also have drawn inspiration from more distant Christian practice. It is intriguing to think of Irish anchorite monks, in their remote Atlantic cells, as occidental desert fathers.

The merest glance at an atlas confirms Ireland's status as a European island. To make a heroic generalization, it is in Europe but not always of it. The civilization that gradually formed around the core of Latin Christianity from the ninth century onwards pulsed strongest at the centre, more weakly at the margins. To take one example, Ireland has no great cathedrals to rival those of Italy, Germany, France or England. As the Latin world grew in confidence, having split from the Eastern Orthodox church in 1054, it created a common culture that embraced most of the continent, including Scandinavia and the Baltic states, west of a line roughly drawn from Helsinki to the heel of Italy.

The great fracture in that civilization came with the Reformation in the early sixteenth century. The intellectual fissure in the Latin Christian church affected Ireland as surely as it affected every other corner of Europe. From the Reformation until the present day, the question of confessional allegiance has been *the* Irish question. In modern times, to be Roman Catholic has been overwhelmingly to be a nationalist, aspiring to weaken or destroy the British connection; to be Protestant has similarly been to be unionist. The exceptions on both sides have been statistically negligible. (From this pattern, I naturally exclude the Protestant population of the modern Republic: times move on.)

The origin of this lies in Ireland's response to the Reformation, a response unique in Europe and beyond question the most complete departure from normative European practice in its history. Previously, Ireland's engagement with Europe was either partial or hesitant or eccentric or, on some occasions as with the early missionaries, formative. But the island's response to the Reformation represented a fracture.

The standard European response to the intellectual and spiritual tumult of the Reformation was summed up in the formula *cuius regio, eius religio*. The phrase is usually translated as 'whose kingdom, his religion', meaning that a king or ruler could choose whether to be Catholic or Protestant and that choice would then be binding on his subjects. It was an indication of the degree to which the Reformation was an elite project, whose confessional passions hardly stirred the indifferent multitude. It was also a German solution to a German problem, for the lands between the Rhine and the Oder were the heart of the Lutheran revolt. By imposing this top-down formula, the Peace of Augsburg (1555) saved central Europe from religious civil war for more than sixty years, until the strain grew too great to bear and the continent collapsed into the horrors of the Thirty Years War, the most destructive and consequential conflict prior to 1914.

Most of Europe followed the German example, which is why France persecuted its Huguenot minority; Spain expelled Jews and Muslims; and Elizabethan England made Catholic martyrs. Religious uniformity became a *raison d'état*. It was a blunt and oppressive instrument but contemporaries could look at the agonies endured in central Europe from 1618 to 1648 and argue that it was better than any available alternative.

And it worked everywhere in its rough and ready way,

except in Ireland. As Diarmaid MacCulloch, the most distinguished modern historian of the Reformation, has written: 'in
Ireland, official Protestantism became the elite sect and Roman
Catholicism the popular religion, in a result unique in the
whole Reformation. In no other polity where a major monarchy made a long-term commitment to the establishment of
Protestantism was there such a failure.'

The causes of this failure need not detain us here: they are
discussed in the body of the text. What needs to be acknowledged is that this was Ireland's one enormous departure from
standard European practice, and that it happened in respect
of the most critical intellectual and ideological fault-line prior
to the French Revolution. I use these modern terms – intellectual and ideological – rather than confessional or spiritual
in order to emphasize that religion *was* the ideology of the
early modern period. Nothing mattered more. And on this
issue of all issues, Ireland was no longer semi-detached from
Europe, or partial or hesitant in its embrace of something
larger. It was an aberration.

At the heart of this exceptional survival of Catholicism in
the archipelagic British kingdoms lay the taproot of modern
Irish nationalism. The Catholic island simply could not be
comfortably accommodated in the greater Protestant British
state. Later on, in the age of enlightenment, there were
attempts to overlay this confessional impulse with secular
republicanism and thus furnish Irish nationalism with a more
modern (and acceptable) philosophical basis. It was not a
total failure, for it created its own myth, but it was always a
tune played in the minor key. The major key was Catholicism:
that was the integrating factor that drove Ireland towards
separation from Britain.

Except, of course, for the bit of Ireland in which Protestantism
was successfully established by the seventeenth-century plantation: Ulster. If confessional nationalism eventually succeeded
in securing an Irish state separate from Britain, it also provided
the essential condition for the partition of the island in 1920. It

is no accident that the line of partition lies where Catholic numbers cease to be overwhelming and bump up against solid Protestant communities. It is the same logic as Cyprus.

In the course of the long struggle to secure toleration for Irish Catholics within the Protestant British state – one that eventually resulted in separation – the island made one other enduring contribution to the world: mass democracy. We take democracy so completely for granted now that it is easy to forget where it happened first. If the roots were French, the plant was Irish. In the 1820s, Daniel O'Connell became the first political leader anywhere in the world to mobilize a mass of people – a mob, in the eyes of his horrified opponents – in a peaceful political cause. Andrew Jackson managed something similar in the United States a few years later with the foundation of the Democratic Party. But Ireland can legitimately claim to be first.

Why Ireland? It is tempting to speculate that the exception to the Reformation settlement was a remote but plausible reason. In all of Europe, the Catholics of Ireland were the one, coherent group possessed of a historical memory and a myth of dispossession who had been left freestanding within a larger political unit. Around that memory and myth, it was possible to mobilize, which is precisely what O'Connell did. The naked sectarianism of his rhetoric makes uneasy reading for modern liberals, but he knew his market.

Islands absorb on the one hand and export on the other. Ireland has been no different, absorbing to a greater or lesser degree ideas and structures from Europe (often mediated through an English filter). It has exported people, as islands do, sometimes heroically as with the early Christian missionaries, sometimes tragically as with the wretched, impoverished survivors of the Great Famine. Yet it was these unpromising people, fleeing from the ruin of their island, who carried the germ of mass democracy – sown by O'Connell – to the New World. They played to their strengths: knowledge of the English language and of how to mobilize people politically. They took over large areas of Jackson's Democratic Party, especially the big city machines. The result – unlovely but brutally efficient – was Tammany Hall.

At the heart of the Irish story there is, therefore, an irony. The island's experience has usually been unexceptional in the larger European context: often partial, occasionally innovative, but rarely outright contrarian. The irony inheres in the one great exception to the rule: the failure to embrace the normal Reformation settlement, which might be another way of saying that England never finished the job in Ireland. The conquest was incomplete. Had it been otherwise, Ireland might have turned out to be another Wales – a playful thought.

MAP OF IRELAND

I

PREHISTORY

What follows is not entirely true. No history can be complete. The sources upon which it is based are always partial, often in both senses of the word. But that opening statement holds especially true for the first two chapters of this book. For here we are dealing with the era before written records – reliable or otherwise – and have only the inferences drawn from archaeology and surviving artefacts to guide us. Irish history proper gasps into life after 430 CE, with the first tentative written evidence that has survived. But by then, the island had already been inhabited for about 7,000 years, or about six times the span of historical time.

This book will, therefore, focus overwhelmingly on about one-sixth of the story of human habitation in Ireland. But before we do so, it seems worth the effort to try to re-imagine the lost five-sixths, albeit through a cracked and distorting mirror.

The last of the various Ice Ages ended about 10,000 BC. This is relatively late in prehistorical time and the reason for that is simply latitude. Ireland lies between 52° and 55° N, roughly the same as the Netherlands, northern Germany, Denmark and Poland. Farther north again lie most of Russia and all of Scandinavia. The ice retreated more slowly this far north. Europe south of the Alps lies in the latitude 35° to 45° N, roughly the same as most of the continental United States. It was in this southern region, focused on the Mediterranean basin, that the earliest European civilizations developed. For most of historical time, until the second half of the second millennium AD, northern Europe lagged behind the south. Ireland was known to the Greeks and the Romans – especially to the latter, whose empire at its greatest extent reached almost to the shores of the island. But it was a remote, faraway place of little importance. In *The Iliad*, Homer had written of it as 'a land of fog and gloom . . . beyond it the Sea of Death, where hell begins'.

The retreat of the ice caused sea levels to rise and cut the British Isles off from the Eurasian land mass. In turn, it cut Ireland off from Britain. Whether the earliest known inhabitants of the island came by land bridge or by sea is unknown, but the earliest date for human habitation suggested by radiocarbon dating and dendrochronology is about 7000 BC.

These first inhabitants were migrating hunter-gatherers. Their most likely point of entry was at the north-east corner, the part of Ireland closest to Britain. From Fair Head at the north-eastern corner, it is less than 20 km (12.5 miles) across to the Mull of Kintyre in south-west Scotland. This is also the region where archaeologists have found the oldest evidence of human settlement. At Mount Sandel near the modern town of Coleraine, where the River Bann becomes tidal, the remains of a Mesolithic (Middle Stone Age) settlement have been discovered and excavated.

This Mesolithic hunter-gatherer society depended on flint for the fashioning of tools. This is a further clue to the relatively rich archaeological finds in the north-east, for in this area – modern Co. Antrim – are the largest and most accessible deposits of exposed flint anywhere in Ireland. Elsewhere, other stones were used by Mesolithic people to fashion weapons and tools, but flint was the most durable of all available stones for these purposes.

The Mesolithic period was succeeded about 4000 BC by the

Neolithic (New Stone Age). That bald statement amplifies the point about historical and prehistorical time, already made at the outset. In a single sentence, we have jumped a period nearly twice as long as that from the coming of Christianity to the present. The people who lived in Ireland in that vast span of time, perhaps a hundred generations by modern calculations, left no permanent mark on the landscape. Their Neolithic successors did.

They did so by introducing agriculture. Rising temperatures encouraged cultivation and advances in cutting tools made forest clearance possible. Porcellanite superseded flint as the cutting stone of choice. It, too, was found in profusion in north Co. Antrim. Manufacturing centres were established at Tievebulliagh on the mainland and on Rathlin Island. Porcellanite axes from these sources have been found as far away as southern England, although most discoveries in Ireland have been, unsurprisingly, in north-east Ulster.

Cultivation of crops not only stabilized the food supply in a manner superior to hunter-gathering, it suggested permanent settlements. The extensive and truly remarkable excavations at the Céide Fields, near Belderg, Co. Mayo, have revealed a large permanent agricultural settlement that subsisted on the site for at least 500 years in the fourth millennium BC. Cereals – wheat and barley – were cultivated and cattle were raised in walled enclosures. The Céide Fields are the most extensive and impressive but by no means the only example of Neolithic agricultural sites excavated by archaeologists.

Neolithic settlement sites have been discovered all over the island. That at Lough Gur in Co. Limerick was a particularly sophisticated example: a circular house of stone and a rectangular one have both been excavated. There were others, many contained behind defensive enclosures.

Stable settlement and a reasonably secure food supply led to a growing population and also to evidence of domestic permanence. While there is no surviving evidence of pottery from Mesolithic times, there is an abundance of it from the Neolithic.

Pottery from this era was not thrown on a wheel but was made by hand before being fired.

Of all the survivals of the Neolithic, by far the most impressive are its burial sites. There are three principal kinds of tombs that survive from this period: court tombs, portal tombs and passage tombs, of which the latter are the most impressive. All three types are covered by the generic term 'megalithic', meaning very large stones, for that indeed is what these monuments entailed. Although the matter is by no means settled, the scholarly consensus is that court tombs are the oldest. They are also the most numerous: more than 300 examples are known, with the preponderant concentration in the northern half of the country. A court tomb was so called because it comprised a series of chambers leading to burial gallery and was approached by a forecourt orientated towards some astronomical feature such as the rising sun. The most impressive example is at Creevykeel in Co. Sligo.

Portal tombs are a variation on the court theme, providing spaces for multiple burials. Their distinguishing feature is a massive horizontal capstone set astride the upright orthostats (stone slabs at the base of a wall) at the entrance. They are also known as dolmens: outstanding examples may be found at Proleek, Co. Louth, and Poulnabrone, Co. Clare.

But it is the great passage tombs that have really caught the eye and the imagination, none more so than Newgrange in Co. Meath. It is the most thoroughly excavated and restored Neolithic site in Ireland. It forms the centrepiece of a complex known collectively as Brú na Bóinne comprising more than forty passage graves and various other monuments and survivals. The site occupies a U-shaped bend in the River Boyne as it makes its way east towards the sea. It makes a near 90° turn south before resuming its easterly flow and then turning back north and then east again to resume its original course. Brú na Bóinne, a World Heritage Site, is contained within the rectangle of land thus enclosed by water on three sides.

Newgrange is the principal passage tomb but its neighbours

at Knowth and Dowth are also important, albeit neither of them is excavated as fully. It dates from about 2500 BC, which means that it is probably older than the Egyptian pyramids. The circular cairn in which the passage grave itself is contained is over 100 m (328 ft) in diameter. It is a construction of genuine sophistication. The roofing stones were provided with shallow, concave channels to act as gutters, carrying rainwater towards the outside of the cairn and away from the burial chamber itself. Sure enough, when the tomb was eventually excavated, more than 4,000 years after its construction, the 19 m (62 ft) passage and the burial chamber itself were found to be dry: this in a landscape that can expect annual rainfall of 75 cm (30 in.). The outside of the cairn is faced in dazzling white quartz and the entrance decorated with a horizontal stone with elaborate spiral patterns.

The burial chamber itself, at the end of the passage, is cruciform. It is here, on the morning of the winter solstice *and on that day alone*, that the rising sun is admitted through a light box positioned with mathematical exactitude on the roof of the cairn. The sunlight shines all the way into the back of the central burial chamber, illuminating the spiral motif at the very farthest back wall. This astonishing symbol of renewal, marking the approaching return of the life-giving sun from its farthest distance in the southern sky, is a moment of spiritual awe for the small number of people who have had the privilege to witness it. The Neolithic people who built this extraordinary structure were not just simple pastoral farmers. They were skilled in construction techniques, in lapidary design, in mathematical calculation and astronomical observation.

Nor is Newgrange a fluke. Dowth is similarly orientated to the winter solstice and Knowth to the spring and autumn equinoxes. Thus the cycle of the agricultural year is symbolized in stone: the return of the light at midwinter (Newgrange and Dowth) and the start of sowing and harvesting (Knowth). The renewal of the year – and perhaps a spiritual promise of renewal in the afterlife – is marked by these astonishing structures.

We know nothing about the people who built Newgrange and the rest of Brú na Bóinne. We don't know who they were, or where they had come from, or what their religious beliefs were, or what god or gods they worshipped, or what language they spoke.

From about 2000 BC, the Stone Age began to yield to the Bronze Age. Mining techniques were developed at sites like Mount Gabriel in Co. Cork, where copper was extracted. Copper, when mixed with other metals, makes an alloy that is both tensile and strong. The principal copper additive was tin, presumably imported from Cornwall. Ireland is particularly fortunate in the number of artefacts that have survived from the Bronze Age, and not just bronze artefacts but also gold ones. Gold mining and panning was an important economic activity. Domestic pottery became ever more varied and sophisticated. Impressive and fearsome bronze swords have survived, as has a profusion of superb gold ornaments: necklaces, pendants and armbands. Other necklaces in jet and amber, dress fasteners, horns or trumpets, shields and axes: all testify to a society growing in sophistication and technological development.

It also, almost certainly, led to a more hierarchical organization of society. The Later Bronze Age yields evidence of the growing occupation of hilltop sites, although frustratingly there is no solid record of defensive structures. Still, it is reasonable to infer that the increase in hilltop settlements suggested sites chosen for purposes of military defence. By extension, we can then infer a kind of early warlord society and perhaps even the beginnings of rival clan structures with territorial disputes along boundaries. The proliferation of bronze swords was hardly for ceremonial purposes. The fact that the most prolific surviving hoards are from the Later Bronze Age further suggests a concentration of wealth – and power – in the hands of a military aristocracy.

Diet in the Later Bronze Age can be inferred from deposits of animal bones in domestic middens. Beef and pork were the meats most commonly consumed and this in turn meant the development of butchering skills as well as the preservation and salting of meat. Butchering alone was time consuming and labour-intensive and the curing and preserving skills required to carry a stable population through the long winter were significant. In addition, cereals were widely cultivated, which suggests that sickles and millstones were required to harvest and grind the crop. Obviously, domestic baking skills and the use of ovens followed.

The growing wealth and sophistication of the Later Bronze Age is evident from the surviving articles of dress and adornment. Pins, fasteners not unlike modern cufflinks in purpose if not in appearance, buttons, necklaces, and gold ornaments like torcs bespeak a prosperous – and most likely a hierarchical and aristocratic – society. Wool appears to be the most common fabric, although here the surviving evidence is very slight and there is no great evidence of sheep having been reared for meat.

Some time from 1000 BC, and progressively from 500 BC, the Bronze Age yields to the Iron Age. And with the change came the incursion into Ireland of the people (or peoples) with whom the island has ever since been associated. The Iron Age brought not just a new metal and its associated technologies. It also brought the Celts, and with them a mythology that has never departed.

2

CELTS

The very word is tricky. Like so many naming of peoples, the term Celt derives from a label which one society placed upon strangers outside its own community. The Greeks referred to certain peoples in western and central Europe as Keltoi. In modern times, the term has referred not to a nation, or a group of related tribes, but to a broad family of similar languages. It is this convergence of language that gives the term Celt its meaning.

By the eighteenth century, scholars had identified certain common linguistic features between two groups of languages which seemed to have evolved from the language of ancient Gaul. The peoples known to the Greeks as Keltoi were known to the Romans as Gauls. They represented the indigenous peoples against which so many Roman armies were launched, most famously those of Julius Caesar. Geographically, their culture spread beyond modern France into the Alpine regions of Austria and southern Germany.

Their common language is now lost and is supposed to be the taproot of the two groups of modern Celtic languages. These are Q-Celtic (Irish, Scots Gaelic and Manx) and P-Celtic (Welsh, Cornish and Breton). The distinction is based on a key consonant shift that can still be seen in cognate words. The word for head in Irish is *ceann* with the initial consonant pronounced like a modern *qu* sound. The same word in Welsh is *pen*. The fact that these two groups of languages almost certainly have their roots in a lost ur-language is further supported by common patterns of decorative design among the Celtic peoples of Europe.

The people thus denominated by the Greeks and Romans had, therefore, a common culture of some kind which expressed itself most strongly in a common language – or, more likely, mutually comprehensible dialects – and distinctive forms of decorative art. They remained outside the reach of the Greek world and of the Roman Empire – except for occupied Gaul. Moreover, they were a constant threat to the lusher civilizations of the Mediterranean. They sacked Rome as early as 390 BC and destroyed the sacred temple of the Delphic Oracle in Greece in 278 BC. And they were persistent: they were a constant presence on the northern and western margins of the empire during the long centuries of Roman hegemony.

It is now believed that there was no sudden invasion of Ireland by conquering Celts. Instead there was a steady influx of these related peoples over decades and centuries from about 500 BC. By 200 BC the pattern is well established. The Celts were an Iron Age people, highly skilled in metalwork, and their superior military prowess caused them to displace the aboriginal population. Quite what became of the latter is uncertain. What is certain is that by 200 BC one group of Celtic people, the Gaeil, had displaced not only the aboriginals but had also imposed themselves upon other Celtic groups antecedent to them. It was these Gaeil who gave the island its linguistic unity through their language that we call Gaelic or Irish. It was they who subsequently carried their people and language across the narrow sea to western Scotland to produce the tribal society of the Highlands and the variation on the Irish language known as Scots Gaelic.

The Gaeil represented a common linguistic and artistic

culture but not a common political nation. There was no insular unity, no central political or national focus, even in embryo.
Nor were such states at all common in contemporary Europe.
Outside the empire, loosely connected warlord and tribal societies were the norm and in that sense Ireland was no exception.
Indeed, no European kingdom in the modern sense emerges
before about 800 CE.

Land communications remained enormously difficult.
Only sophisticated civil engineering cultures such as the
Romans were capable of overcoming the problems, the solu-
tions to which were well beyond the capacities of the Celts
and other tribal societies. But the Irish Celts were able to
establish local warlord kingdoms by building hillforts and
securing as much of the surrounding countryside as possible.
This led to the development of a military aristocracy, but it
was one bound by law and not simply by force. The Celts had
a highly elaborated system of law and a scholarly caste of
lawyers to interpret it.

Gaelic Ireland was a stratified society, in which there no less
than twenty-seven classes of freemen. At the summit were the
local kings, attended by the lawyers, druids and poets who
together comprised the aristocracy. The poets were not simply
versifiers: they were genealogists and memorialists. The body
of laws and customary usages were all committed to memory,
for there was no written literature. It was a legal system of
genuine sophistication. There were specific sanctions for every
crime and no one – not even kings – was superior to the law.
Sagas and epics – many of them echoing mythological foundation tales common across Europe – were likewise transmitted
orally from generation to generation. It was a society with a
strong narrative tradition, with a mythology and a sense of its
own past. But it wrote nothing down. There was a literature,
but no writing.

Nonetheless, the literature was impressive. Ireland can
claim to have the oldest vernacular epic in post-Roman
European history, although Wales has made similar claims.

At any rate, the so-called Ulster Cycle of tales has a fair claim to the title. Its centrepiece, *Táin Bó Cuailnge* or 'The Cattle Raid of Cooley', tells of how Queen Méabh of Connacht raided the territory of King Conchobar Mac Nessa of Ulster. Her purpose was to seize the Donn Cuailnge, a super-fertile bull of legend. Her army comprised many Ulster men who had abandoned their province in protest against the conduct of the king. They spoke of the young Ulster hero, Cúchulainn, and his heroic deeds of valour. Indeed, it was Cúchulainn who arrested the queen's progress. Most famously, he fights Méabh's champions in single combat at a ford on the Ulster border, defeating them all in turn. The emotional climax comes when he fights and defeats his own beloved foster-brother, Ferdia, in mortal combat. The Connacht army is repulsed but at a terrible price.

A very simplified form of writing did emerge around 400 CE. It was called ogham and it comprised horizontal and vertical lines scored as on a tally stick. In most cases, surviving ogham inscriptions are to be found on commemorative standing stones. Given the nature of the script, it was best suited to these simple lapidary inscriptions, identifying the name of an individual. It was not well adapted for continuous writing or script.

The Ulster Cycle was only one of many such extended sagas in the oral literature of Gaelic Ireland. Nor was it the only one to emphasize the cattle raid as an admirable aristocratic activity. In a society where money was reckoned in cattle, it was no crime to steal cattle or slaves from a neighbouring territory. Indeed, successful raiding could facilitate the consolidation of small kingdoms in larger ones by absorbing weak territories incapable of defending themselves.

It is interesting, in view of later developments, that this earliest Irish saga is centred on Ulster defending itself from invasion. The origins of Ulster particularism are deep and ancient, and are helped by the series of natural defences – drumlins, lakes and bogs – that make land access from the south especially difficult. From ancient times, these were augmented by man-made structures along the boundary of south Ulster of which the long, looping defensive earthwork known by various names but most famously as the Black Pig's Dyke is the most celebrated. It meant that ready access was only possible through a limited number of strategic passes. As late as 1600, Elizabethan armies attempting to besiege the province found themselves trapped and defeated in well-laid ambush battles. Later again, the Gap of the North, between Dundalk and Newry, offered the only practical route for the Dublin–Belfast railway and the road that joins the two cities.

Just as Gaelic Ireland did not develop writing, it did not develop towns. This was a pastoral, rural civilization. Only with the arrival of Christianity did proto-towns develop in the form of the early monasteries and even there, as mentioned in the introduction, the analogy is strained. In reality, Ireland had to wait until the Viking incursions in the ninth century before seeing its first urban settlements. The economy was based on cattle rearing, with the work carried on by the various classes of yeoman freemen. Then as now, the wet Irish climate was unfriendly to tillage. So prized were cattle that wealth was measured by the number of the beasts that a person owned. The yeoman freemen were called *bóaire*, literally cattlemen.

Below the freemen, there were slaves. We do not know what proportion of the population was unfree.

There were over a hundred different mini-kingdoms or *tuatha*. In time, alliances of *tuatha* emerged to produce provincial kings whose effective remit ran over a wider region, though seldom without some form of local opposition. Over centuries, these were to develop into two major coalitions: the Connachta in the northern half of the island and the Eóganachta in the southern half. Among the former, the powerful and influential tribal group was the Uí Néill, ancestors of the modern O'Neill family.

By the end of the sixth-century CE, they dominated most of west Ulster and north Leinster. Their southern base was at Tara in Co. Meath, from where they claimed the high kingship of the entire island. This claim was wholly notional: the southern branch of the Uí Néill could not command the full allegiance of their own northern cousins, let alone all the other local kings. As for the southern half of the island, their influence there was minimal. This claim of Tara as the seat of an Irish high king has, however, had a long and persistent history. It is repeated today; in some cases by people who should know better. Tara was almost certainly a religious or ritual site, rather than a political one. There were others like it throughout the island, one of whose important purposes was to serve as the ritual coronation site for kings.

The creation of a historical fetish over Tara is largely due to the desire of nineteenth-century nationalists to claim an antiquity and continuity for an Irish state that never existed. It was a classic case of projecting modern concerns backward on to history in order to serve a contemporary political cause. There were no high kings at Tara and there was no united polity in Ireland. Nor was there any shame in that: it was, as we saw earlier, the norm in contemporary Europe.

Words are often the problem here. The word *rí*, king, did not mean what it later came to mean in Europe. Once kingdoms and states were constituted in a recognizably modern way, the king was variously the most powerful legal ruler and the symbolic incarnation of the state itself. In Gaelic Ireland, he was essentially a warlord and a military leader. He was not the chief legal officer: the law was enforced by the legal class and the king was subject to it. The collective memory of the kingdom – its genealogies and mythologies – was kept in the oral tradition by lawyers and poets. Its religious offices were the domain of the druids. A king could bequeath his immediate personal property to his assigns but his public domain was the property of the community.

Kings were not hereditary. Although primogeniture (the

first-born's right of succession) gradually came to dominate European kingdoms, it was a long, slow development, so once again Gaelic Ireland was not as out of step as a backward reading of history might at first suggest. A king could be succeeded by any of his male relatives who shared the same great-grandfather: thus the contest was open to his brothers, nephews, first and second cousins as well as his sons. This system was not as irrational as it may seem. It did indeed virtually ensure that any succession would be challenged in arms by disappointed candidates. On the other hand, it also increased the chances of the strongest and most capable candidate winning and consolidating his power. It was a kind of trial by ordeal, appropriate to a warlord society.

Gaelic Ireland never embraced primogeniture. It was not alone in this. A number of European crowns were elective into modern times, most famously Poland. While the divisions engendered by elective kingships certainly helped enfeeble the country during its eighteenth-century partitions, it should also be recalled that the Polish–Lithuanian commonwealth dominated north-eastern Europe for almost 500 years until the rise of Russia around 1700. Moreover, the most enduring monarchy of all, the Vatican, is elective.

That said, the logic of consolidated royal states did suggest primogeniture as the most efficient means of succession. Contrariwise, the endless disputed successions in local kingdoms made national consolidation less rather than more likely. This was certainly the case in Ireland where, with the single possible exception of Brian Ború for a few years at the start of the eleventh century, there was no high king worth the name. That is to say, there was no one overlord whose writ ran with authority over the whole island.

One of the great clichés of Irish history is that the Romans never came to disturb the security of Gaelic Ireland. It is true, but that does not mean that they wholly disregarded the island. They traded with it from Roman Britain: there is ample evidence of this in the discovery of Roman coins and other artefacts in Ireland. At the greatest extent of Roman power, in the last days of the republic and the early years of the empire, Roman arms took the fight to the Celtic peoples of north-western Europe. Gaul was conquered and likewise Britain almost up to the Highland line. For almost 500 years, most of Britain was a Roman province: they built roads and towns; they had defensive walls and army barracks. At the mouth of the River Dee, in the north-west of England, they established the fortified town of Chester. The name is derived from the Latin *castrum*, or fortification. From Chester, it was a relatively short voyage to the east coast of Ireland.

Even shorter was the crossing from south-west Scotland to the north-east of Ireland, the ancient route almost certainly taken by the first post-Ice Age inhabitants. In 82 CE, the military governor of Roman Britain, Gnaeus Julius Agricola, prepared to launch a small armada across the straits. The conquest of Ireland would have been the final laurel in a brilliant career. Agricola had been largely responsible for the conquest of Britain. He had participated in the campaign against Queen Boudicca in 61 CE and it was he who carried Roman arms into Wales and deep into Scotland. The conquest of Ireland would have been a logical extension of this policy and of the commander's reflexive aggression.

The details are not completely certain. We have only the histories of Tacitus – who was Agricola's son-in-law and biographer – to rely upon, but he is a more reliable historical witness than any other in this era. He recounts that a disaffected Irish petty king, having lost his throne, made his way to Agricola's camp and offered his help to conquer Ireland for Rome. The general believed that Ireland could be held with a single legion. Events conspired against Agricola's plan. There was a mutiny in the army and a Pictish rebellion to suppress nearer home. From Rome, Emperor Domitian ordered Agricola to deal with the Picts. Once that was done, Agricola was finally recalled from Britain. Subsequently, the

Romans withdrew from southern Scotland to the wall ordered by and named for Domitian's successor, Hadrian. The Romans had done with Scotland and never again contemplated an invasion of Ireland.

It seems to have been one of those close-run things and it is perhaps the greatest might-have-been in all of Irish history.

Just as it was an easy voyage from western Britain to the Irish coast, it was equally easy in the other direction. And the riches of Roman Britain offered an irresistible target for Irish raiders. Well accustomed to cattle raids at home, they had no objection to depredations abroad. Slaves were the most highly prized booty. When Roman Britain was in its pomp, it might have given the Irish pause. But the progressive enfeeblement of the empire from the late fourth century meant the withdrawal of marginal garrisons to face the barbarian threat nearer home.

Emperor Honorius withdrew all Roman troops from Britain in 410, leaving the mainly Christian citizens to fend for themselves. This they managed for a while: Germanus, the bishop of Auxerre and founder of a famous abbey there, visited Britain in 429 and found the Christian community observant and resisting the incursions of barbarian tribes.

This optimistic summary would have been of little consolation to a Roman youth called Palladius Patricius. He had been abducted by Irish raiders from his home in the western town of Bannavem Taberniae and sold into slavery. He was the son of a *decurio*, an imperial civil servant. In all, he spent six years as a slave in Ireland, in locations perhaps as far apart as Co. Mayo and Co. Antrim. Eventually, he escaped and made his way to the coast. Somehow, he managed to take passage on a ship for Britain and eventually found his way back home. He was now in his early twenties. His long ordeal in Ireland had made him deeply religious.

He studied for the priesthood at Auxerre with Germanus. According to his own account – the first written testimony in Irish history in which we can invest confidence – he remained fascinated by Ireland (perhaps in an appalled sort of way) and heard one night in a dream the voice of an Irish man calling him back to the island. He was sent back there as a missionary by Pope Celestine in 431 to serve 'as a bishop to the Irish believing in Christ'. We know him as St Patrick.

3

CHRISTIANITY

With the arrival of Christianity, the Roman world eventually established itself in Ireland, just as it was in general retreat in north-west Europe. The first firm date in Irish history is 431 CE. In that year, according to the *Chronicon* of Prosper of Aquitaine, one 'Palladius, ordained by Pope Celestine, is sent to the Irish believing in Christ as their first bishop.' Prosper was a layman and a scholar, distinguished for his defence of Augustinian orthodoxy. His *Chronicon* is accepted by all scholars as a reliable contemporary account of events.

So who was Palladius? We do not know, for he promptly disappears from history. Indeed, we don't know if he ever assumed his Irish see. He may well have been St Patrick, given that he was originally named Palladius Patricius. But the recording of his appointment in a reliable contemporary document tells us that there was a Christian community in Ireland in the early fifth century and that they were deemed numerous enough – albeit still a minority – to merit their own bishop. Perhaps they were late Roman traders, already Christianized in Britain, who had settled in Ireland for one reason or another. Indeed, it is possible that some of them were slaves as the Christian Palladius Patricius had once been. At any rate, Prosper's clue at least identifies this community.

Although the name of Palladius disappears from view almost as soon as he is introduced, the Gaelic annals – far less reliable as sources than Prosper – do mention the names of other bishops in the 430s. These are Secundinus, Auxilius and Iserninus. All were later associated with churches in the east and centre of the island which were adjacent to royal sites. If these were, as has been speculated, part of Palladius' original mission to 'the Irish believing in Christ', it suggests communities of Christians living under the protection of regional kings in the area immediately west and south of Dublin.

We cannot be certain of any of this. What we can be certain of is that St Patrick also arrives in Ireland around this time – the date traditionally given is 432 – and that he was a genuine evangelist. Rather than providing spiritual leadership for those who were already Christian, he carried the faith to those who were still pagan. His mission almost certainly concentrated on the northern half of the island: nearly all the major Patrician sites are there. There is no evidence of pre-existing Christian communities in this region.

It is impossible to reconstruct the circumstances of Patrick's mission. Equally, it is impossible to imagine its success without royal support, or at least royal tolerance. The later promotion of Patrick as the great evangelizer, the apostle of Ireland, and the consequent annalistic reticence concerning other early Christian figures, is most likely due to Patrick's adoption by the Uí Néill dynasty. As already suggested, this group, originally focused in Ulster, pressed ever harder south into Leinster. The southern branch established its royal status in lands centred of modern Co. Meath. Their coronation site was at Tara, and much of the later mythology about Tara developed from an assertion of Uí Néill control of the whole island, a status they never enjoyed. They were, nonetheless, a very powerful regional dynasty through their two branches.

The fact that the principal primatial see in the Irish church came to be located in Armagh was no accident. Modern Armagh is adjacent to the ancient royal site of Eamain Macha (indeed, Armagh is an anglicization of the Gaelic name), originally dating from the Iron Age. By the fifth century, it lay in the heart of the territory controlled by the northern Uí Néill. As their claims to the notional high kingship became ever more insistent, their patronage of the national apostle became a key weapon in their propaganda armoury.

At any rate, Patrick was clearly a resourceful missionary. Much the same may be said for the other anonymous evangelists who laboured elsewhere in the island. The effect of their various labours was that within a century of Palladius' original appointment 'to the Irish believing in Christ', the island of Ireland was overwhelmingly Christian in its allegiance.

Nonetheless, it is inevitably to Patrick that we return because in all the murk and speculation of early Christian Ireland, here was a definite, living breathing man of whose existence we can be certain. And critically, he left written evidence of himself and his mission. (History is written less by the winners than by the literate and the diligent.) The two surviving documents which we know to have come from St Patrick's hand are his *Confessio* and the *Letter against Coroticus*.

The *Confessio* is an apologia written late in his life, probably in reply to someone who had impugned his fitness for the office he held. In justifying his position, he gives the account of his background and capture with which we are now familiar. His *Letter against Coroticus* is a cry of anguish following the slaughter of newly converted Irish Christians by a raiding party from Britain, themselves almost certainly Christian. Between them, these two documents are the first, tentative chronicles of an Irish life.

The church that Patrick and the other early missionaries established was structured along conventional diocesan lines, with each diocese in the care of a bishop. This arrangement did not last long. Diocesan church organization assumed a network of towns with the principal town in a region becoming the seat of the bishop. As we have seen, Ireland did not have any towns such as there were in the Roman world and instead a different ecclesiastical structure developed in the shadow of local royal centres.

Uniquely in Europe – to the extent that Ireland at this time can be properly considered a part of Europe – a system of monastic church government emerged. The earliest known monasteries date from the middle of the sixth century. By the middle of the seventh, a very considerable network of monasteries covered most of the island, although increasingly sparse as one went farther north and west. The key people in the Irish church were not the bishops but the abbots of the mother houses in this monastic system. It is an exaggeration to insist on a clear divide between bishops and abbots: bishops did not disappear, and indeed the offices of bishop and abbot were sometimes held by the same man, but the preponderant influence in the early Irish church undoubtedly lay with the monasteries.

These monasteries were scattered across an island that comprised about 200 *tuatha* or petty kingdoms. In the absence of towns to act as a diocesan focus, the establishment of monasteries made more sense in Irish conditions. They were much more likely to receive the support of petty kings, for whom towns were not merely alien but would have represented a potential focus of opposition to their secular authority. Monasteries represented no such threat. Moreover, the nature of land ownership in Gaelic Ireland facilitated the establishment of monasteries. Land was held in common by the extended royal family group. It could be leased to a voluntary body such as a monastery without transferring its ownership, something that would have been illegal. A diocese, on the other hand, needed ownership of land both as a source of income and of prestige. While the greatest monastic sites are sometime spoken of as proto-towns they were no such thing. More plausibly, they have sometimes been described as proto-universities, which is a bit nearer the mark, for the greatest of them were indeed centres of scholarship and learning.

The adoption of the monastic model in Ireland set the island apart from the rest of the Latin world but not wholly apart from the greater Christian tradition. In the eastern (later Orthodox) church, which might as easily have become the universal Christian norm as Rome later claimed to be, monasticism and the asceticism associated with it were very common. The great monastery at Athos in north-eastern Greece is simply one of the best-known examples; monasticism was widespread in Syrian Christianity (one of history's great might-have-beens) and most famously in the Egyptian Coptic church and in that other tenacious outpost of African Christianity, Ethiopia. Ireland therefore behaved like many Christian centres on the margins of the Roman world – or outside it altogether – in adopting this form of church governance. Only a perspective that assumes Rome to be the centre of the world and entirely normative can regard Ireland as an aberration.

Asceticism was long to remain a feature of the Irish church. A desire on the part of holy men to flee from the secular world – again, echoes of the east are strong here – led to the establishment of such remote religious centres as Glendalough, deep in the fastnesses of the Wicklow hills, and Skellig Michael, a ferocious triangular sea stack 16 km (9 miles) off the wild coast of south-west Kerry. From time to time, ascetic groups were formed calling for repentance, exceptional rigour and 'reform', in a pattern that was to be repeated throughout the history of Christianity by millenarians and other rigorists. The best known of these groups in Ireland were the Céilí Dé (companions of God), a late eighth-century movement that detected corruption and luxury in the church – another repeating theme – and preached mortification of the flesh, the renouncing of secular pleasures such as music and a regime of severe prayer and penance.

The earliest of the great monastic sites was at Clonmacnoise, on the east bank of the Shannon between Lough Ree and Lough Derg, with a foundation date in the mid-sixth century. The surviving stone buildings on the site – it is now a national monument – date from the ninth century and later. The earliest buildings, mainly of timber, have long since disappeared. All of the surviving artefacts, the round towers, high crosses and church buildings, are from the later period, so we have no remaining evidence of how it looked in its first three centuries of life.

An interesting foundation was that of Kildare, presided over by St Brigid, the so-called 'Mary of the Irish'. At one point, Kildare was a rival to Armagh for primacy in the Irish church. Indeed, there was no reason to suppose that Armagh had any particular claim to primacy except for its repeated Patrician associations, sedulously promoted by the Uí Néill. Brigid is cognate with the Celtic pagan goddess Brigantia, and appears to be a particularly suggestive example of Christian devotion subsuming an older tradition.

The most celebrated of the early abbots was Colm Cille, otherwise known as St Columba. Most of what we know about him derives from a biography written nearly 100 years after his death by Adomnán, one of Colm Cille's abbatial successors. The biography is trusted by scholars because it drew on documents and traditions in Columban foundations, and is less open to the charge of being simply a post facto hagiography. The saint was born around 520, to a branch of Uí Néill with strong connections to the north-west of Ireland. He studied at the great monastery of Clonard, near Clonmacnoise, and founded a number of monasteries in Ireland, including one near the site of the modern city of Derry, before making the move in 563 with which he is forever associated.

In that year, he left Ireland forever. Various reasons have been advanced for his departure. The most common legend is that he copied a psalter (a translation of the Psalms) made by St Finnian. The saint requested him to yield up the copy and Finnian appealed to the legal scholars. They held that ownership of the copy properly belonged to him who had made the original – this is often cited as the first legal judgment establishing the principle of copyright. If so, the concept subsequently had a long sleep, because the first copyright act in the world was not enacted until 1710, in England. Colm Cille refused to obey the judgment and St Finnian went to war. In the battle that ensued, many thousands were killed. In his remorse for his conduct, and on the advice of his confessor, Colm Cille resolved to sail out of sight of Ireland and redeem as many souls for Christ as had been killed in the battle. He established a monastery on the remote island of Iona in the Inner Hebrides. It became the mother house of a network of monasteries in Ireland, Galloway and Northumbria. It is a further reminder of the single culture that came to embrace north-east Ireland and the west of Scotland, with the sea acting as a highway rather than as a barrier to travel.

From Iona, he carried out a wholesale evangelization of the Picts – the indigenes of ancient Scotland – helped by a friendship he established with the Pictish king, Brude mac Maelchon, whose seat was in Inverness. As was the case with successful Christian missionary efforts, the patronage – or at least neutral disposition – of the secular ruler was essential. Moreover, in a pattern that echoed that of the Patrician evangelization of Ireland, Colm Cille was canny enough to preach a Christianity that was as compatible as possible with the existing Pictish religion, building churches at Pictish sacred sites and adapting established festivals to the Christian church calendar.

His reach went beyond the Picts. Columba sent his monks across the lowlands and into Northumbria, introducing Christianity to the Anglo-Saxon tribes who had settled there after the collapse of Roman Britain. One of the great ironies of the Anglo-Saxon triumph in England is that these Germanic conquerors were pagans, whereas the Celtic peoples they had displaced were already Christian because of the Roman presence. Now, however, Christianity was reintroduced into north-east England by Irish monks working from a Scottish base. Indeed, the Columban influence was felt much further south: of the first four bishops of Mercia (roughly the modern

English counties of Cheshire, Staffordshire and Shropshire) three were either Irish or had been trained in Ireland.

The Columban church in Scotland had a profound effect on that country's history, because it opened the way for the Gaelicization of the highlands and islands whose effect persists to this day. It also meant that the heterodox Irish form of church governance, together with heterodox doctrine and practice, became the norm in the early Scottish and Anglo-Saxon churches. This remote Columban church was out of line with Roman orthodoxy on a number of important issues, most notably the means employed to calculate the date of Easter. This was a matter of no little moment, failing to agree the date of the most important feast in the Christian calendar.

Columba died on Iona in 597. In that very year, at the far end of Britain, the Italian St Augustine (not to be confused with Augustine of Hippo, the great father of the church, who was by now more than 150 years dead) arrived from Rome with a party of forty monks. He was charged by Pope Gregory I with the task of converting the Anglo-Saxons to Christianity and bringing them into full communion with Rome. He became the first archbishop of Canterbury. The Augustinian evangelization of England pressed ever northward, eventually colliding with the Columban church. The dispute over the date of Easter was not resolved until the Synod of Whitby in 664, when the Roman line prevailed. This drew the fledgling English church into the Roman orbit and diminished the influence of the Irish church on the larger island.

One further point needs to be noted about Iona. It is almost certainly here, around 800, that the greatest of all insular illuminated manuscripts was composed. The Book of Kells is so called because by the eleventh century, it had been removed to the safety of the monastery at Kells, Co. Meath, to keep it from the depredations of the Vikings. It is a manuscript version of the Four Gospels and other marginalia embedded in a decorative design of astonishing richness and variety. It comprises 340 calfskin folios (each folio makes two pages) and is evidence of a scholarly and artistic culture of the highest achievement. It is not the only great illuminated manuscript of the time – the Irish and Columban churches were responsible for many other distinguished examples, such as the Lindisfarne Gospels and the Book of Durrow – but it is by common consent the finest. Miraculously, it has survived the turbulence of the Irish past and now resides in the Old Library in Trinity College Dublin, the jewel in the college's crown and one of modern Ireland's biggest tourist attractions.

The Augustinian revival did not press beyond England. In Ireland, Roman ecclesiastical orthodoxy was not re-established, at least in part, until the thirteenth century under the influence of the Normans. For the best part of 600 years, therefore, the insular church was to continue in its particular course largely uninfluenced by external events.

In fact, the influence was all the other way. In a burst of creative energy, the Irish church became a missionary instrument, reintroducing Christianity to the European continent where it had declined with the collapse of the Roman Empire, its secular sponsor. From 700 on, Irish missionaries appeared to be everywhere, both within and without the boundaries of the old empire. They founded religious settlements all over northern, central and eastern Europe, even as far away as Kiev.

St Columbanus (c.543–615) was the most famous of these continental missionaries. His Gaelic name was Colmán; the name by which he is remembered is a Latinized version. This is appropriate, for he was a Latin scholar of the first rank and a theologian. He studied at the influential monastery of Bangor, Co. Down. When he first went to the continent, he settled in the region of the Vosges Mountains, where he was awarded a grant of land by the local king. He established a number of religious houses in the region, the best known of them being the abbey of Luxeuil, which was the mother house of a number of later abbeys. Of these, Bobbio in north-west Italy was the most celebrated. Columbanus became abbot there towards the end of his life. He had offended the local clergy in the Vosges by criticizing their wealth, and also by asserting the Celtic dating of Easter in defiance of Roman orthodoxy. He later fell out with the local king by declining to bless the king's illegitimate sons, whom the king wished to legitimize for succession purposes.

Columbanus was a rigorist, ascetic in his rule and combative by temperament. He appears to have made little allowance for human weakness. In this, he was a recognizable type: a holy man of narrow views, albeit deeply learned and possessed of a ferocious energy and sense of purpose.

Other Irish missionary saints are remembered in towns and cities across the continent. In Würzburg in northern Bavaria, the cathedral is named for St Killian; the Swiss town of St Gall is named eponymously for one of Columbanus' companions; in Fiesole, near Florence, the Irish poet Donatus was bishop for more than fifty years in the ninth century.

The missionary impetus was part of a revival of Latin and Christian learning in Ireland that made it, for a couple of centuries, one of the intellectual powerhouses of Europe. Not all the intellectuals were religious. There were Irish peripatetic scholars on the continent as well, some of them at least glad to flee Ireland in the wake of the early Viking raids. Of these, the name of John Scottus Eriugena has lived longest in the historical memory. A ninth-century polymath, he was the most distinguished European philosopher of his time. He settled at the court of Charles the Bald of France and translated many previously neglected texts from ancient Greece. His philosophy was strongly influenced by Greek thought, not always welcome in the Latin west where Augustinian orthodoxy was dominant. Eriugena's work was considered sufficiently subversive to be banned by the papacy as late as 1684.

Eriugena was by no means the only Irish scholar of distinction at a continental court, but he was the one who made the longest lasting mark. Other scholars of genuine distinction included Dungal, a ninth-century imperial astronomer, the geographer Dicuil and the poet Sedulius Scottus. Nor, to be fair, was Ireland unique in furnishing such talent to the continent. In the previous century, Alcuin of York had been a leading scholar at the court of Charlemagne himself. Nonetheless, it is remarkable that in these centuries of concentrated energy, the most remote western island in Europe should have inserted itself so centrally into the religious and intellectual life of the continent. In the eighth and ninth centuries, Ireland was no savage outpost: it was a critical contributor to, and perhaps even the saviour of, the culture of post-Roman Europe.

4

VIKINGS

The term Viking refers to groups of Scandinavian people principally from the south and west coasts of what is now Norway, and the Jutland peninsula to the south across the Skagerrak strait. These people, in possession of their lands from ancient times, had probably been part of successive patterns of migration by Germanic tribes across the Great Northern Plain of Europe, which offered few natural obstacles to such migration.

Quite what impelled the Vikings to their sudden, violent and energetic expansion overseas from the eighth century is uncertain. There may have been population pressures, which would have been particularly severe in Norway with its rocky coastal valleys surrounded by impassable mountains on the landward side. The combination of limited and poor land together with the unforgiving northern climate would have made such habitats especially vulnerable to population growth, with any surplus population impelled to shift for itself. The gradual development of the proto-kingdoms of Norway and Denmark in the early Viking period may also have caused tribal groups alienated from the move towards centralized kingdoms to seek their fortunes elsewhere.

Whatever the reasons, the facts are incontrovertible. The Vikings developed the finest fleet of seafaring craft in contemporary Europe, which carried them to Britain and Ireland, north-west France, and as far east as Novgorod in Russia. The first Viking raid on Britain occurred in 789, but the most dramatic early assault was on the holy island and monastery of Lindisfarne in Northumbria in 793. Lindisfarne was one of the great jewels of the Columban church and was, of course, of Gaelic Irish foundation. Its founder, St Aidan, had been sent from Iona to evangelize the north of England. Like all the great monasteries, it was not simply a centre of piety and prayer but also of scholarship, ritual and high artistic achievement. Its greatest accomplishment, almost a century old at the time of the first Viking raid, was the Lindisfarne Gospels, one of the greatest treasures from the golden age of illuminated gospel manuscripts.

The *Anglo-Saxon Chronicle* records the shock of the Viking raid: 'In this year fierce, foreboding omens came over the land of Northumbria. There were excessive whirlwinds, lightning storms, and fiery dragons were seen flying in the sky. These signs were followed by great famine, and on January 8th the ravaging of heathen men destroyed God's church at Lindisfarne.' Alcuin of York (*c.*737–804), perhaps the most influential English monk of the period, observed: 'Never before has such terror appeared in Britain as we have now suffered from a pagan race ... The heathens poured out the blood of saints around the altar, and trampled on the bodies of saints in the temple of God, like dung in the streets.'

Two years after Lindisfarne, in 795, the Vikings appear for the first time off the Irish coast and attacked the wealthy monastery on Lambay island, just north of Dublin Bay. They were raiding in search of loot and treasure and in this they were not alone, for native Irish raiders did not scruple to emulate their example. Undefended monasteries and their riches made a tempting target. For almost half a century, these Viking depredations continued, with the Norse the principal presence on the east and south coasts while the Danes pushed farther inland in their shallow-draughted longboats.

This so-called 'hit-and-run' period ended in 841 with the establishment of a proto-settlement, known as a *longphort*, on the banks of the Liffey. A *longphort* was a defensible enclosure for shipping which offered adequate berthage and easy access to the open sea. The establishment of the settlement marks the foundation date of the city of Dublin. The towns of Cork, Limerick, Wexford and Waterford all followed before 900, all of them of Viking foundation. Interestingly, the Vikings fared worse in Ulster where the Uí Néill had the measure of them.

The *longphort* was not a town, although a town was to grow from it. Its purpose was to give shelter. It was a safe haven. Shelter suggested some degree of permanence, if only in the winter months. Permanence suggested continuity; the domestication of skills; trade and commerce. The Vikings had established secure control of the sea lanes all around the larger island of Britain, including staging posts in places like the Isle of Man. In 866 they established themselves in the old Roman city of York, from where they controlled the first Norse kingdom in the north of England. In short, Dublin became a link in a chain of Viking trading centres, joined by their secure control of the sea.

The Dublin *longphort* lasted until 902, when the native Irish drove the Vikings out. Quite what that bald statement means is unclear, because the settlement had been under pressure from the beginning. The Vikings did not win all their battles with the Irish. On the other hand, there is evidence of inter-marriage and social intercourse from the earliest days, of linguistic confusion and melding, and of ad hoc military and other alliances both formal and informal. It has been speculated – there is no firm evidence – that the expulsion of the Vikings in 902 only affected the military leadership and that domestic tradesmen and suchlike remained behind.

What is clear is that Viking power on the banks of the Liffey was broken until 917, when the leading families returned from their English exile. In England, where urban settlement and development was more advanced than in

Ireland, they would have seen towns that were sophisticated by the standards of the age. They brought this knowledge back to Dublin. From this point on, it is customary to refer to the Viking city's *dún* phase, from the Gaelic word for fortification. No longer merely a *longphort*, the town now had an early, permanent stockade within which the community could find security. That security was not absolute: there were Gaelic incursions throughout the tenth century. The settlement was burned down in 936 but Norse power was subsequently reasserted and the little town rebuilt.

The Vikings established themselves as part of the Irish experience for the three centuries from their first arrival to their final eclipse by their Norman successors. In that time, they did not conquer Ireland, or any substantial part of it: there was no Irish Danelaw. But they did establish a permanent presence, one that was focused on towns in a country that had never known such things before. Moreover, they had irrupted into an island that had not seen military invasion for a millennium or more and had done so with exemplary violence. That violence was recorded, and perhaps understandably exaggerated, by the scholarly monks who were the prime targets of the Viking assaults.

They turned the Irish Sea into a Viking lake. The new towns, especially Dublin, became part of a trading network which had the effect over time of drawing sites in Britain into a more consistent commercial relationship with Ireland. The contacts between the two islands were gradually quickening. No longer a matter of occasional pirate raids or of missionary outreach, the steady permanence of commerce was effecting a palpable change in the relationship of the two islands to each other.

The Vikings also changed the internal dynamic of Ireland. Faced with a ruthless foreign enemy who did not scruple to plunder and kill, the Gaels gradually discovered that imitation was a form of flattery. They not only acquired the skills needed to contain the military threat of the foreigners, they also practised some of their methods. Under the pressure of conflict, old taboos were breaking down. First, some Gaelic warlords came to regard rich monasteries as fair game for their depredations. Second, throughout the Viking era, petty kings and sub-kings had no scruple about making alliances with the Vikings in order to gain an advantage over a regional opponent. The result of both developments was a ratcheting up of violence.

From the middle of the ninth century, the contest between Gael and Viking began to swing towards the former. Two principal factors influenced this. First, the stronger regional kingdoms expanded and consolidated, enabling them to deliver a more concentrated military threat. In Munster, the Eóganacht dynasty established a provincial dominance and looked to press north out of their heartland. A succession of provincial kings pursued this policy, which meant that Eóganacht power would inevitably collide with that of the Uí Néill, who in their turn wished to project their power to the south. The most ruthless and enigmatic of the Eóganacht kings, Fedelemid mac Crimthainn, was at once an aggressive projector of his own power, a looter and destroyer of monasteries (including Clonmacnoise on more than one occasion, Durrow and Kildare), a bishop and a supporter of the ascetic Céilí Dé movement. The puritanism implicit in the Céilí Dé impelled his hostility to the monasteries, which he regarded as dens of worldly luxury. He held the abbacies of Cork and Clonfert. He even occupied Tara in 840, a particular humiliation for the Uí Néill. His assertion of Munster power was continued by later kings such as Cormac mac Cuilennáin, who continued to press on the southern flank of the Uí Néill. All this seemed like a rehearsal for the later success of Brian Ború.

In fact, it was the eventual defeat of Cormac and his successors by the Uí Néill in the middle of the tenth century that weakened the Eóganacht kings of Munster and allowed the improbable and dramatic rise to provincial power of a hitherto obscure sub-kingdom, Dál Cais. This petty kingdom occupied the northern shore of the Shannon estuary, just to the west of Limerick in what is now east Co. Clare. With the reversal of Eóganacht power, the Dál Cais were able to seize the provincial crown at Cashel in 963.

But by then it seemed that the future lay not with any Munster dynasty but with the southern Uí Néill based at Tara. The relentless to-ing and fro-ing between the major provincial armies in the course of the ninth and tenth centuries had at least reduced the number of serious fighting forces to no more than ten or so. Of these the Uí Néill seemed to hold the strongest hand and to have the best chance of pushing south into the Munster heartland. The possibility of a genuine high kingship, and the insular unity it entailed, seemed closer than ever. It came, if only briefly, but not from the quarter expected.

Máel Seachnaill, king of the southern Uí Néill, claimed the high kingship in 980 (in yet another rhetorical gust) and captured Dublin the following year. He could not hold it but he recaptured it in 990. However, the really key development for the future was the succession of Brian Ború to the crown of Dál Cais in 976 and to that of Munster two years later. He resumed the traditional Munster aggression northward, which inevitably brought him into collision with Máel Seachnaill. Through the 980s and 990s, the contest between them continued. Eventually, in 997, the two adversaries met near Clonfert, a monastic site on the Shannon just south of Clonmacnoise, and agreed to partition the island. Máel Seachnaill was acknowledged as overlord of the northern half of the island, Brian of the southern half. It was a remarkable result for the Dál Cais to come from provincial petty kings to overlords of half of Ireland in a generation.

The second factor in the Gaelic recovery was dissention among the Vikings. The original Viking settlers were Norse. In 851, the Danes arrived in Dublin and attacked the Norse. Soon, the two were at each others' throats. The Gaels learned to distinguish between the two groups by the prevailing colour of their hair: Dubh Ghaill (black foreigners) for the Danes and

Fionn Ghaill (fair foreigners) for the Norse. These terms are the remote origins of the common Irish surname Doyle and the place name for the area north of Dublin city, Fingal.

The Viking misfortunes in Dublin in the early tenth century, already noted above, were a direct consequence of this internal division. In many respects, the Vikings came to resemble the Gaels in their tendency to divisions and splits. Some Vikings were happy to make temporary coalitions with Gaelic forces in order to advance their own cause. Likewise, the Gaels were glad of such Viking support as they could garner. In the confused military politics of the late tenth and early eleventh centuries, it was coalition against coalition rather than simply Gael against Viking.

The commerce of Viking Dublin entailed trade with the Isle of Man and with Viking centres in Britain such as York. The slave trade was a significant feature of both its imports and exports, which also included animal hides, wool and jewellery. The stability of commerce found expression in the development of the urban infrastructure. The ever-increasing pressure from the Irish kings and warlords from the 980s onward was a problem, but also provided an opportunity. For as long as the battle for control was inconclusive, provisional arrangements and compromises in the form of inter-marriage alliances gave the town an increasingly mixed ethnic character. This in turn led to linguistic ambiguity, as Norse and Gaelic borrowed from each other and a hybrid form developed.

However, the pressure from the Gaelic world was persistent and ultimately proved decisive. From around 1000, Viking power in the town was fatally compromised. In part, this was due to the rise of Brian Ború. His partition arrangement with Máel Seachnaill was always going to be a temporary affair. The question was which of them would press on towards the supreme prize. It was Brian. In 999, he defeated a coalition of Máel Seachnaill and the Dublin Vikings and occupied Dublin for more than a month. In 1001, he launched himself against

the southern Uí Néill. Máel Seachnaill found himself abandoned by his allies, including the northern branch of his
dynasty, and was weakened accordingly. His failure to compel
his allies, even his own kin, is a stark demonstration of the limi-
tations of kingly power in Gaelic Ireland. If an outstanding
figure like Máel Seachnaill could not do it, who could?

Máel Seachnaill acknowledged Brian's overlordship in 1002.
In the following years, Brian pressed ever further north. In
1005, he secured the support of the primatial see of Armagh, a
key advance. This was the occasion that first caused him to be
called *Imperator Scottorum*, or emperor of the Irish. The
following year, he made a royal tour of Ulster without any
opposition, although the stubborn little kingdom of Cenél
Conaill in the very west of the province held out on him until
1011. In every year following the submission of Máel Seachnaill
in 1002, Brian had felt required to assert himself in Ulster,
making his royal progress and taking local hostages as an
earnest of the local rulers' submission to his power.

He was the nearest thing Gaelic Ireland had seen, or was
ever to see, to a true high king. But this much abused term – a
back projection from nineteenth-century nationalism –
obscures as much as it illuminates. Brian was not a king in any
common understanding of the word. He did not administer a
territory from a secure, permanent base: a capital. His legal
writ did not run throughout the territory he claimed. He did
not have any central revenue raising powers. These were all
characteristics of early European kingdoms: none were present
in Brian Ború's Ireland. And to be fair, even in Europe, they
were for the most part characteristics of future, not present,
royal kingdoms in the first decade of the eleventh century.

Brian is better described as an over-king, the most accomplished warlord in a warlord society. He had authority but no
legitimacy. He was simply top dog for the time being, and if he
slackened his grip his power would be compromised. Taking
hostages for the good behaviour of his subordinates year after
year was a primitive way of asserting power. It was almost

inevitable that he would meet with resistance from provincial sub-kings and their princely underlings when the opportunity seemed ripe. In order to deal with them, Brian was content to permit Viking Dublin a continuing degree of local autonomy. However, the king of Leinster, Máel Mórdha, outbid Brian with promises of autonomy to Dublin and succeeded in enlisting the support of the Viking ruler, Sitric Silkenbeard, in a provincial revolt against Brian's power.

The issue was joined at Clontarf, on the north shores of Dublin Bay, on Good Friday 1014. The Dublin Norse and their Leinster allies were augmented by Viking troops from Britain, Norway, Denmark and the Isle of Man. Against them was ranged Brian's coalition, principally comprising troops from Munster, Connacht and the midlands.

The Battle of Clontarf, one of the most famous fights in Irish history, is a misnomer. It did not take place on the land now occupied by the modern suburb of that name, but most likely to the west of it in the general area of modern Ballybough. In fact, for those familiar with prominent landmarks in the modern city, the most plausible location for the main battle is in the general vicinity of Croke Park, the city's biggest sports stadium.

Brian won, although the battle cost him his life as well as that of his son and fifteen-year-old grandson. This is important given the context of the battle. It is usually celebrated as the moment that Ireland was rid of the Viking yoke. This is an exaggeration. Norse power was undoubtedly weakened – they had backed the losing side in a major battle – but Sitric remained the ruler of the town until his death in 1036. Vikings then retained the leadership of Dublin until at least 1042 and remained a significant presence until the arrival of the Normans over a century later.

The effective assimilation of the Vikings was complete with their embrace of Christianity in the years after Clontarf. However, in a development that was to be significant in the next century, they refused to accept the authority of the see of Armagh – the primatial Irish see – but placed themselves under

the protection of Canterbury in England instead. This link was
further asserted by the reforming archbishop of Canterbury,
Lanfranc, in 1072, who actually claimed primatial authority
over all of Ireland. As we shall see, the submission of Dublin to
Canterbury was undone at the Synod of Kells in 1152, which
created the archdioceses of Dublin and Tuam to join the existing archiepiscopal sees of Cashel and Armagh. But the
ecclesiastical status of Dublin was contested.

Most significant of all was the failure of Brian's successors,
who gradually assumed the family surname O'Brien (as well
they might), to consolidate his achievements. Instead, Gaelic
Ireland reverted to fissiparous type, which was all it knew,
leaving it politically divided and vulnerable to the next major
invasion from a more sophisticated military society.

5

NORMANS

The period from Clontarf in 1014 to the arrival of the Normans in 1169 is one of the most confused in Irish history. It is usually referred to as the period of kings with opposition. The Gaelic order was incapable of creating a united polity – hardly a disgrace, as it might be argued that no such thing was to exist in Ireland until the 1650s – and such warlord-kings as asserted a notional claim to the high kingship always lacked the means to give substance to their claims. In effect, their problem had been Brian Ború's problem, except that to a man they lacked Brian's talent and ruthlessness.

By the early twelfth century, the power of the Munster kings was exhausted. The south-eastern kingdom of Leinster had asserted itself and had attempted the old Munster tactic of pressurizing the southern Uí Néill, with intermittent success but no permanent gain. By the second half of the century, the kings of Connacht had the best claim to the high kingship but, as ever before, it was largely rhetoric. They were capable of knocking heads together to settle petty provincial disputes but they were nowhere near establishing their power in the whole island.

The impulse towards a sort of unity found more eloquent expression in the church than in the secular world. From the beginning of the twelfth century, a reform movement in the

Latin Christian church was driven forward by three energetic popes in particular: Gregory VII (1073–85), Alexander III (1159–81) and Innocent III (1198–1216). The reforms were designed to accommodate the church to the emerging world of early feudalism and to the nascent royal states beginning to form at the time.

These royal states were the products of the feudal system. Pre-feudal societies had been tribal, depending on extended ties of kinship as the principal integrating force. Feudalism developed a new kind of obligation. In return for a fief or grant of land, given under certain legal conditions by a lord, a vassal gave him homage and an undertaking to perform certain services, usually of a military nature. A local warlord had therefore a client base among his vassals whose allegiance to him was based not on kinship but on shared material interest. This created a hierarchy of values leading upward from the vassal to the lord to a regional overlord such as a count or a duke and ultimately to the king, whose authority derived from God.

This hierarchy of obligations was capable of being expressed in legal terms, with the king as the ultimate guarantor of the law. The effective boundaries of a royal kingdom were defined as those places where the king's writ ran, that is to say where a uniform central law was capable of being applied and obedience to it compelled. Outside these boundaries, even though the territories might be formally part of the royal domain, either customary law or palatinate jurisdiction – in which the law and power to raise armies and taxes was devolved for pragmatic reasons – were the norm. Over time, royal kingdoms were to accrue more and more power at the centre until the process was complete in advanced kingdoms like England and France by the sixteenth century.

The gradual rise of the royal kingdom gave greater stability, legal certainty and administrative consistency than the pre-feudal arrangements whose customary usages were codified, as in Ireland, but were applied only over the small sub-kingdom typical of the time. The royal state, on the other hand, ruled from afar, and the whole story of such kingdoms is the gradual absorption by the royal centre of the autonomous peripheries. The kingdoms of France and England developed in this way. Later, although less successfully, so did that of Spain.

Not only law but also the power to raise revenue was important in this regard. The earliest pipe rolls in England date from the twelfth century. Pipe rolls were financial records kept by the king's treasury, rolled up tight and kept safe in metal tubes or pipes. The ability of the English king to assert his power across all his domain was partial but by no means non-existent: the astonishing Domesday Book of 1086 provided William the Conqueror with a detailed land survey of all the holdings in his new kingdom. England was the most sophisticated royal state in Europe at the time. The Normans had simply taken over an Anglo-Saxon kingdom that was more completely developed as a single political unity than anything else in northern Europe at the time.

The rise of the royal state had implications for the church and for the papal reformers in Rome. The earliest and greatest of these was Gregory VII who for the first time asserted the universal authority of the papacy, not just over the Latin Christian world (the Orthodox church having gone its own way in the Great Schism of 1054) but over all creation! The Pope was claiming title to universal monarchy, superior to that of all temporal rulers. He gave uncompromising expression to his claim in the famous incident at the castle of Canossa in northern Italy in 1077. He had excommunicated the Holy Roman Emperor, Henry IV, and, before a meeting to absolve him from this condition, the Pope made him wait bareheaded (and possibly barefoot) in the snow to show him exactly who was boss.

This new assertive papacy was not able to make all its claims of precedence over secular authority stick. But it realized that if its other purpose, to regulate and control the personal lives of the faithful, was to be best realized then an organizational structure that paralleled that of the royal state was the ideal vehicle. Thus there was a strengthening of the royal centre itself, the papacy, and the diocesan and parish structures through Christendom, with their hierarchy of authority reflecting that of the secular, feudal world. The right of the College of Cardinals alone to elect the pope dates from 1059, and the Roman Curia (or bureaucratic court) dates from 1090s.

These structural reforms were advanced throughout the Latin church. In this context the antique Irish church, with its eccentricities and exceptionalism, looked more anachronistic than ever. Those among the Irish who were most alert to developments in the wider world were already in touch with the reformers. The late eleventh-century Dál Cais kings of Munster were in touch with Rome and also with the two reforming archbishops of Canterbury, Lanfranc (1070–89) and Anselm (1093–1109). Both archbishops regarded the Irish church as full of abuses, and reported as much to Rome. They despaired of Armagh ever tackling the problem and wished to assert their own primacy, the better to accomplish the task. Their beachhead in Dublin, where the Vikings recognized their primatial status before that of Armagh, together with their Dál Cais contacts, gave them hope of extending their influence to the smaller island.

What were the specific complaints of the reformers about the Irish church? That its bishops were lacking in legal and administrative authority; that simony – the selling of ecclesiastical office – was widespread; that the sexual lives of the clergy were a scandal. The reform movement was concerned to exercise increasing control over the private lives of the faithful: marriage was denominated as a sacrament around this time and clerical celibacy insisted upon by the Lateran Council of 1139.

The reform movement in Ireland started in Munster in the first years of the twelfth century and gradually spread north in deference to the primacy of Armagh. By 1111, partial reforms were in place throughout the island, hardly enough to satisfy Rome, but a start. Dublin formally joined the Irish dioceses, acknowledging the primacy of Armagh, in the 1120s as part of this early reform. Without the active support of two successive archbishops of Armagh, Cellach and St Malachy, the Irish reform movement would have stalled. Armagh, with its wealth and its uncontested prestige, was key. The greatest achievement of the reform movement came at the Synod of Kells in 1152, which established the system of Irish church government that has broadly survived to the present. It created two new archdioceses, Dublin and Tuam, to join Cashel and Armagh. The raising of Dublin's status was a reward for the renouncing of its former connection to Canterbury. The creation of a new archdiocese in the west was an emollient gesture towards the powerful kings of Connacht. The smaller suffragan (subordinate) dioceses within each province were identified, creating the basis of the hierarchical provincial-diocesan-parish structure – as neat as any feudal declension – that replaced the old monastic arrangements. Indeed, even the monastic life was changing with the arrival of continental reform orders such as the Augustinians, Benedictines and Cistercians. From now on, the Irish church was in fuller communion with Rome, especially in the emphasis on authority and church law. The process was incomplete but irreversible.

Let us return to the secular world and to an incident that was the product of an intrigue and a turbulent life. In the 1160s, Diarmait Mac Murchada, the king of Leinster, abducted one Degovilla, the wife of a minor regional king called O'Rourke. Whether the lady consented to be abducted or not is unclear, but the upshot was that O'Rourke – understandably humiliated to be made a cuckold – appealed to Rory O'Connor, the king of Connacht and the provincial ruler with the nearest claim to call himself high king. O'Connor's muscle saw Mac Murchada lose his kingdom. He was forced to flee abroad.

Diarmait eventually found his way to the Norman king of England, Henry II, then on campaign in Aquitaine. Henry was sympathetic but could not spare any of his troops to help

Diarmait recover his kingdom. He did, however, give him letters authorizing him to raise troops in Henry's lands back in Britain. In return, Diarmait pledged to hold Leinster as Henry's vassal and to offer his daughter's hand to whatever military leader might be found in Henry's lands.

This possibility immediately secured a potential interest for the crown of England in the island of Ireland. There was already the contested ecclesiastical loyalty of the see of Dublin to confuse the issue, not to mention a papal bull of 1155, *Laudabiliter*, which authorized Henry II to invade Ireland in order to enforce religious conformity. This bull was almost certainly prompted by the see of Canterbury – nettled by the 'transfer' of Dublin to Armagh's jurisdiction under the terms of the Synod of Kells. Moreover, Canterbury would have had a ready ear in Pope Adrian IV (Nicholas Breakspear, the only Englishman ever to hold the office). In fairness, the reform movement in Ireland was partial. For example, there is no evidence of a parish structure having been established before the arrival of the Normans, and the radical reformers would have pointed to the weakness or absence of Irish royal authority to enforce reform. The church needed a strong royal secular power to enforce its will. The net effect was that Henry II had a papal warrant to invade Ireland should it suit him. It did not, but he had no objection to helping Diarmait recover his kingdom.

And so it was done. The story has been told a thousand times. Diarmait raised troops in Wales, returned and recovered some of his lands in 1167, and was reinforced by more Norman troops that landed in 1169 followed an even more formidable force in 1170. Its leader was Richard FitzGilbert, deposed Earl of Pembroke, known to history as Strongbow. It was he who claimed the hand of Diarmait's daughter, Aoife.

Strongbow and his men captured Dublin in that same year. The Anglo-Norman era had begun.

The Normans had originally been a Viking tribe that established itself in north-west France in the tenth century. Under an agreement of 911 CE known as the Treaty of Saint-Clair-sur-Epte, the Carolingian King Charles the Simple granted territory around Rouen for settlement by the followers of Rollo, the Viking chieftain. This was the remote origin of the Duchy of Normandy.

The presence of a Viking duchy across the channel was a worry for the kings of Anglo-Saxon England, for whom the presence of Viking kingdoms in eastern England was a constant anxiety. Gradually, however, the Vikings of Normandy became thoroughly assimilated in their new land and from about 1000 we can speak of them as French. They then emerged as one of the most remarkable expansive forces in medieval Europe. They sent bands of adventurers into the Italian peninsula. By 1130, they had ousted the Saracens and established a kingdom in southern Italy and Sicily, which over time was to mutate into the famous Kingdom of the Two Sicilies. Their own rule only lasted a mere sixty-four years before the kingdom yielded to the rising power of the Hohenstaufen, but they left an indelible mark on the region and were the leading force in the establishment of the Christian kingdom in Palestine in 1099 following the First Crusade.

By the time the Normans' Italo–Sicilian kingdom foundered in 1194, their cousins were long established in England, which they had conquered in 1066. The Norman Conquest wrought the destruction of Anglo-Saxon England and transformed the country. Just over a century later, their knights under Strongbow were in Ireland.

The first small party of Normans, with Diarmait in tow, arrived in 1167 and immediately recovered part of his kingdom. The main Norman force landed at the beach of Baginbun ('where Ireland was lost and won') in 1169. In fact, Ireland was not lost and won there: the Normans were simply regarded as mercenaries, which is what they were, come to help a local king recover his patrimony. Ireland was not lost and won until King Henry II arrived two years later, as we shall see.

By 1169 Rory O'Connor, king of Connacht, had established himself as the most powerful figure in Gaelic Ireland since BrianBorú. In the 1160s, he had successfully subdued his internal enemies and appeared to have ended the long series of dynastic wars that bedevilled the island since the Battle of Clontarf. Whether his ascendancy was anything more than temporary we shall never know, for like BrianBorú he may have been required to reassert his primacy year after year by campaigns against actual or potential recalcitrants, renewing their submission by hostage taking and the promotion of their local rivals' interests over their own. The potential sinews of a royal state were not present in Ireland in the late 1160s any more than they had been 150 years earlier. The absence of an urban network securely in Gaelic hands, with a church diocesan structure in parallel support, suggests that any progress in this direction would have been slow, at best.

The contrast with Scotland was instructive. There, Kenneth MacAlpin had established a Gaelic kingdom north of the Forth–Clyde line and south of Caithness and Sutherland as early as 843. It absorbed the aboriginal Pictish population. By 1018 Malcolm III had pushed this kingdom south into the Borders, where the Anglo-Saxon Northumbrians had previously held sway, and fixed the southern boundary of the Scottish kingdom on the Tweed. The lowlands were now Scottish for the first time. This was a kingdom with a far greater internal unity than Gaelic Ireland. Malcolm's queen, Margaret, was of the Anglo-Saxon royal house and introduced southern influences to the lowlands, the most potent being the Anglo-Saxon language which over time mutated into lowland Scots, the language of Robbie Burns. Following the Norman conquest of England in 1066, Norman influence made itself felt north of the border and eventually Normans settled there by invitation, not by invasion. The Scots kings welcomed the military superiority of the Normans, which could be deployed against the autonomous and troublesome highlands.

With the Normans came feudalism, chartered towns, fortified

castles and a modernized church in full communion with Rome. These elements were absent in Gaelic Ireland, either in whole or in part. Given their absence, it is difficult to see how Rory O'Connor might have asserted himself as a true king, capable of ruling from distance (with the need for the frequent threatening incursions into opposition territory reduced or eliminated) with the rudiments of a national treasury and an administrative bureaucracy.

The question was rendered academic by the arrival of the Normans. Unlike Scotland, where they had been invited to bolster the forces of a more-or-less centralized kingdom, in Ireland they were enlisted in an internecine fight. They quickly imposed themselves, capturing the key towns of Waterford and Dublin. Indeed, so successful were they that King Henry II – whose principal interests lay in England and western France and for whom Ireland was a distraction – was obliged to take control. He feared that Strongbow would establish an independent kingdom in Ireland.

This was no paranoid fantasy on the king's part. Once the Normans had arrived in force, in the summer of 1170, they brought a level of military power unlike anything seen before in Ireland. Their two key military resources were mounted and armoured knights and the longbow. The former, on their huge horses, were irresistible. A disciplined Norman cavalry charge was a terrifying experience. Likewise, the longbowmen could engage and devastate an enemy at distance. The quick military successes of the Normans in Ireland were not accidental.

The capture of Dublin opened the possibility of the Normans establishing a royal kingdom, secure in arms, which with reinforced numbers could then project its power across all or most of the island. This was Diarmait Mac Murchada's grand ambition, not merely to recover his lost provincial kingdom but actually to make himself high king of Ireland. He was frustrated in this ambition, dying in May 1171, with Strongbow succeeding to his Leinster crown as part of the marriage settlement with Aoife.

By the winter of 1170, the Normans held all of south-east Leinster and its three main towns, Dublin, Waterford and Wexford. They had pushed into the countryside to the west to show their military power, and thus far Rory O'Connor had been powerless to stop them. In the summer of 1171, however, he besieged Dublin. He was confident of his ability to starve the city into submission. Indeed, starvation was his only hope, because Gaelic Ireland knew nothing of siege engines. His confidence was shared by Strongbow. In a move that Henry II could only regard as treasonous, he offered to submit to O'Connor – thus betraying his feudal obligation to Henry – in return for keeping the throne of Leinster. Instead, O'Connor offered only the three towns. Strongbow rejected this paltry offer and resolved on a sally.

It was a desperate gambler's throw. In the afternoon, the least likely time of day, the besieged garrison charged forth, catching the Gaelic army by surprise. Indeed, it literally caught the high king with his clothes off for he was bathing in the Liffey at the key moment. The result was a demoralizing rout for the besiegers and the capture of such booty and supplies as to sustain the besieged indefinitely. O'Connor withdrew. This success helped to bring some key Gaelic lords in the midlands over to Strongbow's side. O'Connor was weakened both materially and in prestige.

Having won his victory, Strongbow now needed to mend his fences with Henry. The king did not trust him, nor did he like him. Nonetheless, business is business. When Strongbow presented himself before Henry in the English West Country – the elaborate preparations for the king's journey to Ireland were now in full swing – Henry accepted his submission and granted him the kingdom of Leinster as a fief but not the three towns, which he wished to retain to the crown. Thus Strongbow had to settle for something less than he had acquired in arms. He was glad to do so, for he had little alternative and the king's patience with him – short enough to begin with, and rendered even shorter by the knowledge of his offer to O'Connor – was wearing dangerously thin.

Henry II landed at Waterford in October 1171 with the largest and most formidable army ever seen in Ireland. The whole armada comprised 400 ships. It was an irresistible force. This was also an invasion force. Its purpose was to secure the feudal allegiance, not just of the Norman beachhead, but of the Gaelic kingdoms as well, to the crown of England. This is the moment at which that crown inserts itself into the history of Ireland. It was to be a constant presence in most of the island until 1922 and is still present, in the early years of the twenty-first century, more than 800 years later, in the north-east.

6

COLONY

In the course of his six-month stay in Ireland, the king accepted the submission of the Anglo-Norman lords and of many Gaelic chiefs as well. Whether the latter understood the nature of feudal hierarchies may be doubted. It is as likely that, in submitting to Henry, they imagined that they were securing protection against the further advances of the colonists.

Henry made grants of territory to his leading barons. As we saw, Strongbow got Leinster. Hugh de Lacy, whom the king trusted, was awarded a huge territory in the modern counties of Meath, Westmeath and Cavan. This was a counterweight to Strongbow to the south. Rory O'Connor was not among the Gaelic lords who submitted but an arrangement was later reached between him and Henry in 1175. Henry claimed formal lordship over Leinster, Meath and the three towns. Rory was confirmed as king of Connacht and overlord of the areas not claimed by Henry. This concession was, however, subject to a tribute payable to Henry. This compact is known to history as the Treaty of Windsor. The fluid circumstances in Ireland made it impossible to enforce. Neither party could secure its side of the bargain. Rory could not deliver the chiefs, nor Henry the barons.

There was too much juggling for position among the

Norman colonists struggling to stake their claims to land, while the dynastic disputes among the Gaels, and the cattle raids and other traditional depredations, continued. As with the Vikings in the past, alliances were made across ethnic lines: it was not simply a matter of Norman versus Gael. Rory O'Connor gave his daughter in marriage to Hugh de Lacy. This fateful and confused series of events marks the first direct involvement of the English in Ireland. By 1177, that claim is raised a notch by the designation of Ireland as a separate lordship of the English crown, a status it was to retain until 1541. The title Lord of Ireland was bestowed upon the king's youngest son John, known as Lackland, who was nonetheless to succeed to the English throne in 1199.

In the same year, an impecunious baron called John de Courcy, originally from the English West Country, set out from Leinster bound for the unknown wilds of Ulster and established himself in modern Co. Down. After many vicissitudes, he overcame the king of the Ulaidh and took Downpatrick, believed to be the burial place of the national apostle. He was later chief governor of Ireland in the 1190s, married the daughter of the king of Man (which meant that he could resupply his coastal redoubt by sea), and was later displaced by the expansionist forces of de Lacy from the south. Still, this kind of energetic, ruthless conquistador was typical of the Norman urge for land and territory. The colonial presence that de Courcy established in east Ulster was to prove remarkably tenacious.

The Normans did not have everything their own way, suffering some defeats. These were due as much to topography as anything else, for their war machine was designed to conquer in open countryside where their archers and cavalry could be deployed to best effect. In bogs and swamps, or on rough upland, they were less effective. Moreover, the Gaels gradually found the means to neutralize much of the colonists' initial advantage. It is worth recalling that nearly all the contemporary sources that we have for this period are Norman, including

Giraldus Cambrensis (Gerald of Wales). His two contemporary documents, *Topographia Hiberniae* and *Expugnatio Hiberniae*, are invaluable accounts of the land and its conquest, but they were informed by an inveterate prejudice against the native Irish. Gerald never loses an opportunity to condemn their backwardness in military matters, politics, diet, dress, ecclesiastical affairs, hygiene and sex: he was an unapologetic critic of the Gaelic world. He was an ideologue, providing intellectual cover for the conquest. It suited his purpose to cast the Gaelic world in the worst possible light.

Reading Gerald, one would wonder how this world was capable of producing the scholarship, literature and music that distinguished it. Yet he stands at the head of a consistent tradition that accompanied every stage in the English conquest of Ireland down to the seventeenth century. An English or Scottish newcomer could always be found to anathematize the natives, to represent them as backward and savage and requiring redemption at the hands of a superior and more advanced culture. This consistent assertion of a civilizing mission runs like a leitmotif through the centuries of English writing about its Irish colony. It is not possible for the modern reader to judge whether this constantly repeated theme was pure prejudice employed as ideological justification for conquest or whether it had any objective documentary merit. Each reader must decide according to their general predisposition.

The Normans built. Their imposing stone castles, of which Hugh de Lacy's at Trim was the greatest, asserted their territorial control and were impregnable to Gaelic arms. All across the rich limestone land of the south-east, and in eastern Ulster, these mighty structures, vastly more formidable than anything imagined – let alone seen – in Ireland hitherto, were the physical manifestation of the conquest. In Dublin, the city stood secure after Rory O'Connor's failure in 1175. The walls were augmented and strengthened. Dublin Castle was built in the early thirteenth century, standing astride the ridge on the rising ground just south of the river. Although much added to in later centuries, it remained on the same site. The principal medieval survivals in the Castle complex are the Record and Bermingham Towers. It remained the centre and symbol of English royal power in Dublin until 1922.

The lifeblood of Norman Dublin was trade and manufacture. That meant the introduction of the guild system to the city. Merchant or trade guilds were associations formed by the practitioners of various occupations for mutual protection and the maintenance of standards. They combined the functions of primitive trade unions and producers' monopolies. Unless a person held membership of the relevant guild, he could not practise the trade concerned. Membership of the early Dublin guilds was confined to 'persons of English name and blood', thus further emphasizing ethnic exclusivity. This latter prescription was flexibly interpreted, because the Dublin guild merchant roll listed members not just of English provenance but from continental Europe as well. But the bottom line was: no Gaels.

The two cathedrals of Christ Church and St Patrick's stood within a mile of each other, the former within the city walls, the latter without. Christ Church was originally a Viking establishment dating from 1038, St Patrick's a collegiate foundation built by Archbishop John Comyn and dedicated in 1192. Built on the site of a Patrician well on what was then an island in the River Poddle, it was raised to cathedral status in 1213 by Archbishop Henry de Londres following a dispute with Christ Church.

By the early thirteenth century, the colonists had settled much of Leinster and Munster. Connacht was a marchland, endlessly contested although the de Burgos established a consistent presence west of the Shannon and eventually drove all the way to the Atlantic. Richard de Burgo was confirmed as king of Connacht in 1234. Galway was an uncompromisingly Norman walled town. Most of Ulster, outside the eastern coastal enclave, was still solidly Gaelic although at its apogee the colony pressed hard on the lands of the O'Neill (as we shall refer to the Uí Néill from this point on) in the centre of the province. In the settled lands, King John created the beginnings of an Irish administration. English law was introduced and a justiciar, or chief governor, was appointed. The king himself visited in 1210, spending nine weeks in the country and enjoying a military triumph that secured the integrity of the colony. The royal writ now ran in the greater part of the island. The first Irish parliament sat at Castledermot, in south Kildare, in 1264. A network of inland and coastal towns, developed by the Norman magnates, facilitated the spread of commerce. New Ross, Drogheda and Athenry all date from this period. Kilkenny Castle was started in the early thirteenth century as the centre of the vast south-eastern landholdings of William Marshall, the most powerful of the early magnates who had married Strongbow's daughter, Isabella. The medieval city that developed in its shadow became, and remains, one of the more important inland centres in the country.

The population of Dublin grew rapidly and by the first half of the thirteenth century more than half the inhabitants lived outside the walls. The city pushed west towards Kilmainham, north into Oxmantown and south towards St Patrick's. Some suburban areas without the walls were denominated as Liberties, that is palatinate jurisdictions under the rule of local magnates to whom specific privileges were granted. These included the administration of justice and other functions normally exercised by the municipal authorities. There were a number of such Liberties in the early Dublin suburbs, of which the most prominent were those of St Sepulchre – granted to the archbishop – and of St Thomas Court and Donore which belonged to the abbey of St Thomas. Indeed, the suburbs themselves tended to cluster around powerful religious foundations.

The economic boom of the thirteenth century enabled conspicuous displays of wealth, none more obvious than the endowment of religious houses. The new orders of friars – Franciscans, Augustinians and Dominicans – were introduced from the continent and generally established themselves in or close to the new towns.

By the close of the thirteenth century, the Normans had established themselves on more than 60 per cent of all Irish land, including nearly all the fertile and productive land. These land holdings were governed by English feudal law and acknowledged the ultimate, if remote, authority of the English king. The conquest was not complete, but it was an unambiguous success. At its margins, it had nearly all the forward momentum. These successes were to be overturned in the fourteenth century.

The fourteenth century was a disastrous time in Europe. One distinguished historian, Barbara Tuchman, has written that 'its disorders cannot be traced to any one cause; they were the hoofprints of more than the four horsemen of St John's vision, which had now become seven – plague, war, taxes, brigandage, bad government, insurrection, and schism in the Church.'

In Ireland, the headline story in the fourteenth century is the shrinking of the colony and the revival of the Gaelic lordships. Many factors contributed to this, but the early weakening of English royal authority was more important than most. After the thunderous reign of the bellicose Edward I (1272–1307), he was succeeded by his son Edward II. He was unable to consolidate his father's gains, especially in Scotland where the old king had quite spectacularly snuffed out Scots independence in 1296. Yet here was a kingdom that was a vast distance from London, whose independence had been a fact of life for 500 years. Although it had never held all of what is now Scotland, the kingdom of Scots had consistently been the biggest political unit since the ninth century. Its heartland and traditions were secure; its royal succession had been orderly for the most part. Robert Bruce regained Scottish independence by defeating the army of Edward II at Bannockburn in 1314.

The following year, Bruce's younger brother Edward invaded Ireland, landing at Larne and marching south to capture Dundalk. In 1316, he was proclaimed as high king, an empty gesture. He spent the next three years to-ing and fro-ing across Ireland in a campaign of mounting incoherence. He drew less support from Gaelic kings than he had expected, for they combined caution with internal division. The fact that the Bruce campaign in Ireland coincided with a three-year famine across north-west Europe compounded the potential misery. The famine is estimated to have killed one in ten of the population of Europe.

Bruce came closest to success in February 1317 when he presented himself in the western approaches to Dublin – in the region of modern Castleknock – with the clear intention of capturing it. The response was decisive, ruthless and perhaps a bit panicky. To block his approach, the walls were strengthened and the suburbs burned. This was no small undertaking. The suburbs were more populous than the compact walled centre. They generated more tax revenue for the municipal authority. The retreat of such a number of citizens into the already crowded walled city must have created all the pressures that one can readily imagine in a medieval siege. Sanitation alone would have been a nightmare.

But the great fire did the job in the short run. Bruce hesitated. And as he did, an English force under Sir Roger Mortimer landed at Youghal and began to push towards Dublin. Bruce decided not to besiege the city. Instead he withdrew, to continue what remained of his campaign. The end came at the Battle of Faughart, near Dundalk, in 1318. Bruce had come full circle. He died in the battle.

The Bruce invasion was the clearest evidence that the highwater mark of the Norman colony was in the past. Gradually, colonists began to assume Gaelic customs, to learn the language and to adopt Irish usages. They even substituted Irish law for the common law, either in whole or in part. In modern parlance, they began to go native. This tendency was remarked on by all contemporaries and was a source of endless anxiety to the colonial leadership. The parliament of 1297 passed a statute condemning the 'degeneracy' of those colonists who adopted Irish fashions. It was the first of many such legislative plaints (legal statements of grounds of complaint), the most famous of them the Statutes of Kilkenny of 1366. The process revealed two things that coexisted uneasily with each other. First, there was genuine antagonism and cultural hostility between the colonists and the Gaels, and it was a two-way street. Second, and notwithstanding that, life on the Irish marchlands required the give and take that facilitated porous cultural exchange, however much purists might deplore it.

Why this reversal after the self-assured expansion of the previous century? First, there was the tyranny of numbers. The colonists were few relative to the size of the Gaelic population and had been weakened by Edward I's raising of a number of armies from the colony to fight his incessant wars. Moreover, the Gaelic succession laws tended to throw up ruthless and capable warlords. There were always plausible candidates to succeed a fallen king: it was easier to defeat the kings than the kingdoms. Nor was it simply a matter of Gael versus colonist and vice versa. There were internecine quarrels within the two communities, which were often more vicious than anything that passed between them. Many of the Norman marcher lords were effectively beyond the reach of the king's government in Dublin, and very pleased to be – behaving like palatinate hidalgos and dispensing frontier justice as circumstance allowed and demanded. One of the most notorious, Maurice FitzThomas, the first earl of Desmond, was a recklessly lawless and violent desperado, but it did not stop him from ending up as the king's justiciar.

By the middle of the fourteenth century, all of Connacht except Galway and its environs and all of Ulster except Carrickfergus and the Lecale area of south-east Co. Down, with its huge castle, had been recaptured by the Gaelic kings. The Norman colony was diminished accordingly, focusing ever more on the rich limestone country of the midlands, east and south. In this regard, two branches of the FitzGerald family gradually grew in power, possessions and influence. The Kildare branch was centred in the modern county of that name, with strongholds at Maynooth and Kilkea. The Desmond (*Deas Mumhan*: south Munster) branch consolidated its earldom in a great arc that ran from west Kerry to east Cork and took in some of the richest agricultural land in the country. Between them, controlling the rich river valleys of the southeast, lay the earldom of Ormond, in the control of the Butler family, who succeeded to the lands of William Marshall when his line died out. (Failure to produce male heirs was a recurring problem for the colonists.) This shrinking of the colony was relentless through the fourteenth and fifteenth centuries.

Worse again, from the government's point of view, was the shrinking of the space in which the royal writ and the common law ran. By the 1480s, this area had contracted to a pale (an area in which local laws can be applied) surrounding Dublin, in a loop that went inland from the Wicklow hills to Trim or thereabouts before meeting the coast again around Dundalk. Outside this English Pale, there was a mixture of magnate jurisdiction, such as that of the FitzGeralds and Butlers, and Gaelic kingdoms.

The Genoese trading port of Caffa (modern Feodosiya) in the Crimea is about as far as one can go from Ireland and still be in Europe. It was here that the deadly plague bacillus first announced itself in Europe in 1347. It had probably been carried along the Silk Road from China and central Asia. It was better known as bubonic plague – because its physical symptoms were the presence of buboes or swellings, generally in the armpits and the groin. Most people who contracted it died within a week, which made it a terrifying presence. It was carried along trade routes by rats which transmitted it to humans. This made port cities especially vulnerable to the pandemic.

From Caffa, it was carried west by fleeing Genoese traders who introduced it to Italy. From there it spread like a bush fire across the continent. It is estimated to have killed about a quarter of the total population of Europe – perhaps as many as twenty-five million people – although its effects were generally more lethal in the Mediterranean lands than in the north and west. Still, casualty rates in England are estimated at about 20 per cent of the entire population and there is little reason to doubt that the Irish figure was very different.

The populations of Europe were in a poor condition to resist. The climate changes – colder, wetter winters – which were typical of the early fourteenth century had reduced crop yields and contributed to the famine of 1315–18. This was a classic subsistence crisis arising from a preceding period of economic expansion. Populations had grown in the thirteenth century; now the climate had turned and famine was the consequence. Even when the famine passed, nutrition levels generally were poor in the first half of the century. People's systems were ill equipped to deal with any plague, let alone one as virulent as this.

The Black Death reached Ireland in August 1348. In a malignant example of medieval globalization, it had taken barely a year to travel the trade routes from one end of Europe to the other. By Christmas that year, it is estimated to have killed 14,000 people in the city of Dublin alone. Its effect on towns was more severe than in the countryside, meaning that its devastation fell more heavily on Norman colonies than the Gaelic kingships. It is impossible to estimate the total mortality, but scholarly estimates reckon that at least a third of the Irish population died.

7

KILDARE

With this mixture of demographic disaster and Gaelic revival, not to mention the ever-contracting Pale, one might wonder where the king's government was in all this. Ireland was wondering just this, as there had been no effort on behalf of the English crown to reconquer the country, or to tackle the autonomy of the marcher lords, or to recover the gains made by the Gaelic kings.

The fact was that the kings of England had bigger fish to fry. Ireland was not that important. In the century after the Black Death, the English crown found itself fighting that series of campaigns in France known as the Hundred Years War. It arose from the crown's claim to about a third of modern France, one that went back to the Plantagenets. The claims of the English crown were opposed by the emerging kingdom of France, pushing outwards from its heartland in the Île-de-France. Eventually, it was to result in total victory for the French in 1453. But in the meantime, it was the compelling overseas preoccupation of the English kings.

To be fair, the crown did not completely ignore Ireland, and spent considerable resources – drawn from English taxation – on military support for the Irish colony. But the crown could neither pacify the country nor reconquer it nor turn it into a source of profit. It was the usual problem of too little and too late.

The progressive decline of the colony, together with its mutation in the areas beyond the Pale into a series of marcher lordships, continued steadily from 1350 to the 1530s. We have already noted the alarm expressed in the Statutes of Kilkenny (1366), a series of legislative prohibitions which attempted to arrest the 'degeneracy' – i.e. Gaelicization – of the colony. The necessity for the legislation was evidence of the problem it purported to address. It enjoined the colonists to speak English, to ride their horses in the English fashion, to use English personal names and to have recourse only to the common law. It forbade marriage between colonists and natives. All these prohibitions were ignored. The tide of Gaelicization was flowing too fast. Given that nearly all of Ireland was now outside the Pale, the purity demanded by the Statutes was simply impractical. Two communities thrown together were inevitably going to borrow from each other, if only to facilitate the smooth running of social life.

The Anglo-Irish, as we may now call members of the colony, had always deplored the Gaelic practice of 'coign and livery', whereby soldiers were quartered on helpless farmers. But gradually the practice was adopted by crown troops themselves. Their pay was often disastrously in arrears and they employed summary justice in order to compel bed and board. This adoption of a despised Gaelic custom – prompted by terrible necessity – is a good illustration of the permeability of the two cultures.

In the late fourteenth century, the Pale itself came under pressure, with Gaelic tribes from the Wicklow hills immediately to the south of the city attacking the suburbs. The chief instigator of these raids was Art MacMurrough Kavanagh, a lineal descendant of Diarmait Mac Murchada and, like his ancestor, king of Leinster. The revival of the title was itself evidence of the Gaelic resurgence. MacMurrough Kavanagh assumed the throne in the 1370s and was a thorn in the flesh of the colony until he died forty years later. He was one of the first, but no means the last, of the Gaelic lords to exact 'black rent' from the more vulnerable margins of the colony. This was a polite term for blackmail, protection money or frontier taxation. He was even able to press the city of Dublin for this tribute, and his harassing of its southern boundaries was a constant reminder of the threat he posed.

Leaders of the colony had made repeated pleas to the king, either to come himself or to send a formidable force under a capable general to address the situation. Tellingly, it was due to a respite in the French wars that Richard II felt able to come to Ireland in 1394. He stood at the head of a formidable army of 5,000 men, by far the largest fighting force seen in Ireland in the medieval period. It had the desired effect, and in short order. Various Gaelic kings, including MacMurrough Kavanagh, submitted to him. But the new order foundered partly because of the cynicism of the Anglo-Irish magnates, who used the relative calm to expand their own lands at the expense of the Gaelic lords. This ensured that the Gaels promptly returned to their old ways, although no doubt many were glad to do so. The king came again in 1399 but this second expedition was cut short by the need to return to England to deal with the Bolingbroke rebellion. This he failed to do; he lost his crown and his life and Bolingbroke became Henry IV.

As the fifteenth century advanced, the progressive 'degeneration' of the Anglo-Irish community had the effect of creating a hybrid society in the marcher lands beyond the Pale. There were marriage and military alliances made across the divide, with the result that the greatest of the Anglo-Irish magnates established a web of social networks with reciprocal obligations over a wide territory. This did not completely collapse the distinction between colonist and Gael – the gap narrowed but never closed, and the Anglo-Irish rejoiced in their difference. The marcher lordships were effectively independent of the crown, but the ancestral tug of loyalty to that crown never disappeared. No such loyalty, residual or otherwise, was felt in the Gaelic world. The fifteenth century, therefore, comprises three cultures coexisting, overlapping, colliding and melding: the 'land of peace' within the Pale; the 'land of war' under the Anglo-Irish palatinate marcher lordships; and the Gaelic world, mainly in the west and north, which increasingly came to seem antique and anachronistic – and would seem utterly so to the horrified 'New English' of the next century.

In the long series of English dynastic struggles known as the Wars of the Roses, both sides – the houses of York and Lancaster – welcomed the support of the great Anglo-Irish families. The three dominant families in the marcher lands were the two branches of the FitzGeralds, those of the earldoms of Kildare and Desmond, and the Butlers of Ormond. The FitzGeralds, both branches, were Yorkists; the Butlers, Lancastrians. In 1461, the Yorkists triumphed in the person of King Edward IV. He appointed the earl of Desmond as chief governor of Ireland, a strange choice because the Kildare FitzGeralds were geographically and culturally closer to the business of government than the more Gaelicized Desmonds.

Desmond proved to be a distinctly mixed bag. He permitted the spread of some Gaelic practices – most notoriously, coign and livery – into areas previously free of them. On the other hand, he came down hard on the Gaelic lords in the matter of black rent and made the communities remit equal sums to the Irish treasury. Fatally for him, however, he was defeated and captured by the Gaelic O'Connors in the midlands in 1466. He was replaced by an Englishman, Sir John Tiptoft, a man of humanist learning, wide administrative experience and a formidable reputation for violence against the English enemies of York. He convened a parliament at Drogheda and, in what appears to have been a well-rehearsed coup, attainted (that is, passed a judgment of death or outlawry upon) both branches of the FitzGeralds.

What happened next was without precedent and shocked the whole country. Tiptoft had the Earl of Desmond summarily executed. The late earl's brother, Garret, went on the rampage north into Leinster with a menacing army of gallowglass (ferocious Scots mercenaries, a key feature of the age whose arms had played an important part in the Gaelic revival). Kildare was released from prison and gradually appeased Garret, but the incident was a watershed. Tiptoft reversed his position, undid Kildare's attainder, and effectively acknowledged that Kildare's great influence was needed to pacify a situation that threatened to run out of control.

With Desmond neutralized and Ormond in the Lancaster camp, the house of Kildare now rose towards its eminence. It acquired the chief governorship in 1470, lost it briefly and then was then threatened with having to share it with another Englishman. All these partial expedients failed, and by 1478 Gearóid Mór FitzGerald, 8th earl of Kildare, was chief governor. He might as well have been called prince of Ireland, so complete was his authority.

The FitzGeralds of Kildare were enormously rich and well connected, related by birth and marriage to a huge network of Anglo-Irish and Gaelic families alike. The rule of Gearóid Mór, the Great Earl, was the high-water mark of Anglo-Irish magnate power. His support in Ireland was such that he could defy an early attempt by the king to appoint an Englishman in his place: the king backed down in the face of relentless opposition in Ireland. He calculated that a stable administration could best be provided by Kildare's ability to command the loyalty of his clients and followers, who would otherwise be a chronically disruptive element. With a few exceptions, this rule was followed by the English crown until the crisis of the 1530s. So successful was Kildare in securing this status that he was effectively able to bequeath the office of chief governor to his son on his death in 1513.

A Yorkist, Kildare was able to survive the final Lancastrian triumph in 1485. In that year, Henry Tudor established the dynasty that bore his name by overthrowing the last York king, Richard III. This might have given hope to the earls of

Ormond, traditional supporters of the red rose, but Kildare endured. No one could possibly have realized that the Tudors would occupy the throne undisturbed for over a century: there was good reason to suppose that Henry VII's reign might be brief. This might explain Kildare's uncharacteristic endorsement of two Yorkist imposters.

The first of these, Lambert Simnel, appeared in 1487, purporting to be the earl of Warwick and legitimate heir to the throne. The Duchess of Burgundy, sister of the last Yorkist king, Edward IV, had schooled the boy in the role. The real Warwick – who was a prisoner in the Tower of London – had a more legitimate claim to the throne than Henry VII. The obvious ploy behind all this was to effect a Yorkist restoration. The Simnel plot was so well organized and funded, with mercenary troops sent in support, that the Irish colony was convinced. Simnel was feted in Dublin by Kildare and other Anglo-Irish magnates, traditionally allies of York, and crowned king of England in Christ Church cathedral. The Dublin mint issued coinage in the name of the new 'king'. A council was summoned by Kildare in the name of Edward VI and a royal seal was issued. The pretender then sailed to England to press his claim, sustained by an army provided by Kildare. He was defeated and lived out his life ingloriously as a kitchen scullion in the royal household. The incident proved two points: first, that the whole royal succession was so fluid and uncertain that the magnates placed little faith in the security of the new dynasty; second, that Kildare's position in Ireland was so solid that he was able to survive even this treasonous effrontery.

In 1491, however, another Yorkist imposter turned up in Cork, claiming to be Richard, duke of York, who had in fact been one of the princes murdered in the Tower of London by Richard III in 1483. The imposter's name was Perkin Warbeck. As with Simnel, the Duchess of Burgundy was behind this plot, assisted by the kings of France and Scotland, each of them pleased to make trouble for the English crown. The Holy Roman Emperor himself, Maximilian I, even lent his support.

It is worth emphasizing this point, because it underlines the seriousness of these threats to the Tudors. Simnel and Warbeck have often been treated as ludicrous figures of fun. That was a judgement formed with the perfect hindsight afforded by their failures. They were in fact a deadly threat to the dynasty, with its uncertain legitimacy. Their impostures had the active support of some exceptionally powerful and influential people.

Warbeck found an ally in the house of Desmond, the other branch of the FitzGeralds. It was later claimed that Kildare had given his support to the pretender, something the earl hotly denied. Not everyone believed him. This time Henry VII took no chances. He sent the illegitimate son of the earl of Ormond to Ireland with an army, designed to place himself in the traditional Ormond position between Kildare and Desmond. Warbeck left Ireland in early 1492. He was to return again in 1495 before finally trying to raise the Yorkist standard in Cornwall in 1497. He was defeated and hanged.

In the meantime, Henry had finally had enough of Kildare for the time being and dismissed him in June 1492. He was eventually replaced by an Englishman, Sir Edward Poynings, who was furnished with a small army in the hope of pacifying Ireland once and for all. As ever, it was too little. Poynings is best remembered for the law that bore his name, passed by the Irish parliament at his bidding in 1494. The act stated that no Irish parliament could convene without royal consent, nor any bill be introduced there unless it had prior approval of the king and his council. Poynings would have been astonished to discover that this legislation would become a constitutional cause célèbre in the eighteenth century. Its purpose was immediate and simple: to ensure that there could be no repetition of the Simnel coronation at the behest of an Irish parliament acting unilaterally.

Kildare was back as lord deputy in 1496, having briefly been under arrest the previous year. As ever, he simply could not be excluded from the picture for long. In his absence, his followers had threatened a Geraldine rebellion and relations between the Geraldine and Ormond factions had brought Ireland to the point of civil war. Once more, it was clear that Kildare alone had the authority to stabilize the situation. Moreover, Henry VII – always of necessity parsimonious – had spent huge sums of money in his brief experiment with direct rule. He simply could not afford any more of that luxury.

Gearóid Mór FitzGerald, 8th earl of Kildare, was now the undisputed ruler of Ireland. He survived the succession of the young king Henry VIII to the English throne in 1509, being confirmed in his office by the new king the following year. When the Great Earl died three years later, the post of lord deputy passed seamlessly to his son, Gearóid Óg, the 9th earl. Geraldine power was now so entrenched that it passed, as if by royal succession, from father to son. In fact, it was the new king in England who accomplished the fall of the house of Kildare.

8

HENRY VIII

The young King Henry VIII was England's – and Ireland's – first experience of a Renaissance prince. He was the younger son of Henry VII but became his heir on the death of his brother Arthur in 1502. He was the first English monarch to be influenced by the Renaissance, that revival of classical and secular learning that marked a break with the overwhelmingly religious sensibility of the medieval era. The new learning placed an emphasis on individual consciousness, intellectual enquiry, the beginnings of the modern scientific method and humanist scepticism. It also coincided with the great age of European exploration: America had only been discovered seventeen years before Henry ascended the throne in 1509. It was only eleven years since Vasco da Gama had sailed around the Cape of Good Hope to open up India and the Far East to European commerce. In the course of Henry's reign, Ferdinand Magellan would complete the first circumnavigation of the globe.

What Henry was to achieve in church and state was a revolution from above. There was a new theory of kingship abroad in Europe in which the personal glorification of the king was asserted with unprecedented emphasis. It was all of a piece with the Renaissance ideal of the autonomous individual, best expressed in the new portraiture with its isolation of the unique physical and psychological features of the sitter. In governance, it implied a movement towards enhanced royal authority in centralized royal states. This meant unitary kingdoms and the weakening of regional magnate power. France was the most conspicuous example of this new development: Henry's contemporary François I was the *beau idéal* of the Renaissance monarch, flamboyant in the physical display of his power. The fullest expression of the process would not be seen until the seventeenth century and the doctrine of the divine right of kings, but the movement towards the integral royal state was already under way in the early 1500s. Henry VIII wanted to move his kingdom in the same direction. This meant clipping the wings of great magnate palatines such as the Percys in Northumberland and the Kildares in Ireland.

At first, just like his father, he found that he could not do without the Kildares. He first tried to do so in 1519, when he summoned Gearóid Óg to London, held him under conditions of close confinement and supplanted him as lord deputy in Ireland by Thomas Howard, earl of Surrey. Once again, an English king put his own man in place finally to subdue the Irish only to discover that the resources, both military and financial, required to do the job properly were way beyond the reach of his purse. Kildare returned to Ireland in 1523 and to the lord deputyship in 1524. Normal service, it seems, had been resumed.

It was one thing for Henry to hanker after a more assertive and integrated monarchy. It was another thing to find the means to achieve it. As Surrey had proved in Ireland, a wholesale conquest of the country would have been ruinously expensive. He had told the king that a ten-year plan to settle Ireland properly would have entailed a huge castle building programme and a standing army of anything from 3,000 to 6,000 men. Similar, if less acute, problems faced him in the north of England. It was difficult for an impecunious monarch to project his power as he would wish in every corner of his realm.

The means of asserting royal power was found accidentally

through religion. The German religious reformation, prompted by Martin Luther's pinning of his ninety-five theses on the door of Wittenberg cathedral in 1517, tripped off an intellectual firestorm that was to fracture Latin Christendom beyond repair. At first, England was unaffected: indeed, Henry himself was so staunch in support of Rome that he was awarded the honorific title *Fidei defensor* (Defender of the Faith) for an anti-Lutheran tract of 1521 that he may or may not have written but for which he claimed credit. There had, however, been a persistent undercurrent of rigorist reforming zeal in the English church. It went back at least as far as the Lollards, the name given to the followers of John Wyclif, a radical Oxford theologian of the late fourteenth century. The Lollards deplored luxury in the church, denied the clergy's right to hold property and questioned the authority of the Pope.

This underground current in English religious life sprang to the surface in the wake of the Reformation, which echoed many of its concerns. In 1526, the publication of William Tyndale's great vernacular translation of the Bible – the linguistic forbear of the Authorized Version – caused a panic in English church circles. Tributary streams were converging: religious dissent, scepticism born of humanism, theological turmoil in the wake of the Reformation and the democratization of the Bible. All this might have been contained had it not got caught up in Henry VIII's marriage difficulties.

His queen, Catherine of Aragon, had suffered a series of miscarriages and had only given birth to one daughter, the future Queen Mary, in 1516. He wished to divorce her and marry the younger (and hopefully more fruitful) Anne Boleyn, whom he genuinely loved. Henry is often caricatured as an old goat, and he may well have been, but he had good reason to fret over the succession. His father's legitimacy to the throne had been challenged often enough, and the memory of the chaotic Wars of the Roses was a recent one. The birth of a healthy male heir was essential to the security of the Tudor dynasty.

Normally, a divorce would not have been a problem. The

Pope understood these dynastic imperatives and would, in the
ordinary way of things, have given Henry the necessary dispensation. Unfortunately, in 1527 when the matter came to a head,
Pope Clement VII was a prisoner of the Habsburg Emperor
Charles V, nephew of Catherine of Aragon. Following the
notorious Sack of Rome by imperial troops, the Pope was
incarcerated in the Castel Sant'Angelo. Charles did not wish to
see his aunt humiliated, so he encouraged the Pope to dig in his
heels with Henry. The consequence was the break with Rome
and the establishment of the royal supremacy in the years
1533–6. Thus was born the Church of England, with the
Church of Ireland following suit in 1537. Although this was
not a theological break – Henry died still believing himself a
Catholic – it laid the indispensable foundation for the
Reformation in both islands.

The royal supremacy in the church was all of a piece with
the drive towards the centralizing royal state. In Ireland, the
earl of Kildare began to feel the heat. In 1530, he was nominally
replaced by Sir William Skeffington, although Kildare was still
the real power in Ireland. In acknowledgement of this Kildare
was reappointed in 1532. It seemed like another of those irri-
tating interludes, as with Poynings in 1494 and Surrey in 1520,
where the English monarch had to relearn the lesson that only
the Kildare interest could keep Ireland in some sort of order. In
1534, however – the year that Henry was excommunicated by
Rome – Kildare was once more summoned to London.

Henry's chief minister, Thomas Cromwell, was already
intriguing against the Kildare interest and had allies in the Irish
Council in Dublin. Kildare left his son Thomas, Lord Offaly,
in charge back home with instructions to be wary of the Irish
Council and to ignore any instruction to go to London. Kildare
was in poor health when he travelled over as a result of gunshot
injuries previously sustained. Offaly, better known to history
as Silken Thomas, was able to maintain contact with his father.
Kildare gave him regular advice, although also informing him
that he had been forbidden to return to Ireland. In the

meantime, the summons to London duly arrived and with it the belief on Thomas's part that his father had been disempowered by Henry.

What followed was the famous revolt of Silken Thomas. In the words of one historian, 'Thomas was not the immature and headstrong fop of legend: the silken epithet was a piece of bardic whimsy.' In association with his advisers and the traditional network of Kildare allies, he was attempting to demonstrate that Ireland could not be ruled without the cooperation and support of the traditional Kildare power base. Still, his defiance of the king went beyond anything that the Kildare faction had ever attempted previously. They were soon to discover that Henry and Thomas Cromwell were not men to be defied.

On 11 June 1534, Silken Thomas and a retinue of over 100 horsemen burst in upon a meeting of the Irish Council in St Mary's Abbey, on the north bank of the Liffey. He resigned as vice-deputy, handing over the ceremonial sword of office to the lord chancellor. He then withdrew to Oxmantown, where he had troops billeted. This action was taken on the direct advice of his father and with the support of his advisers in Ireland. When word of this action reached London, Kildare was promptly clapped in the Tower, where he died – whether from the injuries previously sustained or from poison is unknown – in September.

What made the rebellion of Silken Thomas different was the religious issue. Thomas denounced Henry as an apostate and called for allegiance to the Pope and emperor, to whom he sent emissaries soliciting aid for his cause. He also called for the expulsion of all Englishmen from the lordship of Ireland. This led to the capture of the archbishop of Dublin, John Alen, who was indeed English and who was duly murdered.

This was a direct challenge to the Henrician settlement in both church and state. In October 1534, Henry sent Skeffington to Ireland with a substantial army and with formidable artillery. Thomas, now 10th earl of Kildare, made an alliance with the O'Briens of Thomond and sought Spanish aid. Almost none was forthcoming. The result was the total defeat of Silken Thomas and the destruction of Kildare power for ever. Their hitherto impregnable castle at Maynooth fell to the royal guns (and to treachery: the chief guard was bribed). Silken Thomas and five of his uncles were shipped to London and executed. The Kildare power was broken and their vast land holding forfeited to the crown. It was the end of the Middle Ages.

The fall of the house of Kildare meant a fundamental change in the government of Ireland. Henry could not revert to magnate rule and there was nothing for it but to commit English governors to the task and supply them with the military means to enforce the law. The problems, as always, were money on the one hand and the incompleteness of any victory on the other. Lord Leonard Grey, appointed chief governor in 1536, was a believer in main force and had some genuine successes before falling foul of King Henry's ever-growing paranoia and going to the scaffold in 1540. His successor, Sir Anthony St Leger, pursued a different policy, known to history as surrender and regrant.

This was a more emollient approach to Ireland. The basic transaction involved Gaelic lords surrendering their lands to the king, who would then grant them back to the lords under the usages of the common law. In return for the lords recognizing the king's sovereignty over them and over Ireland, they would acquire the full protection of the law and a royal charter confirming the grant of the new lordship by the crown. They had to acknowledge the king as their lawful sovereign from whom they would receive a peerage, renouncing their ancient Irish title in return. They undertook to attend parliament and to abjure the jurisdiction of the Pope in church or state. They also had to adopt the English language and customs and to encourage their spread through their territories.

What all this implied in law and logic was a single sovereign political entity under the king. The ambiguity of magnate rule and palatinate jurisdiction, together with the indulgence previously shown to Irish law, were all to be swept away. In 1541, Ireland was declared a kingdom, no longer a mere lordship. It was united to the crown of England but was otherwise regarded as a separate entity with its own Houses of Lords and Commons and its own courts system. Its people were to be regarded as one, subjects of the king without regard to ethnic origins. This, at least, was the theory and the aspiration. The reality would prove more intractable.

An essential plank of the Henrician revolution was the church settlement. The Church of Ireland was established as the state church under the king as its supreme head. This was accomplished in parliament with relatively little fuss. Likewise, the dissolution of the monasteries and the friaries was not as contentious as it might have been: they had long been regarded as corrupt. Anglo-Irish lords, as well as English parvenus (but not Gaels), profited from the confiscated lands. There was unease, to be sure, but it was reserved for attempts to enforce doctrinal change. The question of authority was not the source of dissent. That of doctrine was much more material.

The Henrician reforms were not themselves driven by doctrinal changes, but they inevitably embraced them. All those who wished for real church reform in England, whether drawing on old Lollard traditions or wishing to promote Reformation ideas, were naturally drawn to the new religious settlement. Although Henry died still thinking of himself as a Catholic, the move to Protestantism was already advanced in England. It did, however, meet with violent resistance. As early as 1536, the north of England rebelled in the name of the old religion in the movement known as the Pilgrimage of Grace. It was the most serious challenge to royal authority in the whole of the sixteenth century. Interestingly, in view of the centrality of religious difference in the future history of Ireland, there were no such rebellions and no martyrs in the early days of the Reformation in the smaller kingdom.

It is no accident that the Pilgrimage of Grace was a northern phenomenon. In general, Protestantism appealed more readily to urban, literate, relatively well-to-do people. Distance conduced to conservatism. And so it was in Ireland, as the leaders of the Anglo-Irish colony gradually retained their allegiance to the Pope and the Catholic Church and, for the greater part, did not embrace the Reformation. From now on, we may refer to this community by the name by which they are best known to history: the Old English.

The three social and ethnic groups that now began to emerge in Ireland were the Old English, descendants of the original Norman colony; the Old Irish, or Gaelic population; and the New English, recent arrivals (and new ones were coming all the time as the sixteenth century wore on) who were adventurers, administrators and new colonists. The first two groups retained their allegiance to Catholicism. The New English were not just Protestant, but disproportionately Puritan. There would be no union of hearts and minds between the Old Irish and the New English, despite the aspirations incarnate in the policy of surrender and regrant. The religious quarrel simply ran too deep: the division between Catholic and Protestant was to place all of European Christendom on an intermittent war footing for over a hundred years. It was not possible for Ireland to escape the infection, once allegiances were declared.

The Old English were the ones caught in the middle, loyal subjects of the king who nonetheless declined to abjure their spiritual loyalty to the Pope. They were still the richest, most coherent community in Ireland, dominating the towns and holding most of the good land in the south and east of the island. They welcomed the Jesuit mission to Ireland – the first Jesuits arrived as early as 1542, shock troops of the Counter-Reformation, and a sure sign that, even at that early date, the doctrinal issue had been well and truly joined in Ireland. The Gaels, meanwhile, preferred the ministry of the Franciscan friars, which tended towards the gloomy spirituality of Spain. Where the Jesuits appealed to apologetics and reason, as befitted a highly educated and literate order, the friars focused on an often dark spirituality. This difference of emphasis within the emerging Irish Catholic community overlay and gave emphasis to its twin ethnic constituents. This was to be important in the seventeenth century.

Why did the Reformation fail in Ireland? First, there is the question of language. There was no Irish language translation of the Bible available until 1603. (The contrast with Wales is instructive: the earliest Welsh translation of the *Book of Common Prayer* dates from 1567.) Indeed, the fonts required to print in Irish did not exist and had to be specially cut. Even then, the 1603 translation was of the New Testament only. A translation of the Old Testament, based on the Authorized Version, did not appear until the 1630s. In a country where Irish was still the vernacular of the great majority, this absence alone subverted the possibility of a mass conversion. In addition, kinship ties between Gaelic lords and the clergy were very close, and antique irregularities in the Gaelic church still persisted, much to the impotent fury of reformers. These included married clergy and hereditary succession to benefices. One sixteenth-century bishop of Clogher was eulogized on his death as 'a very gem of purity and a turtle dove of chastity', this despite his leaving behind at least fifteen children.

The conservatism of the Gaelic church in doctrinal matters mirrored the conservatism of the Gaelic lords in the secular world. Despite the theory of surrender and regrant, Gaelic titles, succession rites and inauguration practices still continued as before with chiefs living in parallel worlds simultaneously. Thus 'The O'Neill', the traditional title for the scion of the greatest house in the Gaelic world and bearer of its most ancient name, was simultaneously the earl of Tyrone.

The failure of the Reformation among the Old English is better explained by distance. Like many English recusant communities (Catholics who refused to attend Church of England services), their relative remoteness from the Protestant centre in the south of England is a factor. So was the early arrival of the Jesuits, although their immediate impact was not as great as it was later to prove. The appointment of Englishmen to clerical office under the new regime was a source of bitter resentment among the Old English, who regarded themselves as the Irish elite. On the other hand, the existing clergy of the towns were now obliged by law to conduct services by the reformed rite, simply being reappointed under the auspices of the Church of Ireland without showing much evidence of theological conversion. It is not surprising that, in these circumstances, traditional observances crept back into use and reform was but thinly rooted. And in all this, there was the old problem of where the king's writ ran. Outside the Pale, it was impossible to enforce religious conformity completely. In the Old English parts of the island, there was some chance of success (not actually realized) but in Gaelic Ireland it was a lost cause from the start.

The failure of the Reformation in Ireland was arguably the most momentous single event in the island's history, for it has marked every major development to the present day. It meant that Ireland stood outside the standard European solution to the early religious wars, formulated at the Peace of Augsburg in 1555: *cuius regio, eius religio* – 'whose kingdom, his religion'. This meant that the king or prince could choose the confession of his choice and that allegiance would be binding on the population under his care. Ireland was part of the king's domain, a sister kingdom. Yet as England and Wales embraced Protestantism and Scotland redefined its nationality as a specifically Calvinist enclave, Ireland alone clung to the old religion.

9

RUPTURE

Henry VIII died in 1547 and was succeeded by his sickly son, Edward VI. He only survived six years on the throne before succumbing to tuberculosis at the age of sixteen: for most of his reign, his government was in the hands of regents. Of these, the dukes of Somerset and Northumberland were the most important. They were staunch reformers and under their direction the English Reformation really acquired momentum. This momentum was thrown into reverse by the young king's death because it brought his half-sister Mary, daughter of Catherine of Aragon, to the throne in 1553.

Mary was a Catholic. Not only that, she was married to Philip II of Spain, the most powerful Catholic prince in Europe and the man who, years later, would dispatch the Armada against her half-sister and successor Elizabeth. Mary had to overcome strenuous efforts by reformers to deny her the throne: her short reign was marked by an attempted Protestant counter-coup in the shape of Thomas Wyatt's rebellion. Unsurprisingly, this was centred on Kent whereas Mary's support was strongest in the recusant areas farthest from London. Ireland was among these regions, and the Old English of Kilkenny, among others, celebrated her accession to the throne as if it were a liberation.

Mary entered the demonology of English by her vigorous persecution of Protestants for heresy. John Foxe's *The Book of Martyrs*, a partisan but vivid account of those burned at the stake during her reign, became part of the English Protestant imagination thereafter. If Mary's co-religionists in Ireland expected a softer hand from the queen, they were disappointed. Mary had as little time for the recalcitrant Irish as she had for English Protestants. She supported military action to extend the 'land of peace' westward. To this end she sponsored the plantation of Laois and Offaly. These lands were shired, given the names of Queen's and King's County and settled with reliable English colonists. The Gaelic lords were expelled. The plantation was only a limited success but it pointed a way for future Irish policy.

Mary longed for a child that would secure the Catholic succession. Cruelly, the illness that she first felt in early 1558 was not a sign of pregnancy, as she hoped, but of the stomach cancer that would claim her life before the year was out. She was succeeded by Elizabeth, the daughter of Anne Boleyn.

With Elizabeth on the throne, the pendulum swung back towards Protestantism. Never again, except for the short interlude at the end of the 1680s, would the Catholics of Ireland look optimistically to a co-religionist on the throne of England to redeem their interests. The future was Protestant.

Ireland continued to be troubled and disturbed throughout most of Elizabeth's forty-five-year reign. The traditional Ormond–Desmond rivalry in the south reignited and led to the Battle of Affane in Co. Waterford in 1565. Here, the forces of 'Black Tom' Butler, 10th earl of Ormond, defeated those of Gerald FitzGerald, 14th earl of Desmond. It was the last such battle in Irish history between private magnate armies. Butler was a distant relative of the queen, and when Elizabeth bound both nobles to the peace he kept his side of the bargain. Indeed, so secure was he in his new gains that he built a manor house for himself at Carrick-on-Suir that still stands. It was remarkable for being built without any thought to military defence, unlike the defensive tower houses that were the norm up to then.

Desmond, however, was another matter. He was an erratic character and was regarded as so unreliable that he was imprisoned in the Tower of London for five years. In his absence, his cousin James FitzMaurice FitzGerald effectively ran the earldom as captain-general. He was an adamant supporter of the old faith, and he used a personal dispute over land succession to foment a full-scale rebellion in the name of 'faith and fatherland', not the last time that conjunction would echo in Irish history. The rebellion was met with exemplary brutality by Ormond and Sir Humphrey Gilbert, the queen's commander in Munster. The earl was released in 1573 and immediately reverted to Gaelic ways. At the same time, James FitzMaurice FitzGerald went to the continent to seek help from the Catholic powers – another practice that was to be repeated in the future.

He found no interest in France or Spain but received a better hearing in Rome, where the Pope, Gregory XIII, promised troops. He was as good as his word and furnished 1,000 Italian infantry. FitzGerald sailed from Corunna with these men and made landfall at Smerwick harbour, on the northern shore of the Dingle peninsula, in the far western margin of the Desmond lands. There they built a fort, known then and ever since as Dún an Óir, the fort of gold. They bore papal letters absolving the Irish lords from allegiance to the queen and calling for a religious war to re-establish Catholicism in Ireland. This was the great ideological fault-line of the age. It was all or nothing for both sides, which helps to explain the horrors of the war as state violence rose to unprecedented levels.

The papal force was trapped at Smerwick by Lord Grey de Wilton, the chief governor, and massacred. The English response to the Desmond rebellion was pitiless: famine, together with wholesale slaughter of people and livestock.

Attaque à l'outrance (attack to excess) was the means employed and it reduced that fertile earldom to a barren, starving shambles. Desmond himself was outlawed and finally murdered in 1583. The power of the southern FitzGeralds was now as thoroughly broken as that of their Kildare cousins had been in the 1530s. The earl's lands were confiscated and Munster was planted with New English. Plantation was becoming the preferred policy choice.

At the other end of the island, events in Ulster were just as chaotic. The medieval earldom of Ulster was long a thing of the past. By the time of Elizabeth's reign, all of the province, except for a few coastal places that could be supplied and secured by sea, was in Gaelic hands. Indeed, Ulster was the most thoroughly Gaelic of the four provinces.

Conn Bacach (the Lame) O'Neill, chief of his ancient clan, had accepted the title of earl of Tyrone under the terms of surrender and regrant. His son Matthew inherited the title on his death and, although probably illegitimate, this succession was deemed to be good in English law. Irish law, however, was quite another matter. The Gaelic laws of succession enabled all of Conn Bacach's sons, at a minimum, to contest the succession. The most ruthless and able of these was Shane O'Neill, the eldest of Conn's sons whose legitimacy was not in question. He had Matthew murdered in 1558 and joined the earldom to the title of The O'Neill, which he had made his own.

Shane O'Neill was by far the most powerful Gaelic warlord in Ulster. He faced no internal opposition in his Tyrone heartland and pressed hard on adjacent lordships. English expeditions against him proved futile, and perhaps for one reason more than others: there were no maps of Ulster. The earliest maps of Ireland which were reasonably reliable were only made in the 1570s, usually by Italian cartographers such as Baptista Boazzio working in the Low Countries. Given the absence of modern surveying techniques, their accuracy was impressive. However, Boazzio's map was inconsistent. The folio is folded in two and the line of the fold runs horizontally across the map, almost exactly along the Dublin–Galway line. Most of the map's accuracy is located south of the fold. The farther north you go, the more it is clear that Boazzio was guessing.

Ulster was terra incognita. Lough Erne, close to the northwest margin of English power in Connacht, is shown as a far greater body of water than distant Lough Neagh, deep in enemy country. The cartographers knew of its existence but made a totally wrong guess as to its relative size. Pieter van den Keere's map of 1591 makes a similar error. The English expeditions sent against Shane O'Neill were not the last ones to get lost in Ulster and find themselves exposed to ambush attacks from the Gaelic natives who knew every rock in the countryside.

Elizabeth could not beat Shane, so she tried to tame him. She invited him to London where he turned up with a retinue that appeared to Londoners to be both savage and exotic. A compromise was reached in which he was recognized as a captain but not as earl of Tyrone. When O'Neill returned, he proceeded to attack the various Gaelic lordships until he had effectively reduced the whole province. But he had overreached himself and made too many enemies. He was defeated by the MacSweeneys and O'Donnells of Tír Chonaill (Donegal) in 1567 and forced to flee east. He took refuge with the MacDonnells of the Glens, whom he had humiliated only two years earlier. Why he thought that he might be safe with people whom he had reduced to tributary status is unclear, but it was a misjudgement that cost him his life. They killed him.

His death made little difference to English fortunes in Ulster. Indeed, Shane's whole life had been lived by Gaelic rules and he died in a characteristically Gaelic quarrel. The succession was a text-book example of the failure of surrender and regrant, at least among the most Gaelic parts of Ireland. The title of The O'Neill passed to Turlough Luineach O'Neill and remained with him until 1593, when he surrendered it voluntarily. The English title of baron Dungannon, later to lead to the earldom of Tyrone, was vested in Hugh O'Neill, son of Matthew. He was to prove the coming man and one of the greatest figures in Irish history.

His background was a world removed from that of Shane O'Neill. From nine years of age, he had been educated in England, at Sir Henry Sidney's castle in Ludlow and later at Penshurst in Kent and in London itself. In ennobling him in English law, the crown hoped to have someone formed culturally and religiously in their shadow as a reliable bulwark in the heart of Ulster. He would be a counterweight to the ambitions of Turlough Luineach. In fact, Hugh O'Neill proved to be a master of ambiguity. He was a reliable harasser of neighbouring Gaelic lordships, which the crown found reassuring. On the other hand, the threat from the O'Donnells to the west and the Scots MacDonnells of the Glens to the east meant that he had to develop a formidable military force, based on a large influx of gallowglass, to thwart this twin threat. Nor did he scruple to play by Gaelic rules when it suited his book, as when he personally executed one of the sons of Shane O'Neill. This Tyrone liked to keep everyone guessing

That said, Hugh O'Neill cannot possibly have planned the war that established his place in history. He was drawn in to it involuntarily as much as anything else. But the outcome was the Nine Years War in Ulster from 1594 to 1603. In 1593, he had united the Gaelic title of The O'Neill in his own person with that of the earl of Tyrone which he had held since 1587. It gave him a new legitimacy but also exposed him to obligations that he did not altogether welcome.

The English had been pressing on the southern margins of Ulster for some years, breaking up minor lordships and reallocating the divided lands among local families under English law. It was classic divide and conquer. But when the process was pushed west into the Maguire lands in Fermanagh, Hugh Maguire rebelled. He was abetted by the lord of Donegal, 'Red' Hugh O'Donnell. In 1591, Tyrone had engineered a dramatic escape by O'Donnell from Dublin Castle. It was a strange thing for an O'Neill to do for a traditional tribal enemy, and was further proof of Tyrone's ambiguity. It was an ambiguity born of trying to maintain a balance between two incompatible worlds.

At first, Tyrone joined the English commander in Ulster, Sir Henry Bagenal, in suppressing the Maguire rebellion. Relations between the men were strained because Tyrone had eloped with Bagenal's sister, Mabel, in 1591, and made her his third wife before displaying a lordly infidelity to her with at least two other women. Bagenal extruded Maguire from his stronghold, Enniskillen castle, and garrisoned it. At this point, for reasons unknown, Tyrone changed side. The most likely explanation was that this shrewd, intelligent man, with his close knowledge of the English, realized that the Gaelic heartland in Ulster would come under ever-increasing and relentless pressure. He had to choose to be the earl of Tyrone or The O'Neill. He could no longer be both. In rebelling he made his choice.

Tyrone proved a formidable adversary for the crown. He won two celebrated ambush battles at Clontibret (1595) and most famously at the Yellow Ford (1598), where he routed his father-in-law, Bagenal, who lost his life. Maguire and Red Hugh O'Donnell recaptured Enniskillen. The earl of Essex was sent to Ireland by Elizabeth and proceeded to lose battles in the midlands, in country supposed to have been settled by the Laois–Offaly plantation. His mission ended in failure. The English met with other defeats in Wicklow and in north Connacht. By now, Tyrone was receiving supplies from Spain and felt strong enough in 1599 to call upon the Old English of the southern and eastern towns to join the rebellion. Significantly, they stood aloof: the two nations were not yet one, despite their shared Catholicism.

Tyrone's links to Spain raised the stakes. A widespread rebellion now proclaimed in the name of religion and supported by the great continental power that, only a decade earlier, had sent the Armada to English waters, represented an existential threat to the English crown. As in the Desmond rebellion, only more so, it was all or nothing. The new English commander, Charles Blount, Lord Mountjoy, applied a scorched earth policy as he pushed north towards Ulster. Simultaneously, Sir Henry Dowcra sailed into Lough Foyle and established a beachhead on the western shore of the lough, abutting O'Donnell territory. It later developed into the town of Derry.

By late 1600, the English counter-offensive had recovered much of the island outside Ulster. But the northern fastness still held firm and, for as long as it did, the contest was still uncertain. Finally, Spanish troops appeared off the Irish cost in response to Tyrone's appeals. The admiral of the fleet wanted to put ashore in Kinsale, Co. Cork, whereas the military commander Don Juan del Águila wanted to honour Tyrone's request that they disembark at Killybegs, securely in O'Donnell country in west Donegal. The admiral got his way. The Spaniards invested Kinsale. They were promptly surrounded by an English army under Mountjoy. Tyrone and O'Donnell marched south, the whole length of the island, in the depth of winter through often hostile territory, to join their Spanish allies.

They surrounded the English who had surrounded the Spaniards. Tyrone was cautious in his tactics but Red Hugh O'Donnell persuaded him to attack at dawn on Christmas Eve. It was a shambles. Mountjoy's cavalry, able to deploy in open formation and no longer facing ambush battles in unknown country, routed the Irish. The Spaniards were left as bystanders. It was all over before they could come to the aid of their allies. Even more so, it was all over for Gaelic Ireland.

There followed a treaty made at the abbey of Mellifont, near Drogheda. It granted extremely lenient terms to the Ulster lords, who were permitted to retain their lands and titles. This hugely annoyed the New English administration in Dublin and the English military in Ireland. In their eyes, they had risked their lives against the greatest ever threat to English rule in Ireland, only to see the culprits get away lightly. They applied relentless pressure on the Ulster lords. The stone chair at Tullaghoge, Co. Tyrone, on which The O'Neill had been inaugurated since ancient times, was destroyed. (It was the O'Neill equivalent of the Stone of Scone.) A highly prejudicial commission was established by the Dublin administration with the clear intention of finding legal pretexts to dispossess the lords. In the face of this pressure, they resolved on flight. On Friday 4 September 1607, in what is known as the Flight of the Earls, O'Neill, Rory O'Donnell (Red Hugh's father), Maguire of Fermanagh and a number of other Ulster lords boarded a Spanish ship at Rathmullan, on Lough Swilly in Co. Donegal. It had been sent specially to spirit them away to the Spanish Netherlands, there to seek military reinforcements for a reconquest of Ireland and a Catholic restoration. They were blown off course, landed in France, proceeded to Flanders and from there eventually to Rome. They were well received everywhere but no one was willing to meet their demand for an army. It might be said of them that they received every assistance short of help. They would never see Ireland again.

Their lands in Ulster now lay at the disposal of the crown. The result was plantation, that favoured policy. But this plantation was different. Unlike the feeble effort in the midlands or the incomplete effort in Munster, the Plantation of Ulster was a decisive, transformative event. Although sponsored by the crown, it was partly financed by private capital through the various merchant companies in the city of London: thus the name awarded to the western urban outpost of the plantation, Londonderry. The raising of adequate capital, together with the wholesale forfeiture of large tracts of land, allowed for the attraction of new landowners and, just as important, tenants. A significant Anglo-Scottish population thus established itself in Ulster, Protestant to a man and woman.

Antrim and Down were excluded from the official plantation area but were the subject of individual settlement efforts which ran in parallel with it. The net effect was the transformation of the Ulster population and the gradual establishment of the settlers on the best land, leaving the poorer uplands for the remaining natives. It was a more thoroughgoing success than any previous plantation but was precarious nonetheless and required continued financial inputs from the larger island. There is no sense in which the Plantation of Ulster was an instant success.

There were internal tensions between English colonists (generally Anglican, albeit many with a Puritan tendency) and the Scots (ferociously Calvinist), which have never completely disappeared from Ulster Protestant life. The Scots were regarded with suspicion by the New English administration in Dublin, for Scotland had traditionally been an enemy kingdom. Even though Elizabeth's successor in 1603 had been James VI of Scotland who now united the two crowns as James I of England, the two kingdoms remained separate constitutionally for another hundred years and even when formally united in 1707 retained separate settlements in law, religion and education.

The early Scots settlers were not obviously more sophisticated in agricultural techniques and land development than the Gaels they replaced. But the English were markedly more advanced. Gradually the colony cleared land, opened up woodland, built towns and improved communications. English law was now the sole law of the land and a form of early capitalism, alien to its previous population, began to take root in Ulster. A money economy developed. The private plantation schemes in Antrim and Down – not part of the official plantation and under way prior to the Flight of the Earls – were especially successful.

The Plantation of Ulster – together with the Anglo-Scots migration into Antrim and Down – represented the last concentrated movement of people into Ireland in its history. Vikings and Normans had arrived centuries earlier and had disturbed the pattern of the Gaelic world that had been stable for centuries. In whole or part, however, they had been assimilated and had contributed to the creation of a hybrid Irish culture. The Ulster Protestants, on the other hand, came as the vanguard of a religious-ideological movement that convulsed all of Europe. That, together with their regional separation from the rest of the island, meant that to some degree they would always remain a people apart.

10

TRANSFORMATION

The collapse of the Gaelic world and the new dispensation in Ulster placed the Old English of the south and east in an ever more precarious position. Their new masters in the Dublin administration were Protestants – and ardent Protestants at that. The new colonists in Ulster were likewise Protestant. That was the normal European arrangement worked out at the Peace of Augsburg. As the king went in religion, so went his people. King James I, who ascended the throne in 1603, had no intention of affording toleration to Catholics. His was a Protestant realm and that was that. Thus it was in England and Wales and Ulster. But outside Ulster, the traditional elite – the Old English – were recusant. They were caught between two loyalties.

They were also a powerful economic and political interest. Most of the productive land was still in Old English hands and in an age when ownership of land was the key determinant of the political nation, this meant that their influence was still potent. Nonetheless, they faced an administration openly hostile to their interests. A parliament with a rigged Protestant majority collapsed in farce. The Old English of the towns faced economic discrimination if they failed to take the sacrament in the Protestant manner and to attend Protestant church services.

James I died in 1625 and was succeeded by his son Charles I. The Old English had hopes that the new king might be more accommodating than the old. He had made an unsuccessful attempt to conclude a marriage with the Spanish infanta and instead married Henrietta Maria of France. He had therefore attempted one marriage and concluded another with the two greatest Catholic royal houses in Europe. This gave rise to deep suspicions in England. Contrariwise, it suggested to the Old English of Ireland that in the new king they might find a friendly ear, or at any rate one more friendly than that of his late father.

It was not the religion of France or Spain that most influenced Charles I. Rather, he wished to adopt their theory of kingship, the doctrine we know as the divine right of kings. It is based on an assertion of hierarchical values, with God bestowing authority directly on the monarch. Consequently, since the source of royal authority is not of this world the monarch cannot be subject to any earthly power. He is therefore absolute. It had a certain glamour in the early seventeenth century, since the two greatest powers in Europe, France and Spain, were absolute monarchies. States like England that aspired to the top table were naturally tempted to adopt the theory.

However, the divine right of kings sat awkwardly with English constitutional history. Parliament was already an ancient institution and one, moreover, that had real and well-defined powers. Unlike the consultative assemblies at continental royal courts its authority was required to approve certain actions, most obviously the raising of state revenues. Charles' desire to bypass parliament was potentially ruinous for him because he had no other legal means of raising funds. Looking to Ireland, he promised concessions to the Old English in return for a grant of funds in 1626. The concessions were known as the Graces. Vaguely and loosely formulated, the Graces were a promise of toleration for Catholics in return for the money the king desired.

The Irish parliament, still dominated by the Old English, approved the money, whereupon the king dragged his heels. He prevaricated for years, so that by the 1634 parliament he was able to effect a similar ruse, with the Old English still hoping for the full implementation of the Graces: religious toleration, secure land titles and full Catholic access to the higher professions.

By then, he had installed Thomas Wentworth as lord deputy of Ireland. A martinet, Wentworth managed to alienate every interest group in the country. He governed Ireland as if it were a laboratory for the king's desired personal rule in England, and was ruthless in appropriating land for the crown. He established a commission for defective titles which had only one object: to find evidence of illegal or semi-legal land grabs by New English parvenus and to sequester them to the profit of the crown. This likewise alarmed the Old English, for they themselves had not been wholly innocent in these matters; more to the point, however, was a general sense of hysteria relating to the security of land titles. Nor was Wentworth's never-realized plan for a plantation of Connacht at all reassuring to Irish landed interests, as it would have entailed wholesale confiscations and the forfeiting of existing titles. He also tried to force Anglican conformity on the Calvinist Scots of Ulster through the notorious Black Oath (whereby everyone over the age of sixteen had to swear allegiance to the king and reject the Scottish National Covenant, which contested the crown's absolute religious and state authority). This merely added that flinty community to the growing number of the king's enemies.

Wentworth had no intention, anymore than the king or his father before him, of granting religious toleration – both he and the king knew that such toleration could not become a political reality anyway, given the weight of opposition it would engender in England. In 1640, with the king at last forced to convene parliament amid the gathering crisis that would lead to the Civil War, Wentworth was recalled to shore up the tottering royal regime. Instead, he became a lightning rod for parliamentary revenge and was executed.

By the start of the 1640s, the royal government of Charles I had managed to create profound instability in three kingdoms. In England, a vengeful parliament had reassembled, loathing the king's years of personal rule, dominated by Puritans and deploring what they regarded as his crypto-Catholic policies in the Church of England. The Scots had been outraged by such enormities as re-consecrating the kirk of St Giles in Edinburgh to cathedral status and appointing a bishop to it, about as provocative a thing as could be imagined in a country whose national self-image was Calvinist. There was a riot in St Giles in 1637 against what was seen as an alien imposition in the church. The result was the Scottish National Covenant of 1638, signed by over 300,000 people, in which Presbyterianism was declared the national church in fact if not in law. In Ireland, the king, through Wentworth, had alienated all interest groups with equal insouciance.

In the larger island, the result was the tangled Civil War between parliament and king, in which the Scots – after securing their own early victories against the king's forces – tried for a time to stay aloof but could not. It ended with the king stepping out on to a scaffold in January 1649. In Ireland, the island was set aflame in 1641.

This is a key date in Irish history and one that led to the most confused sequence of events. Catholics, Old English and Gaelic alike, feared the new Puritan radicalism of the English parliament which they knew to be an enemy to their church. Wentworth and the king had been bad: parliament threatened to be a lot worse (and proved to be so in the fullness of time). The Scots Covenanters' military success against the crown, which effectively preserved the Presbyterian settlement in that country from further southern intrusion, was also noted, albeit the Scots were even more implacable in their dislike of Catholicism than the English parliament.

The Old English dithered, caught as ever between religious loyalty and devotion to the crown. The Old Irish had fewer qualms. A plot was hatched among the increasingly marginalized Gaelic lords of Ulster – some had survived the plantation – to follow the example set by the Scots. The leader was Sir Phelim O'Neill who had lands in south Co. Tyrone. The plan was that O'Neill would rise in Ulster while his southern allies would seize Dublin Castle. The Ulster rebellion quickly succeeded in every area west of the Bann other than Enniskillen and Derry. In the east of the province, Lisburn held out against the rebels and bought time for the fortification of the coastal towns.

The plot against Dublin Castle failed, however. It was betrayed by a spy and the leaders of the revolt in Dublin found themselves held prisoner in the Castle rather than masters of it. The Dublin administration, with cynical mendacity, blamed all Irish Catholics for the rebellion: this was a chilling judgement for the Old English and a sign of things to come. Increasingly, radical English Protestants were deliberately eliding the ethnic differences within Catholic Ireland. In brazenly ignoring this reality, they were adding fuel to the sectarian fire by implying that the struggle was a religious war of Protestant against Catholic. The Old English, in particular, were being pushed towards a corner they did not want to occupy.

With the failure in Dublin, the rebellion was now focused wholly on Ulster. O'Neill lost control of his followers. Given the speed of their victories in the centre and west of the province, the Catholic insurgents found themselves in possession of large numbers of Protestant settler prisoners. It was all too easy to recall the sundry humiliations that Ulster Catholics had endured since the plantation. Now they had the enemy at their mercy. What followed has haunted the Ulster Protestant imagination to the present day.

Prisoners were massacred. The total number is unknown: the more cautious estimates give a figure of 10,000 dead. It is highly probable that the numbers were later exaggerated for propaganda purposes. That is hardly the point. Men, women and children, without regard for age and sex, were butchered or turned out on the roads naked in the depth of winter. Houses, farmsteads and other holdings were destroyed in an elemental outburst of revenge. This was the work of the marginalized Catholic masses, not of their leaders: a people who had been reduced to penury in their own land, impoverished and disregarded. Their vengeance had an almost biblical quality to it. The horrors of the Thirty Years War, still raging in Germany, had come to Ireland.

The Ulster Catholic army now turned south. They besieged Drogheda. Nearby, however, they met with Old English leaders of a royal army sent against them by the Dublin administration. The Old English decided to change sides, to make common cause with their co-religionists and to look to their arms for the protection of their own community. In their own eyes, they were king's rebels, for it was really the radical Protestantism of parliament (and of the Dublin Castle regime) that they most feared. Nonetheless, it was an absolutely seminal decision. They may have hoped for a reconciliation with the king – indeed, they earnestly desired it – but no one knew how the king would fare in England. In Ireland, the two Catholic communities, anciently suspicious of each other, had now made common cause. The cause was the Catholic religion. For the Old English, they had abandoned their allegiance to the English connection for the first time since their ancestors' arrival on the island nearly five centuries earlier.

Thus was established the Confederation of Kilkenny, with headquarters far from the turbulence of Ulster and deep in the Old English heartland. It maintained a full representative assembly within the territory it controlled. It functioned as a normal administration, raised taxes, minted coins and kept an army in the field. It also maintained links to the king, and sought assurances – similar to those long promised in the Graces – of secure land titles and religious toleration on the return of peace. These negotiations dragged out until the Battle of Naseby (1645) firmly tilted the English Civil War towards parliament.

The king had an army in Ireland under the command of James Butler, earl of Ormond, scion of the greatest surviving Old English house. Unlike most of his community, he had conformed to the state church. Weakened by defeat, the king now desperately wanted the royal army to cross to England to help him recover his position. But any serious attempt to realize this hope would have been fatal for Charles: the cure was worse than the disease, for it would have confirmed a suspicion long held by parliamentary radicals that the Irish army was being held in reserve specifically as an engine of royal coercion. Even Ormond so deplored the king's overtures to the Irish Catholics that he surrendered Dublin to Michael Jones, the parliamentary general. Better parliament than the Confederation of Kilkenny.

Meanwhile in Ulster, a Scots army under General Robert Munro had come to the aid of their beleaguered countrymen in the wake of the 1641 massacres. On the other side, the Confederate army acquired the services of experienced Irish officers from the Catholic continental powers, notably Thomas Preston and the Ulsterman Owen Roe O'Neill, nephew of the great Hugh O'Neill. O'Neill routed the Scots under Munro at Benburb, in his ancestral county of Tyrone, in 1646.

A papal nuncio, Gianbattista Rinuccini, was sent by the Pope to the Confederation of Kilkenny. He was a Counter-Reformation rigorist who saw the struggle in simple Catholic–Protestant terms, eerily similar to the analysis of the parliamentary radicals in England. He deplored the Old English approaches to the king, whom he regarded as a heretic. He did nothing to hold the Confederation together and everything – in his misplaced zeal – to open wider the fissures between Old Irish and Old English that were never far from the surface.

The entire bloody mess was resolved by the final victory of parliament in England and the execution of the king at the start of 1649. With a clear winner at last on the larger island, it now fell to the victors to settle matters in the smaller. On 15 August 1649, the parliamentary commander, Oliver Cromwell, landed his troops at Ringsend in Dublin harbour. He was bent on revenge for Catholic atrocities committed during the 1641 rebellion. He too made no distinction between one kind of Irish Catholic and another.

By the time he left Ireland less than a year later, he was well on the way to doing what no English ruler since 1170 had managed: the effective subjugation of the entire island and the projection of English law and power into every corner of the land.

Cromwell first besieged Drogheda, which he took. He proceeded to conduct a massacre that has lived as long in the Irish memory as anything that happened in 1641. Indeed, Cromwell made no bones about the fact that this exemplary slaughter was both revenge for 1641 and a warning to the Irish – 'these barbarous wretches' – as to their future conduct. The massacre at Drogheda was considered a sensation even in a world desensitized to extreme violence by the excesses of the Thirty Years War. In Irish terms, it was without precedent that English military forces should conduct themselves with such utter lack of restraint, and should be encouraged to do so. Cromwell then went south to Wexford, where another 2,000 were put to the sword in case the message had not got home the first time.

He then turned west into Munster, meeting ever diminishing resistance. There was one exception. The town of Clonmel, in south-east Tipperary, was ably defended by Hugh Dubh O'Neill who, like his kinsman Owen Roe, was an Irish veteran of service in the Spanish Netherlands. He mounted such a spirited defence that he inflicted the biggest defeat – in terms of casualties – suffered by the New Model Army in the wars of three kingdoms. But in doing so, he exhausted his supplies and materiel. He and the garrison slipped away by night and Clonmel formally surrendered the next day.

By the time Cromwell returned to England early in 1650, the rest of the campaign was in the nature of a mopping-up operation. In the end it took longer than it should. Still, by 1652 the Cromwellians had even taken the remote island of Inishbofin off the coast of Co. Galway.

Cromwell now determined upon a wholesale revolution in Ireland unlike anything seen before. He dispossessed the vast majority of Catholic landowners. Eleven million acres of land were confiscated. On them were settled a mixture of adventurers and soldiers, the former having been investors whose money had supported the parliamentary armies and who were now due their dividend. By the mid 1650s, not a single Catholic landowner remained in possession east of the River Shannon, an area where twenty years before over 80 per cent of land had been in Catholic hands. Most of Connacht west of the Shannon – some of the poorest land in the country – was kept as a reservation for those displaced Catholics who had neither escaped to the continent nor been shipped off to the West Indies as indentured servants, a polite name for slaves. The new Cromwellian elite now in control of the land of Ireland would, in time, mutate into what became known as the Protestant Ascendancy.

In technical terms, the Cromwellian plantation was a remarkable achievement. It was made possible by the brilliance of Sir William Petty, the surveyor-general of Ireland, whose survey of the whole country was the most accurate mapping of the island up to that time. It was known ever after as the Down Survey, because it set down on maps what had only been expressed in verbal and numerical descriptions in previous surveys.

The Cromwellian plantation set the pattern for Irish land ownership until the early twentieth century. Cromwellian politics proved less durable. England wearied of Puritan rule. Cromwell died in 1658. Two years later the son of the executed king, Charles II, was bid home from his travels to take his place upon his father's throne. The Stuarts were back.

* * *

The new king was cynical, worldly and genial. Most of all, he was of a mind to keep his head on his shoulders and his throne beneath him, unlike his father. That meant not offending powerful interest groups. Accordingly, he had long since agreed with the Scots that their Presbyterian church organization was acceptable to him, thus abandoning the attempt to enforce Anglican uniformity throughout his realm, the lost cause that had started Charles I on his slide to disaster.

As with Scotland, so with Ireland. Charles may not have found the new Cromwellian landlord class very congenial, but there was no possibility of his ever being able substantially to dispossess them or to reverse the land settlement generally. This was a sore disappointment to many people, most of all to those Old English who had stood by the king and who were now to be denied their reward. Of course, there were some who simply could not be ignored. Most obviously, James Butler, the great survivor, was restored to his historic patrimony and created 1st duke of Ormond. He was to dominate Irish government for most of Charles' reign.

Ormond began the development of Dublin as a proper royal capital. For 300 years, since the Black Death, it had been a neglected backwater. Hardly a single civic building survives in the city from those three centuries. From the early seventeenth century, it had become the permanent seat of the Irish parliament. The medieval parliament had been peripatetic, meeting as often in Drogheda or Kilkenny as Dublin. The seventeenth-century peace also brought the gradual return of economic growth. Dublin began to expand again, with notable suburban development on the north bank of the Liffey and to the west of the walled city towards Kilmainham. A city that had only ever had one bridge acquired four more between 1670 and 1683. Three of these bridges still exist, although all have been reconstructed over time.

The finest of these was on the site of the modern Capel Street bridge and represented a shift of the city's centre of gravity eastward towards the bay. It created a new north–south axis from the Castle and made the development of the northern suburbs beyond a tempting prospect. This is exactly what happened in the great eighteenth-century building boom, with the earliest fashionable Georgian developments located north of the river.

Perhaps the most enduring legacy bequeathed the city by the Duke of Ormond is the Phoenix Park. On his arrival in 1662, he took up residence in the Phoenix Manor which stood on the site of the modern Magazine Fort. He acquired 2,000 acres around the Manor as a vice-regal deer park. One of the previous owners from whom he bought the land was Sir Maurice Eustace, the speaker of the Irish House of Commons, whose name lives on in a street in the Temple Bar district in the city centre. The duke stocked the park with deer, whose descendants are still to be seen there today.

Another notable Ormond legacy is St Stephen's Green. This had existed from medieval times as a pasture area for cattle and horses in the distant south-east reaches of the small town. By 1664, when its twenty-seven acres were denominated by the Dublin Corporation as a public leisure area, it was still distant from the city centre. Building lots were sold to enclose the green and were gradually developed for townhouses. There was a problem, however. The route linking Trinity College and the Green was deemed to be 'so foule and out of repair that persons cannot pass to the said Green for the benefit of the walks therein'. Something had to be done and in 1671 the Corporation set about the improvements that in time led to the development of Grafton Street. Dublin owes the beginnings of its modern shape to Ormond's benign patronage.

To the extent that he had any strong religious feelings, Charles II was a moderate Anglican and for the most part he left the Catholics of Ireland in peace. He was suspected of being a closet Catholic (he may indeed have died as one) and like his father he had a French Catholic wife, although his marked preference was for his English Protestant mistresses, who were legion. Only the hysteria following the so-called Popish Plot in England brought a brief persecution – although this was enough, in 1681, to see the judicial murder of St Oliver Plunkett, the archbishop of Armagh and a member of one of the oldest Old English families of the Pale.

The religious wars of Ireland were not quite over. The promise of the Caroline peace was to be betrayed by the final act of the long drama that had carried Ireland from the end of the medieval world, with the destruction of the house of Kildare, to the brink of modernity and the final, complete triumph of the new Protestant interest.

II

ASCENDANCY

Charles II died in 1685. He had no legitimate heirs – although well provided with bastards – and so was succeeded by his brother James. The new king was a Catholic. Even worse, he had some of his father's hankering after absolutism, now at its continental zenith at the court of Louis XIV in France. For Irish Catholics, and for the Old English in particular, it seemed like a moment of deliverance. Not since Queen Mary 130 years earlier had one of their co-religionists been on the throne.

For equal and opposite reasons, James II was an object of intense suspicion in Protestant England, to say nothing of Scotland where he reigned as James VII. But in Ireland, the Old English had reason for their optimism. One of their leading men, Richard Talbot, was appointed duke of Tyrconnell and given charge of the army with instructions to strengthen it. He was also given the position of lord-in-general and quickly moved to replace Protestants with Old English Catholics in the Irish administration. Most of all, he held out the hope of restoring Catholics to their lost lands.

In England, Tyrconnell's Irish army was viewed as a potential means of establishing royal absolutism, just as the parliamentary radicals had regarded Charles I's Irish army at the start of the Civil War. This fear turned to conspiracy when the queen produced a male heir, thus securing the Catholic succession. A *coup d'état* in the Protestant interest brought the Dutch *stadtholder*, William of Orange, husband of James's daughter Mary, to the throne in 1689, an event later dignified as the Glorious Revolution. James fled first to France, and then – with the greatest reluctance – to Ireland, where he at least had a natural power base. He summoned the so-called patriot parliament which was, in fact, an assembly of the Catholic Old English. It was their swansong.

The Glorious Revolution was welcomed in Protestant Ulster and among the Cromwellian New English. They watched in horror as the patriot parliament disendowed the Church of Ireland and began the process of undoing the land settlement. At the same times, James's forces gathered themselves and moved north into Ulster. Soon the whole province lay at their mercy except for the walled plantation towns of Enniskillen and Derry which, as in 1641, held out.

On 18 April 1689, King James II presented himself before the walls of Derry. He was fired on by the Protestants gathered within, their numbers already swollen by refugees from the countryside. The gates were slammed against the Jacobite army and the siege of Derry began. The defence of Derry seemed a hopeless undertaking. The Jacobites had effectively taken Ulster: a month earlier, at Dromore, Co. Down, on the far side of the province, they had easily defeated a Protestant army. Now the tiny walled town of Derry, at the very western margin of the British Protestant world, bursting with civilians, children and old people as well as troops, was supposed to hold out against a conquering army.

But they did, helped, it must be said, by the ineptitude of the besiegers. Conditions within the walls were vile. The defenders were, for example, reduced to eating vermin. But they held out for 105 days. In the meantime, a Williamite army had landed at Larne, Co. Antrim, and eventually Williamite ships broke the boom that the Jacobites had thrown across the Foyle estuary and allowed supplies into the starving town.

This war between William and James was to be crucial for the future of Ireland, but in European terms it was simply a sideshow. It was a distant theatre of action in the greater European conflict known as the War of the League of Augsburg. The contending forces were the French under Louis XIV, looking to establish their absolute hegemony in Europe, and a coalition of interests put together by William of Orange. Louis was quite happy to see Anglo-Dutch troops tied up in Ireland, a place of no strategic importance in European terms. It was, however, possible to be the means of restoring James to the throne of England: the ensuing problems that this would create were not displeasing to the French. Accordingly, French troops were provided to bolster the Jacobite army.

After the Jacobite failure before Derry, however, the tide began to turn against them. In June 1690, William of Orange landed at Carrickfergus and made his way south. On 1 July, he met James at the Battle of the Boyne, just west of Drogheda. William won what was the largest, most fabled and arguably most important battle in Irish history. James retreated in haste to Dublin, then to Waterford and from there took ship for France, to live out the remaining ten years of his life.

William, likewise, found little to detain him further in Ireland. The Boyne had settled the question of the English kingship, so he left the conduct of what remained of the Irish war in the hands of his capable Dutch general, Godert de Ginkell. The Williamite progress was steady, although they met heavy resistance at Limerick, which they were forced to besiege. The defence of Limerick was led by the French General Boisileau but it was his Old English second-in-command, Patrick Sarsfield, who most distinguished himself. The first siege of Limerick was raised but then there came the Battle of Aughrim, Co. Galway. This was what finally broke the back of the Jacobite cause and with it the remaining Old English influence in the history of Ireland. It was a close-run thing. The Jacobites, under the command of the French General St Ruth, believed that they had won the day when a stray cannonball decapitated the general. In the confusion that followed, Ginkell routed them. The Jacobite cavalry, mostly Old English, retreated in good order and fell back on Limerick. The Gaelic infantry was slaughtered.

A short second siege followed at Limerick, followed by a surrender and a treaty on generous terms. The treaty contained military and civil articles. The former allowed the Jacobite officers to leave for the continent in a great diaspora of the Old English: these were the Wild Geese of fable. The civil articles promised religious toleration. In a re-run of the treaty of Mellifont, the king saw no advantage in a punitive peace now that his victory was secure. The Protestants of Ireland, newly delivered from an existential threat to their community, thought differently. It was the post-war Irish parliament, now an exclusively Protestant assembly, that dishonoured the civil articles of the treaty.

The English conquest of Ireland was complete.

The long wars were over. Ireland was at peace because one side had achieved a decisive, overwhelming victory. The Protestant interest was everywhere secure, although the memory of its recent insecurities was strong enough to make it ungenerous and unyielding in its hour of triumph. King William – and maybe even the English parliament – would have been content to honour the civil articles in the Treaty of Limerick. But the Irish parliament, now composed only of the British colonial beachhead in Ireland, was not. The memories of 1641 and 1688 were still too fresh.

This was the group who were to become known as the Protestant Ascendancy, although the term was not to be coined for another century. The eighteenth-century Ascendancy consisted of major landowners, mostly Cromwellian settlers, who subscribed to the Church of Ireland, an Anglican church but one with a pronounced Calvinist streak which influenced its worship and liturgical practices, if always the secular behaviour of its members. The real Calvinists, of course, were the

Ulster Presbyterians (or Dissenters), a separate regional sub-group for whom the Ascendancy had little affection.

The Irish parliament passed a series of penal laws against Catholics and Dissenters alike in the early years of the eighteenth century, of which those against the Catholics were more onerous. These were directed against Catholic ownership of land, already reduced to barely 10 per cent of the island, in the hope of further diminishing residual Catholic influence. Land ownership meant power and access to power through politics. Catholics were also forbidden to practise law, to hold public office or to bear arms. Younger sons who conformed to the established church could disinherit elder brothers who did not.

These penal laws were not part of any proselytizing effort. Protestants had no desire to convert Catholics – except perhaps for the occasional elite Catholic – wishing simply to neutralize them in the public sphere. Despite formal prohibitions against the practice of Catholicism, there was little actual persecution. What there was resulted not from any state policy but from the exertions of local bigotry. Indeed, the Catholic Church maintained its institutional structures in remarkably good order during the eighteenth century, all the more so as the century went on. And it was a changed church, for under the impact of defeat, Catholics were now seen and saw themselves as a single, coherent community. The distinction between Old English and Old Irish grew weaker with time. Rather, Catholics were the dispossessed.

The feeling of dispossession is a constant feature of Catholic life from this point forward. It took different forms as social and political circumstances changed, but its essential proposition was constant: the land of Ireland had been stolen from its rightful owners and given to strangers whose title to it might be good in English law but was morally illegitimate.

The penal laws were not rigorously enforced, especially after the 1730s as Protestants grew more relaxed. Still, they left a poisonous legacy for the future. In the short run, their effect on the Ulster Dissenters, who were excluded from public office and subjected to various forms of minor discrimination, was more pronounced. Many of them simply left for the more congenial atmosphere of Puritan America, to the later benefit of what became the United States.

The eighteenth century was the age of the Ascendancy. Gradually recovering confidence as their dominance stabilized, the new elite began to leave its mark on the land. They built themselves fine country houses in the neoclassical style, none finer than Castletown, in Co. Kildare, built for Speaker William Conolly of the Irish parliament in a style that mimicked the Palazzo Farnese in Rome. But it was in the cities that their imprint has lasted longest, and especially in Dublin. Georgian Dublin, with its mixture of noble public buildings and wonderfully coherent streetscapes, was their masterpiece. It still stands, although much knocked about in places by latter-day vandals. It was a uniquely Irish variation on the great European theme of classical architecture. In the turbulent seventeenth century, only one public building of note – the Royal Hospital (1684) – was built in the city. In the eighteenth, all the great buildings of classical Dublin were either completed or set in train.

The first half of the century saw an explosion of public building, some of it of the very highest quality. The new Parliament House opened to the design of Edward Lovett Pearce in the 1730s, although the additions by James Gandon and others from the 1780s give the building its modern appearance. Pearce's original structure was one of classical purity and dramatic confidence.

Across the street, Trinity College, dating from 1592 and at that time still the only university in Ireland, began to assume its modern form. The oldest surviving structure in the college, the Rubrics, dates from the first decade of the eighteenth century. In the second, Thomas Burgh designed the Old Library. There are still prints that show it in the form in which Burgh left it, but its modern form derives from Thomas Deane and Benjamin Woodward's addition of the sensational barrel-vaulted ceiling in the 1860s. It is an ironic thought that while modern planning laws might have spared us the 'restoration' of Christ Church and St Patrick's cathedrals in the nineteenth century, they would also have robbed us of what one authority has described as 'the finest secular interior in Ireland'.

Trinity was a work in progress for most of the century. The Printing House – a pretty building in the style of a Doric temple, the work of the German Richard Cassels – dates from 1734. The Dining Hall followed in the next decade. The 1750s brought the great west front of the college that gives on to College Green. Front Square itself was gradually completed in the 1780s. The Provost's House (1759) is the only private Georgian house in Dublin that still serves its original function.

The establishment of the Wide Streets Commissioners in 1757 was the most enlightened piece of planning legislation in the city's history. The body it set up was charged with widening existing narrow streets and proposing standards for new ones. It was empowered to buy land and property where necessary. The Commissioners – there were usually twenty-five in number – were all men of substance and influence. What they created was a city re-imagined as an aristocratic display space, no longer simply the random, twisting pattern of streets dictated by ancient pathways and commercial necessity.

The modern city of Dublin is unimaginable without their work. All the classic Georgian squares and streets on both side of the river felt their influence. Merrion Square is the prime example: the view along the south side of the square and down Upper Mount Street to the perspective point of the Pepper Canister church is the best formal testimony to their purpose. But every district felt their influence. They had real powers – they could override the Corporation in those areas within their remit – and they did not hesitate to use them.

James Gandon was *the* architect of Dublin's golden age. He designed the two finest buildings in the city: the Custom House (1791) and the Four Courts, built farther upstream on the north bank of the Liffey. This monumental structure dominates the upper reaches of the river. The foundation stone was laid in 1786 and the building was finished in 1801, although it was sufficiently advanced by 1796 for the courts to use it. Gandon was also responsible for the brilliantly successful eastern addition to Lovett Pearce's Parliament House. This created a new entrance to the House of Lords with its portico and Corinthian columns projected over the street pavement.

Many of the anxieties and contradictions in Ascendancy Ireland were captured in the person of Jonathan Swift. He was born in Dublin in 1667. Both parents were English, although his maternal grandparents had themselves lived in Ireland in the 1630s. Swift's father was an official in the King's Inns in Dublin. The family was well connected: they were related to the Duke of Ormond on Swift's mother's side and were close to the Master of the Rolls in London, Sir John Temple, whose son, Sir William Temple, would become Jonathan Swift's influential patron as a young man. He was also related to John Dryden, the leading English poet of the age.

The Swifts were therefore typical of many English families that established themselves in Ireland following the Restoration – the Ormond connection, in particular, would have done them no harm – and prospered. The elder Swift died a few months before his son was born but the family memory of persecution by the Puritans in Cromwell's time – what Swift himself described as 'the barbarity of Cromwell's hellish crew' – inclined them towards an orthodox mainstream Anglicanism. This was the tradition into which Jonathan Swift was born. He was educated at Kilkenny grammar school, a preferred academy of the Old English since pre-Reformation times and by now a reliable centre of Church of Ireland conformity. He was ordained in the church in 1695.

He was an ambitious clergyman and his ambition was firmly fixed on the larger island. In the first decade of the eighteenth century, he was in London and was an influential figure in literary and political circles. He wrote for the *Tatler*, and was a friend of Alexander Pope and other leading wits and writers.

Politically, he hitched his star to the Tories under Harley and Bolingbroke, but the death of Queen Anne ushered in the long Whig hegemony and Tory sympathizers were out of favour. Swift had backed the wrong horse. Instead of an appointment to the bench of bishops in the Church of England, for which he had hoped, he was returned to Dublin as a mere dean, albeit Dean of St Patrick's cathedral.

For Swift, this was exile. He had harboured thoughts, not unreasonably, of a glittering career in the metropolis – the greatest city in Europe except for Paris – but had to settle for provincial Dublin instead. The ripening of Swift's satirical genius had this background for context. The Swifts were nominally Irish, but really English in Ireland and thinly rooted there. And the patriotism that Jonathan Swift was to espouse and personify from the 1720s on was that of the frustrated provincial, the creole abandoned by the metropole, condescended to and dismissed as of lesser account. Much of what was denominated patriotism in the eighteenth century – culminating in Grattan's Parliament in the last two decades – was of this kind. When an existential threat to this settler community arose in the wake of the French Revolution, the facade collapsed with suggestive ease.

Nonetheless, the fact that a truculent colonial patriotism did develop was a testimony to the increasingly confident position of the New English elite in the early eighteenth century. They represented barely 10 per cent of the Irish population; they were observant Church of Ireland Protestants in their confessional allegiance, surrounded by a sea of Catholics and – in their Ulster redoubt – Presbyterians. In a manner typical of pre-industrial states, this elite alone constituted the political nation. Their victory in the Williamite wars at the end of the preceding century had delivered them the security that made their position seem impregnable. This sense of security was the essential condition for their patriotism, because a nervous or insecure community could not have afforded the luxury of anti-English sentiment.

And of that sentiment, there was no shortage. The colonial parliament chafed under restrictions on its discretionary powers that dated from medieval times. Such restrictions were perfectly usual in provincial or subordinate assemblies in pre-modern Europe but they were a source of tension none the less. In Ireland, this tension was increased in 1720 by the passage of the Declaratory Act in London, which stated that Westminster could pass legislation binding on Ireland over the head of the Dublin parliament. Then came the controversy known as Wood's Halfpence.

William Wood was an ironmaster in Wolverhampton, near Birmingham. In 1722, he was awarded a patent to mint £100,000 worth of copper coin for Ireland. This patent aroused immediate and spirited opposition in Ireland, where there was no national mint. It was alleged that he received the patent by paying £10,000 to the Duchess of Kendal, one of the king's mistresses. The total amount of currency in circulation in Ireland was about £400,000, so there was an understandable fear that Wood's coins would flood the country and cause a severe inflation.

That was the primary objection to the coinage, but there was also a sense of resentment that the Irish parliament had been bypassed yet again. The entire Irish establishment united against the coinage and refused to circulate it. In 1725, the London government admitted defeat and withdrew the patent. In the meantime, Swift had established himself as a master satirist by writing the six pamphlets collectively known as *The Drapier's Letters*. Assuming the disguise of M. B. Drapier, a respectable shopkeeper, Swift attacked the patent, but reserved his most acid and brilliant ridicule for the demeaning and subordinate position in which the colonial parliament was held.

The letters were addressed quite self-consciously to a Protestant audience, in an age when Dublin was still a Protestant city. Swift should not be confused with the later tradition of patriotism in the Irish nationalist context of the nineteenth and

twentieth centuries. There was a common anti-English sentiment, but there the similarities end. Swift would almost
certainly have been a unionist in the nineteenth century: the
vast majority of the descendants of those he addressed in his
satires were unionists. Where he does represent the beginning
of a tradition, however, is in the literary sense. He is the first in
a line of Irish – usually Dublin – writers who have, whether in
Ireland or overseas, been the island's glory. He stands at the
head of a great tradition, one of the writers of true world
importance that the country has produced.

The contrasts that are characteristic of any country at any time
were never far away. In 1740 and 1741, the whole island was
gripped by a famine which proportionally was almost as severe
as the Great Famine of the 1840s. It is estimated that up to
400,000 people died of starvation and consequent illnesses in
these years, out of a total population of about 2.5 million. But
just a year later, in 1742, Dublin played host to one of the great
first performances in the history of European music. On 13
April, in the New Musick Hall in Fishamble Street and under
the direction of the composer, Handel's *Messiah* was first given.

As the century progressed, the self-confidence of the new
Protestant elite grew. The campaign against Wood's Halfpence
had been evidence of it, because a defensive, nervous community would not have dared such self-assertive defiance. The
Hanoverian dynasty seemed secure. All the same, for as long as
James II's son lived, the danger remained because the legitimist
Stuarts, for all their faults, had a better title to the throne than
anyone else. Known to history as the Old Pretender, he would
have become king in any Stuart restoration. It was in support
of precisely that objective that *his* son, Charles Edward (Bonnie
Prince Charlie or the Young Pretender) had mounted the
Jacobite rising of 1745, known as the 'Forty-Five', in Scotland.
It ended in the slaughter at Culloden and the prince's romantic
flight back to France and later Italy, there to live out his days
in an alcoholic stupor.

It is interesting that Ireland did not stir, let alone rise, in 1745, anymore than it had done thirty years earlier when the Earl of Mar had first raised the Jacobite standard in Scotland. This was testimony to the completeness of the Protestant triumph and also perhaps to the devastating aftermath of the 1740 famine, whose enfeebling effects were still being felt five years later. It was yet another indication of Protestant security and victory.

12

GRATTAN

King James VIII and III died in 1766. The Old Pretender was the son of King James II. His regnal numbers were those of Scotland and England respectively, but they had become as meaningless as the man himself. The union of England and Scotland in 1707 had long since superseded the mere union of crowns effected by his Stuart ancestor, James VI and I, in 1603. It made Great Britain a single insular polity first under Queen Anne, the last Stuart to occupy the throne, and then definitively under the Hanoverian dynasty beginning with the first of the Georges in 1714. The Hanoverian succession survived two Scottish attempts to restore the Stuarts.

So James VIII and III cut a rather Ruritanian figure, dependant as he was on the kindness of strangers. Foremost among these was the Pope. Clement XI provided him with a Roman residence where he set up and maintained an ersatz court, complete with the customary formalities and observances. He married into the Polish royal family, taking as his bride the granddaughter of King John III Sobieski who had been the hero of the relief of Vienna from the Turks in 1683. This was a conspicuously Catholic union, blessed by the pontiff and binding the house of Stuart to one of the great Catholic families of Europe. If there had been any doubts about Stuart confessional loyalty before, there was none now. A Stuart restoration in Britain would mean a Catholic restoration – or at least a mighty attempt at one. The Pope and the Whigs both understood what was at stake. From polar opposite perspectives, their analyses agreed.

The eldest son of the marriage, Charles Edward, became the last hope of the Stuarts. The Old Pretender mouldered away in Rome, but the son went off to head the Forty-Five in Scotland and to become a folk hero in defeat. He scarcely deserved this status, for he was a whingeing sot who never ceased to blame his loss on the highlanders who had fought so courageously for him and whom he had abandoned so blithely. Fourteen years later, in 1759, with the Seven Years War still (but not for much longer) in the balance, the French duc de Choiseul was planning an invasion of England. He hoped to install Charles as a symbolic figurehead, if not actually as king, and to that end the two men met. The Young Pretender turned up drunk and made a poor impression on Choiseul, whose invasion plans were in any event scuppered by British naval victories.

Thus it was, in 1766, when the Old Pretender finally died, that the pretence of Stuart legitimacy died with him. Pope Clement XIII, as little impressed by the prince as Choiseul had been, declined to recognize him as king and instead acknowledged that the house of Hanover, in the person of George III, was the proper and actual royal house of Britain. The papacy had finally acquiesced in the Glorious Revolution and the other Catholic powers of Europe had followed suit.

It was a moment of psychological release for the Protestant interest in Ireland. The Pope himself had effectively thrown in the towel. Any attempted Stuart restoration would have had as logical a base in Ireland, where Catholic numbers might tell, as in Scotland. The Protestants in Ireland, a people to whom the mythology of the siege came all too readily, now recognized a new deliverance: the enemy had folded his tents and gone away. When a siege is lifted, the defenders can breathe more easily and behave more liberally. And so it was to prove.

Protestant fears had not been groundless. Irish Catholics had, for the previous 150 years, been strong supporters of the house of Stuart, which they saw as a bulwark or protection against parliamentarians, Puritans and Whigs, all of whom they correctly identified as being hostile to their interests. Even when Stuart kings were formally Protestant, it was a less ardent version of the Reformation, as with the two king Charles. Charles I was married to Henrietta Maria, sister of King Louis XIII of France. His queen was, not unreasonably, believed to wield her interest in support of French and Catholic ambitions. Moreover, Charles was a supporter of the so-called Arminian tendency in the Church of England which the Puritans regarded as little better than disguised Catholicism. These tensions were eventually to lead to the Civil War and the execution of the king.

His son, Charles II, also married a Catholic – Catherine of Braganza, the royal house of Portugal – and almost certainly died a Catholic, to be succeeded in turn by his brother James who was openly so. None of this did anything to shake the confidence of Irish Catholics in the Stuarts, even when they proved a disappointment in reality, as with the failure of Charles II to overturn the Cromwellian land settlement. The decades after the battles of Aughrim and the Boyne, roughly the seventy years from the 1690s to the 1760s, saw the high-water mark of Jacobite mythmaking in Gaelic literature. A tradition of expected Catholic deliverance – an ironic mirror image of the Protestant siege – found its fullest expression in Gaelic poetry.

The preferred form was the aisling. In this highly allegorical verse – the allegory required to conceal the treasonous politics – the poet describes a dream or vision. Typically, a young woman wronged (Catholic Ireland) is lamenting the loss of her true lover or husband. Indeed, in some poems she complains outright of rape at the hands of a cruel stranger. The young woman of the aisling expresses her dream of hoped-for reunion with her true love in what are almost millenarian terms.

The aisling poems dominated Gaelic poetry throughout the eighteenth century. Interestingly, the greatest concentration of aisling poets was in north and east Munster, precisely the locus of the Whiteboy agrarian disturbances of the 1760s, the tithe war of the 1830s, the heartland of Daniel O'Connell's campaigns and later of the War of Independence and – in what may be no more than a coincidence – the centre for the game of hurling to this day.

The aisling poets were carriers of an underground tradition. The wronged Catholics of Ireland looked to the Stuarts – assisted by the Catholic powers of Europe – to deliver them from their bondage. This mythmaking survived the final demise of the Stuarts in 1766. It was displaced into a general myth of deliverance which would later look to revolutionary France as foreign saviour and even – less probably – to 'gallant allies in Europe' in the form of the Kaiser's Germany in 1916. The consistent thread running through this tradition was the illegitimacy of the Cromwellian land settlement and, by extension, of Protestant rule in Ireland. This is important: the focus of opposition was not the rule of the British crown per se but of the British colony. The distinction between crown and colony would be lost in the course of time. But for the moment, in the eighteenth century at least, there is a submerged nation which finds its voice in a confessional cause, not a national one. Nationalism had to await the effects of the French Revolution, and even then it could never disentangle itself from the older confessional tradition sustained for so long by the aisling poets.

Protestant Ireland may not have been privy to the serpentine allegories of the poetry, but it was well aware of the underlying sensibility. It was also aware of the unsettled nature of the Irish countryside, animated as always by agrarian grievances grounded in the hated land settlement. The Whiteboys – so called because they wore white sheets to disguise their identities – were the most famous but not the only secret society to ravage the Irish countryside in the second half of the eighteenth and the first half of the nineteenth centuries.

Defenders, Ribbonmen, Shanavests and Caravats all at one time or another represented rural alienation and engaged in acts of cruelty and violence against persons, property and farm animals. A particularly unpleasant practice was the houghing of cattle – cutting the hamstrings of the poor beasts to render them unsaleable at market.

Disturbances such as the Whiteboy campaigns in Munster induced hysteria among the authorities, understandably. The spectre of Catholic numbers mobilized in pursuit of what could only be regarded as a counter-revolution was quite enough to give full expression to the siege mentality. One conspicuous victim was Father Nicholas Sheehy, a parish priest from Co. Tipperary. Like most eighteenth-century Catholic clergy, he was a well-travelled man – unlike the insular and monoglot Anglican clergy – having been educated in Santiago and Salamanca. He was charged with Whiteboy offences. Fearing the prejudice of an all-Protestant Tipperary jury, he succeeded in having the trial moved to Dublin, where he was acquitted, only to be immediately arrested on his return on a trumped-up murder charge, convicted and hanged. It was a simple case of judicial murder, born of hysteria and panic.

Father Sheehy went to the scaffold in March 1766. He was unlucky, for the Old Pretender had died on New Year's Day and the papal recognition of the Hanoverians that followed took some heat out of the situation. He was the last victim of the worst of the penal era. In breathing that bit easier, Protestant Ireland could also breathe more liberally. When the siege is in process, security is the only watchword. When it is lifted, the defenders can afford a more generous temper.

The next thirty years, roughly from the mid 1760s to the late 1790s, were dominated by an internal debate within the Ascendancy caste. In very broad terms, the debate lay between a reform party that favoured the relaxation of the legal disabilities on Catholics, now that the Jacobite threat was finally gone, and those who wished to retain them in whole or in substance.

These views intersected, but did not completely overlap, with a debate between those who wished to end the parliamentary subservience of Ireland to Westminster (but not the royal connection to the crown, which no Protestant even contemplated diluting). In general, those in favour of greater autonomy for the Irish parliament tended to favour Catholic relief and vice versa. That said, it is one of those generalizations that should be deployed sparingly, for there were many significant exceptions to the rule. The Ascendancy started to behave like a classic creole colony, both dependent on the formal link to the motherland through the crown but also resenting the excessive interference of the metropole in their domestic affairs.

These differences were played out in the Irish parliament, an institution that could – with a certain amount of intellectual elasticity – trace its origins to 1264. But unlike the English parliament, it had enjoyed no continuous existence but instead a sporadic one. Nor was it established as a central and fixed element in the constitution, as in England. The condition of Ireland up to the start of the eighteenth century had been too turbulent and uncertain to permit the king's government to be mediated through representative institutions. Only with the coming of the Protestant peace after 1691 did the parliament begin to meet on a regular basis.

The main reason for this was money. Traditional sources of revenue – many of which were voted for the lifetime of the monarch – were inadequate to meet the growing costs of the state, so that the crown in Ireland had by constitutional convention recourse to parliament to vote the necessary revenues. By time-limiting such grants of revenue, parliament ensured that it would need to reconvene on a regular basis, if only to renew the grants. By the 1720s, the Irish parliament had so established itself as a stable element in the Irish political firmament that it built itself a permanent home in College Green in Dublin, on the site of the old Chichester House where it used to sometimes meet in the previous century. It is a Palladian masterpiece, one of the finest buildings ever put up in Ireland. It was, in truth, far too grand for such an exiguous assembly as the Irish parliament.

This parliament was really no such thing, at least as understood in the modern sense. That is to say, it was a not a sovereign assembly untrammelled by external authority. On the contrary, as mentioned, under the Declaratory Act of 1720 Westminster reserved the right to legislate for Ireland over its head. Moreover, there was one of the great examples of the law of unintended consequences: Poyning's Law of 1494, originally enacted to limit the discretionary autonomy of late medieval viceroys like the Great Earl of Kildare by ensuring that no Irish parliament could meet or any bills be introduced without royal consent. What was intended to deal with an immediate crisis in the 1490s was still being quoted as constitutional law 250 years later. As it waxed in importance and confidence, the Irish parliament naturally resented these restrictions on its independence of action. But it was not until the more relaxed atmosphere of the 1770s, with the siege receding into memory, that it felt able to address these shortcomings in a meaningful way.

There was another reason for the quickening of Irish colonial politics from the 1770s on. Britain had achieved a stunning victory in the Seven Years War against the French, which opened the way for the first British Empire. Britain was now firmly established in the Indian sub-continent. Canada had been seized from the French thanks to the heroics of General James Wolfe on the Heights of Abraham in 1759, that *annus mirabilis* for British arms. Combined with their continuing control of the eastern seaboard of what is now the United States, Britain was at last a serious world power.

But power brings problems, and the revolt of the American colonies from 1775 onwards required a further huge military effort. That meant soldiers; suddenly Ireland became a desirable recruiting ground. This had not been the case earlier in the century: Catholics were simply not trusted with arms and Protestants, other than officers, were discouraged lest too many recruits depleted the colony. Moreover, the Catholics showed their unreliability throughout the first half of the century by enlisting in significant numbers in continental Catholic armies – above all the French – where they distinguished themselves. The French victory at Fontenoy in 1745, during the War of the Austrian Succession, was a fabled success for the Irish Brigade.

Thirty years later, the situation had been transformed. The vastly increased British requirement for recruits meant that discriminatory practices against Irish Catholics were no longer sustainable. Not only did recruiting pick up in earnest, the changed atmosphere led to the first significant legislative breach of the Penal Laws, the Catholic Relief Acts of 1778 and 1782. These acts were sponsored by Luke Gardiner MP and permitted Catholics to hold land tenancies and inheritance rights on a basis of equality with Protestants. But there is no doubt that the legislation was actively encouraged from London; indeed, the greatest opposition to these and subsequent relief acts came from Protestant conservatives in Ireland. We can observe a mixture of Ascendancy liberalism and British necessity in the relaxation of the Penal Laws. We can also observe, in the more restless members of the Ascendancy, men of a temper similar to the American revolutionaries, a point noted by Benjamin Franklin when he visited Ireland in the early 1770s. The man whose name came to stand for all such people was Henry Grattan. A lawyer-politician, he established himself from the mid 1770s as the leading advocate of the 'Patriot' opposition, that is to say of the parliamentary opposition to the king's Irish government in Dublin Castle.

The Irish administration had been transformed by the permanent residence of the viceroy since 1768 and the consequent development of a muscular administrative structure. Previously, viceroys were as often as not absentees and the job of managing the Irish parliament and ensuring that it did London's bidding had been left to 'undertakers', Irish grandees who undertook to deliver London its desired results in return for personal preferment. With that system now superseded, there emerged a 'Castle party' of tough administrators, generally hostile to growing calls for a more autonomous (and therefore less manageable) parliament. In opposition to this development, there was a growing number of parliamentary 'Patriot' MPs under Grattan.

The war in America was going badly for the British. The French, glad of an opportunity to avenge their losses in the Seven Years War, gave their support to the colonists. The British requirement for more and more troops meant drawing men away from the Irish garrison for service across the Atlantic. This in turn alarmed Irish Protestants, who began to form companies of Volunteers to defend their kingdom. The Volunteer movement developed from the Irish militia, a reserve force of Protestants that had mobilized from time to time throughout the century in response to perceived threats of invasion.

The possibility of a French invasion was present again in the late 1770s and by mid 1779 the Volunteers were a national organization, a reserve dedicated to national defence. Having established itself as a force, however, it could be used for political ends as well as military ones. First, the Volunteers agitated for the removal of trade restrictions which Britain had imposed on Ireland. These restrictions were bitterly resented by Irish Protestants of every opinion, whether Castle supporters or Patriots. This meant that the latter group in parliament were able to take advantage of the pressure generated by the Volunteers, while the Castle's normal supporters had little enthusiasm for a counter-attack. A mass rally of Volunteers outside the Parliament House on College Green – captured in a celebrated painting by Francis Wheatley – added to the pressure. Parliament buckled before this intimidation and only voted funds for six months, a clear indication that unless substantial concessions were made, Ireland might become ungovernable. The system of administration so carefully assembled after 1768 was in danger of collapse by the winter of 1779.

London and the Castle regime gave up. All trading

restrictions were lifted and Ireland now enjoyed the same
rights in colonial trade as the larger island. But this concession,
while naturally welcomed in Ireland, had been part of that
larger claim of sovereignty that Britain had asserted over
Ireland and which had found expression in the Declaratory
Act and Poynings' Law. The pressure to do away with the
political restrictions that had sustained the now departed trade
restrictions grew in strength. In February 1782, a convention
of Volunteer leaders meeting in Dungannon, Co. Tyrone,
called for the repeal of the laws in question and the establishment of 'legislative independence' for the Irish parliament. By
May, the process was in train. Westminster passed the necessary legislation and the subordinate status of the Irish
parliament was ended. It now stood, at least in theory, in the
same relationship to the crown as the British parliament.

Thus was instituted 'Grattan's Parliament', named for the
most illustrious of the Patriot leaders. It was to last for a mere
eighteen years in its reconstituted state. The Volunteers had
extorted the constitutional concessions from Britain at a time
when her fortunes in America were at their lowest ebb: the
defeat at Yorktown in the autumn of 1781 had effectively
settled the war in favour of the colonists and American independence was soon to be a reality. It was a humiliating moment
for Britain. But for this humiliation, it is unlikely that legislative independence could have been secured.

The very public nature of the agitation for free trade and
legislative independence created a sphere of public discourse
and excitement in Ireland that was without precedent. The
growing influence of the Dublin press was material in all this.
Even more so was the fact that a further major Catholic Relief
Act was passed in 1782, so that Catholic public opinion now
began to be heard through the voices of Archbishop John
Thomas Troy of Dublin and of bourgeois leaders of the
Catholic Committee – hitherto a deferential body, far too
respectable for its own good – like John Keogh, a wealthy
merchant. However, the question of further concessions to

Catholics was to divide the Irish parliament for all of its short life. When all was said and done, this was still a Protestant assembly for the Protestant people of Ireland. Passing gusts of liberalism on the religious issue were all very well but the entrenched suspicion and fear of popery was never far from the surface. It is interesting that the major piece of legislation passed in this area during the life of the parliament – the Catholic Relief Act of 1793, which allowed some Catholics to vote for the first time – was forced through by London (by now embroiled in the French Revolutionary wars) despite being deplored by parliamentarians and Castle officials alike in Dublin. It was a re-run of the 1770s: Britain's need to avoid trouble at its rear trumped the doubts of its Irish creoles.

The end of the American war robbed the Volunteers of their *raison d'être*. They tried to prolong their life by agitating for parliamentary reform. But any such proposals were absolute anathema to London – and to many Irish parliamentary grandees as well, whose political and pecuniary interests were invested in the existing system. The whole panoply of rotten and pocket boroughs (parliamentary areas controlled by one man or family) in both islands would stay in place until the Reform Act of 1832. It was unthinkable that Ireland might act unilaterally in a matter that touched so centrally on the British political system. With the failure of parliamentary reform, the Volunteers fade from history for more than a decade, only to reappear in the violence of the late 1790s as the Irish Militia and the Yeomanry – literally the cutting edge of Protestant reaction.

The 'constitution of 1782' may have delivered legislative independence to the parliament in College Green, but half a mile away, at the western end of Dame Street, Dublin Castle remained the centre of British administration in Ireland. It was still an arm of the London government in Ireland, one of its primary purposes being the management of parliament to ensure that measures opposed by the British government were not carried there. In general, with some exceptions, it succeeded in this, so that the trumpeted legislative independence was not matched by administrative independence. This disjunction between parliament and Castle symbolized the anomalies in Anglo-Irish constitutional relationships in the late eighteenth century. It was one which was thrown into stark relief by the Regency crisis.

King George III was prone to a mental illness that struck him in 1788. It rendered him deranged and unfit to fulfil his duties. The prime minister, William Pitt the Younger, wished the Prince of Wales to assume the regency but with limited powers. Pitt's rival, Charles James Fox, wanted an untrammelled regency, confident that his friend the prince would invite him to form a government. In Ireland, the Patriot party in parliament supported the Foxite position, as much to assert its independence as anything else. It resulted in a famous speech by John FitzGibbon, Lord Clare – the lord chancellor of Ireland and the most lucidly intelligent conservative in the country – in which he warned of an existential crisis should Dublin assume the right to offer the crown of Ireland in a manner that effectively detached the smaller island constitutionally from the larger. If parliament could invest the Prince of Wales with royal powers, it could do the same for the Pope or the king of France, he said. In short, it was claiming the right for the parliament to detach itself from the British connection. Was that what the Protestants of Ireland wanted?

It was a good question, but one that did not have to be answered immediately, for the king made a sudden and full recovery and the regency crisis disappeared. The question that Lord Clare had put would be answered – and answered definitively – ten years later.

13

REBELLION

Eighteenth-century Ireland had been an *ancien régime* society, in which assumptions of inequality were uncontested, in which the political nation was a landed and military minority, and in which authority flowed downward from God to the monarch and thus through such representative institutions as existed to the people. The French Revolution proposed a new paradigm: a sovereign people, living in a nation state – not a royal state – in which power flowed upward from the governed to the governors. This was a thrillingly new idea and it took Europe by storm.

The French Revolution received its most enthusiastic Irish reception in Presbyterian Ulster. The two coastal counties of Antrim and Down, immediately north and south of the city of Belfast, were the areas of densest Presbyterian settlement. It was here, just across the North Channel from Scotland, where the levelling principles of the Revolution found their loudest Irish echo. French principles appealed to Presbyterians, accustomed as they were to their own democratic forms of church government and their dislike for the insolent impositions of the Anglican landed elite. Precisely because of its existential threat to traditional hierarchical authority, the Revolution had less immediate appeal for the majority of the Anglican Church of Ireland.

The third element in Ulster's confessional quilt was, of course, the Roman Catholics. Even more than Anglicanism, Catholicism was a staunch supporter of *ancien régime* values and hierarchies: the Vatican was an enemy of the Revolution from the start. This was hardly to be wondered at, for the Revolution made no secret of its enmity for the church, which it regarded not simply as umbilically joined to the monarchy but also a locus of superstition and ignorance. This characterization was entirely in tune with the Ulster Presbyterian view of Catholicism. However, while the Catholic hierarchy may have watched developments in France with dismay, many of the faithful in Ireland rejoiced in the gradual consolidation of the new regime in Paris and its military successes. The famous cannonade at Valmy on 20 September 1792 threw back the forces of the First Coalition of European powers ranged against revolutionary France and inaugurated an era of French military dominance that was to last until the Battle of Waterloo in 1815.

Few Irish Catholics were indifferent to these continental developments, for on to revolutionary France were projected some of the old Jacobite ambitions, now diverted into a new course. The dreamed-for deliverance by England's continental enemies lived on.

Ironically, these hopes were in part triggered by the ambitions of idealistic Anglicans caught up in the heady idealism of the early Revolution. At first, the Revolution appealed to everyone impatient with the ways of the *ancien régime* state. In England, the opposition Whigs who clustered around Charles James Fox were prominent in this regard, although the outstanding intellect in this grouping, Edmund Burke, soon became the most trenchant and the most devastating critic of the changes across the Channel. In Ireland, likewise, all reformers who chafed under the rule of the Castle and its parliamentary supporters were early champions of the revolutionary cause. This was to dilute as the 1790s progressed and the Terror took hold in France, but a committed minority of political radicals remained steadfast. Of these, the most significant figure was Theobald Wolfe Tone.

Tone was one of the most attractive and elusive figures in Irish history. The son of a prosperous Co. Kildare coachmaker, Peter Tone, his name honoured his father's landlord, Theobald Wolfe. Tone had charm but few connections, and although a barrister he was not one of the gilded legal elite. Moreover, his father's business failed when the boy was fifteen. Nonetheless, his obvious talent carried him to Trinity College Dublin and a legal qualification, although his fantasy ambition was to become an army officer. In one of history's more intriguing might-have-beens, he had tried to persuade his father to finance him to volunteer to fight the American colonists: Tone could have ended up a career officer in the British army.

Instead, he immersed himself in college life, becoming auditor of the Historical Society in his final year. He was already a fine speaker and an accomplished pamphleteer. Like many a brief-less barrister, he had a flair for writing. In September 1791, five years after qualifying at the Bar, he issued one of the most influential pamphlets of the century. Entitled *An Argument on behalf of the Catholics of Ireland*, it proposed the novel idea that not only was toleration of Catholics desirable and timely, it was an essential condition for Irish liberty in general. This placed Tone at the cutting margin of Irish radicalism, on a shore occupied by no Anglican before him. It was the product of a revolutionary ferment on an acute and quicksilver intelligence, impossible to imagine in circumstances other than those tripped off by events in France. In earlier pamphlets, Tone had been content to sign himself 'an independent Irish Whig'. *An Argument . . .* went well beyond Whiggery.

He was not entirely alone, however, within the wider world of Irish Protestantism. Radicals among the Ulster Presbyterian community were gradually losing their hitherto reflexive disdain for Catholicism. One of their number, William Drennan, a doctor originally from Belfast but now settled in Dublin, had already floated the idea of a political alliance

between Presbyterians and Catholics against the common
establishment enemy, which was, of course, wholly Anglican.
This represented a considerable step change for Drennan who
had previously shared in full measure the Presbyterian dislike
of Catholicism, something he never fully shook off. For
instance, he rather glumly wrote to his sister that 'the Catholic
spirit is the soil of Ireland and must be cultivated or we must
emigrate', hardly a ringing piece of ecumenism. Perhaps he was
open to liberal possibility because of his background: his father
had been a minister in Belfast of the so-called New Light
tendency in the church, although some historians have doubted
Drennan's enthusiasm for this tendency. The New Light liberals dominated the Synod of Ulster in the eighteenth century,
not yielding to the Old Light Calvinist conservatives until the
1820s and 1830s when Daniel O'Connell's aggressive Catholic
nationalism helped create a defensive mentality among Irish
Protestants of every hue.

Drennan and Tone were the moving spirits behind the
founding of the Society of United Irishmen in Belfast in
October 1791. The society was born in Peggy Barclay's tavern
in central Belfast and its manifesto included the following: 'In
the present great era of reform, when unjust governments are
falling in every quarter of Europe, we have no national government. *We are ruled by Englishmen, and the servants of
Englishmen.*' It also called for 'a cordial union among *all the
people of Ireland*', thus echoing Tone's *Argument*, and a reform
of the Irish Parliament so thoroughgoing that it must 'include
Irishmen of every religious persuasion'.

This manifesto bears some consideration, because it may be
regarded, among other things, as the foundation document of
the Irish republican revolutionary tradition. It acknowledges
that its context is that of the French Revolution, with unjust
governments falling under French pressure: its ambitions
would be unthinkable – certainly unrealizable – in any other
context. It then deplores the absence of a *national* government,
a typically revolutionary distinction between the nation and

the royal state. In the royal state, the ethnic origins of the rulers were of little account: the Spanish throne, for example, had been occupied successively by dynasties of Habsburgs and Bourbons. In the nation state, this was the supreme question, because national solidarity was invested in the sovereign people, not in the monarch. And by extension, the people must embrace all of the nation regardless of confessional allegiance. This was an existential challenge to the old regime.

Enthusiasm amounting to euphoria and utopian optimism informed radicals' response to the Revolution across Europe. William Wordsworth, who was to live long enough to die a reactionary Tory, nonetheless recalled in rhapsodic verse (*The Prelude*, 1805) the universal fervour that the Revolution inspired in liberals and reformers:

> Bliss was it in that dawn to be alive,
> But to be young was very heaven! – Oh! times,
> In which the meagre, stale, forbidding ways
> Of custom, law, and statute, took at once
> The attraction of a country in romance!
> When Reason seemed the most to assert her rights,
> When most intent on making of herself
> A prime Enchantress – to assist the work,
> Which then was going forward in her name!
> Not favoured spots alone, but the whole earth,
> The beauty wore of promise, that which sets
> (As at some moment might not be unfelt
> Among the bowers of paradise itself)
> The budding rose above the rose full blown.

The principles of the Revolution were amplified in the anglophone world by Thomas Paine's *Right of Man*, one of the wonders of the age. It went through seven editions in Ireland alone in 1791 and 1792, selling more than 40,000 copies. Nowhere was its message more congenial than in Presbyterian Ulster, with its instinctive dislike of hierarchies of every kind.

Tone, the Anglican-Deist from Dublin, may have been the prime mover of the United Irishmen but the early days of the society drew the support of a disproportionate number of Ulster Presbyterians: Drennan, Henry Joy McCracken, Samuel Neilson, Robert Simms and many others drawn from the ranks of Belfast's mercantile bourgeoisie.

In its first few years, the United Irishmen represented the radical wing of the parliamentary reform movement. They were excited by the French Revolution, but their demands remained carefully within constitutional boundaries – if only just. What changed the society, or at least its radicals, from reformers to revolutionaries was the entry of Great Britain into the European wars.

After the Battle of Valmy, the French army under Charles François Dumouriez consolidated its victory at Jemappes, swept the forces of the First Coalition out of north-east France, annexed the Austrian Netherlands (modern Belgium) and occupied parts of the Rhineland including Mainz. Thus by the autumn of 1792, the Revolution had not simply defended itself in arms: it had exported itself aggressively and asserted France's 'natural border' on the Rhine. In January 1793 Louis XVI and Marie Antoinette went to the guillotine. This event horrified Europe and was the proximate cause of Britain joining the coalition. Britain was to be at war with France intermittently for the next twenty-two years.

Tone's dream of the union of Catholic, Protestant and Dissenter in the common name of Irishman was not easily realized. Despite the optimism of their more liberal members, Presbyterians had traditionally harboured a deep hatred and contempt for Catholicism. This was hardly surprising given their Calvinism: they represented, after all, that Protestant theology farthest removed from Catholic practice and most hostile to it. Moreover, Catholics had no illusions about the Presbyterians. Idealism was all very well, but realism dictated caution on both sides. For the Catholics, the entry of Britain into the war revived the hope that military necessity might once more prompt London to ameliorate their disabilities in Ireland, as it had done under pressure of the American war in the 1770s and 1780s. It made sense to keep lines open to London rather than embarking on political adventures with a movement dominated by a hereditary enemy. This calculation was well judged. Pitt's government did indeed put pressure on the Irish parliament to pass Catholic Relief Acts in 1792 and 1793, of which the latter was the more substantial measure.

The 1792 act allowed Catholics to practise law. The 1793 act admitted some of them to the franchise for the first time, and also allowed some of them to hold a variety of public and military offices previously denied to them. The 1793 act was forced through the Irish parliament by the chief secretary, Robert Hobart, over the embittered protests of the Protestant ultras, who regarded the concessions as a betrayal of their interests. It was not the last time that Irish Protestants suspected London's intentions and looked to themselves as the best defenders of their own interests.

In a sense, the ultras were right because London was not just concerned to drive a wedge between any possible junction of Catholics and Presbyterians. The government had also been lobbied by a revived and vigorous Catholic Committee in the early 1790s in support of Catholic relief. This committee, which hitherto had been a genteel, aristocratic affair, was taken over by more robust and assertive mercantile interests and pursued a more aggressive policy of trying to influence government policy. In a sense, it found itself pushing an open door, especially once Britain entered the war with France. The committee's interests and those of Pitt's government suddenly overlapped hugely.

The United Irishmen were now presented with a choice between reform and revolution. The Relief Acts had satisfied immediate Catholic demands and confirmed to the mainstream leadership, both secular and lay, that their best interests were served by positive engagement with the British government. This detached many Catholics, especially the wealthier classes who provided social and political leadership, from any alliance with the United Irishmen. Similarly, the pressure of war convinced moderate United men of the political impossibility of parliamentary reform in any foreseeable timescale. Radical ambitions had to be placed on hold.

Sentiments such as these had the effect of isolating and further radicalizing the revolutionary core within the Society of United Irishmen. From 1794, it moved towards an openly separatist and republican position. Its obvious admiration for the French republic, now at war with Great Britain, left it with no other intellectual option, albeit it exposed United men to the charge of treason. These developments convinced the Dublin Castle authorities in their long-held suspicions of the society, which they had always regarded as a radical wolf in reformist sheep's clothing. Repressive measures were taken against the United Irishmen to prevent them forming assemblies or volunteer corps on the lines of the 1770s. Moreover, leading figures in the movement were harassed by the authorities. Many were arrested, including the editors of their newspaper, the popular and influential *Northern Star*.

Then the government found itself a chance to suppress the society altogether. An English clergyman, Revd William Jackson, who had been infected with an enthusiasm for French revolutionary ideals, was sent from Paris to London to gauge the prospects for a successful French invasion of the British Isles. He was quickly betrayed to the authorities by an acquaintance of his, one Cockayne. This shadowy figure promptly earned himself a pension and the remission of his debts by accompanying the still unsuspecting Jackson to Ireland and reporting on his movements and, more importantly, on whom he met and what they discussed.

In Dublin, they met one of the city's most prominent United men, Leonard McNally, a barrister who was to defend (and betray) many of his leading colleagues in the coming years. He was deeply influential in the society, as well as being a British informer. Whether he was already a spy when he first met

Jackson or became one in panic after the discovery of his association with the clergyman is unclear. What is clear is that he
was perhaps the most proficient and successful spy the British
ever had in Ireland. No one suspected him and he died peace-
fully in his bed in 1820, his treachery undiscovered until later.

McNally introduced Jackson and Cockayne to Archibald
Hamilton Rowan, a leading United Irishman whom McNally
had unsuccessfully defended against a charge of seditious libel
and who was languishing in Newgate prison. He in turn
suggested that they contact Tone, who drafted a paper proposing an optimistic prognosis for a French invasion of Ireland
subject to at least 10,000 troops being sent for the purpose.
Jackson was arrested on 28 April 1794 with a copy of Tone's
memorandum in his possession. Only the pleading of influential friends saved Tone's neck, for he was undoubtedly guilty
of treason in the eyes of the law. Instead of the gallows, he was
allowed to emigrate to America. There was no such escape for
Jackson. He was tried and committed suicide by taking poison
in the dock.

The Society of United Irishmen was suppressed by the
government and thus became an underground revolutionary
body. Even before suppression, some elements in the society
had been making advances towards a Catholic agrarian secret
society, the Defenders, and this union of interests was to prove
fateful in 1798.

The Defenders were a kind of Catholic vigilante movement,
strongest in south Ulster and north Leinster, and had emerged
as a result of the unstable and violent sectarian situation in Co.
Armagh. This small county had a tripartite confessional division. In the north and east, centred on the linen manufacturing
towns of Portadown and Lurgan, the Anglicans were ubiquitous with only a small and marginal Catholic minority.
Surprisingly, there was almost no Presbyterian presence in this
region. It was confined to a middle buffer zone, running horizontally across the county south of Armagh city. South of that
again was a solidly Catholic and Gaelic-speaking area known

as the Fews, which ended in the ring of southern hills and drumlins that separates south Ulster from Leinster.

The tensions between these confessional enemies living in such close proximity were not helped by the presence of many former Volunteers, whose arms became available to Protestant gangs. These gangs, of which the best known was the Peep o' Day Boys, rampaged across the countryside from the mid 1780s. The Defenders were formed as a Catholic counterbalance and organized themselves in Freemason-style lodges, something the Orangemen were soon to copy. Both sides committed horrible outrages, but it can hardly be denied that the principal volition was on the Protestant side. Competition for land leases may have sparked off the first attacks, but they continued sporadically and violently for a decade and more.

The Defenders' stronghold, the Fews, was relatively remote and introverted. It had a rich tradition of Gaelic life and poetry and was an area where older Catholic traditions subsisted. Jacobitism, aisling poetry, dreams of deliverance from abroad: all remained a living presence. The area was rural and poor and the Defenders, just like the Peep o' Day Boys on the other side, were largely a demotic phenomenon, shunned by the embarrassed well-to-do.

The prospects for a union of interests between the United Irishmen – most of whose leaders were Protestants and whose inherited dislike of Catholicism was constantly wrestling with their professed non-sectarianism – and violent, rural proletarian Catholics were unpromising. The full extent of the interaction between the two groups will never be known. The Defenders had what the United men lacked: numbers, and concentrated numbers at that. This raised the prospect of a revolutionary movement with a Protestant (or nominally non-sectarian) head and a Catholic body.

Ironically, this ambition mirrored the structure of the Militia, an army reserve established by the Irish administration on a county basis from 1793 onwards. The majority of its members were Catholics; the officers were Protestant. They numbered about 30,000 men by 1798 and were always deployed outside their own county, as with the notorious North Cork Militia in Wexford in 1798. The United Irishmen devoted some effort to suborning members of the Militia and swearing them into the society. On the basis of exaggerated successes in this endeavour, Wolfe Tone was later able to persuade the French that an invasion of Ireland would be greeted by a popular uprising.

As the decade progressed, the authorities further strengthened their security hand by forming the Yeomanry in 1796. Unlike the Militia, they served in their local areas in support of the magistrates. They were little more than licensed vigilantes and they acquired a ferocious reputation for violence in 1798. Memories of depredations by the Yeomanry – the 'Yeos' – long survived in the popular memory of that fateful year.

The sectarian violence in Co. Armagh came to a head in 1795. An affray known forever after as the Battle of the Diamond took place just outside the village of Loughgall. It represented a resounding victory for the Peep o' Day Boys and left at least thirty Defenders dead. The Boys celebrated their victory in a tavern owned by James Sloan in nearby Loughgall and reconstituted themselves as the Orange Order, with Sloan becoming the first grand master.

The Orange Order and the Defenders represented the persistence of ancient rural atavisms, with memories of historic sectarian animosities constantly refreshed in each generation. Rival historical myths were sedulously cultivated. If the United Irishmen represented the Enlightenment and by extension the optimism of revolutionary France, the Orange Order and the Defenders represented indigenous traditions rooted long and deep in the Irish countryside. For Catholics and Protestants alike, the tensions and contradictions between tradition and modernity were to prove acute and enduring. This was especially so on the Catholic side, where a version of nationalism was forming in the crucible of the 1790s whose twin streams were secular republicanism and Catholic solidarity. They made for a turbulent confluence.

In the same year that the Orange Order was founded, another institution was established by the Irish parliament: St Patrick's College, Maynooth, just west of Dublin, a Roman Catholic seminary for the education of diocesan priests, only the second such academy established in Ireland since the Reformation. St Patrick's, Carlow, had opened two years earlier. Both colleges reflected a general loosening of the Penal Laws, a greater spirit of toleration and also enlightened self-interest. For all of the eighteenth century, Irish priests had been educated in continental seminaries, but with the continent now gripped by French fervour – not to mention the French army – it was hoped to insulate the Irish priesthood from revolutionary contagion. It was further evidence of a growing community of interest between the Catholic Church and the authorities in Dublin and London. And Maynooth may be said to have kept its part of the bargain, for while it was to develop a robust nationalist culture in the coming century, it was a profoundly conservative nationalism.

Catholic hopes were further raised, only to be dashed, by the impetuous viceroyalty of Earl Fitzwilliam, also in 1795. A reformer in too much of a hurry, he summarily dismissed high-ranking Dublin Castle officials of long standing and also raised the possibility of Catholic Emancipation – the total removal of all remaining disabilities against Catholics. Political and administrative chaos ensued. Emancipation never stood a chance politically: it was undeliverable in the circumstances of the day, given both the war on the continent and the rising sectarian tensions in the countryside. (When Emancipation eventually came in 1829, it was only after a titanic political struggle at Westminster.) Fitzwilliam was a loose cannon, and he was recalled to England after a mere fifty days in office. He was a warning to his successors to be neither innovative nor imaginative.

*   *   *

Theobald Wolfe Tone did not skulk around Dublin after his
reprieve. Indeed, he made a point of showing himself openly,
especially during the trial of the wretched Jackson. Still, he had
to keep his part of the bargain with the authorities and sail for
the United States in 1795. Three years earlier, in 1792, in his
role as assistant secretary to the Catholic Convention, he had
been secretary to a group of Catholics who had presented a
petition to King George III in London. Before he left for
Philadelphia, a meeting of the Catholics of Dublin resolved
unanimously, 'that the thanks of the meeting be respectfully be
presented to their agent, Theobald Wolfe Tone, for the readi-
ness with which he accompanied their deputies to England,
and the many other important services rendered the Catholic
body – services which no gratitude could overrate, and no
remuneration overpay.' His final visit prior to departure was to
his friends in Belfast, as he recalled in his journal:

> I remember particularly two days that we passed on Cave Hill.
> On the first, [Thomas] Russell, Neilson, Simms, McCracken
> and one or two more of us, on the summit of Art's Fort, took a
> solemn obligation – which I think I may say I have on my part
> endeavoured to fulfil – never to desist in our efforts until we
> had subverted the authority of England over our country and
> asserted her independence.

Within a month of this dramatic tableau, Tone was on his way
to Philadelphia. There he met two old friends: Dr Reynolds,
who had been chairman of the Dublin United Irishmen at the
time of the Jackson imbroglio, and Hamilton Rowan, who had
escaped from Newgate and subsequently fled to France, where
he had tried to interest the Committee of Public Safety in an
Irish invasion. The fall of Robespierre scuppered that scheme.
Disenchanted, Rowan sailed for America. There was a French
minister in Philadelphia whom Rowan had known in Paris and
he gave Tone an introduction. After much to-ing and fro-ing,
Tone – bolstered by letters from Keogh, Russell and Simms in

Ireland painting a rosy picture of revolutionary potential – sailed for France with a note from the minister in Philadelphia commending Tone and his enterprise to the government in Paris.

He arrived in France on 1 February 1796 and as early as 24 February he found himself in the Palais du Luxembourg talking to Lazare Carnot. Known as 'the organizer of victory', Carnot was a military engineer but his real talent was for raising, equipping and provisioning armies. He was one of the five members of the Directory that governed France after the fall of Robespierre. This intensely practical man – we would probably now refer to him as a technocrat – clearly believed Tone's estimates of Irish revolutionary potential. He agreed to send an army to Ireland, with his enabling instruction making a significant reference to the secret arming of the Defenders. The commander of the expedition was to be General Louis Lazare Hoche. Tone was commissioned as an adjutant-general in the French revolutionary army. He had always dreamed of a military career. Now he had one.

At this point, Hoche was a mere twenty-six years old but he had already established a formidable reputation as an officer. He was a classic product of the Revolution: a poor boy from Versailles who had risen through the army ranks through sheer ability. Under the old regime, he would have been ignored. He had been principally responsible for the brutal destruction of the Chouans, royalist enemies of the Revolution in the Vendée in western France. Ironically, the deeply Catholic Chouans probably had more in common with the Defenders than with the United Irishmen. At any rate, by 1796, Hoche's reputation as a rising star in the French army stood second only to that of Napoleon Bonaparte. His appointment to Ireland was proof of the Directory's seriousness. The French were going for broke in Britain's vulnerable back yard.

It was a high-risk affair and the risks were soon evident. The expedition was scheduled for December 1796, in order to catch Royal Navy ships tied up for the winter in port, but that meant gambling on the mid-winter weather. Moreover, the port of departure was Brest in Brittany. There were three channels to carry shipping out of Brest, all of which presented navigational difficulties of some sort. In addition, these exit channels were all capable of surveillance by the Royal Navy. Not all its ships were in port and spies had reported on the rather obvious preparations in Brest. However, the British misinterpreted the signals, believing that the French were bound for Portugal and would be frustrated by contrary winds. For the most part, French luck held. The expedition avoided any contact with the British and made it to the open sea with the wind in its sails. There were almost 15,000 crack troops aboard, equal in number to the entire regular British army strength in Ireland, most of it billeted far from the south-west towards which the French were aimed. One ship foundered on leaving port and, fatefully, Hoche's ship, the *Fraternité*, got detached from the main convoy and never rejoined it.

Nonetheless, by 21 December the French were lying off Cape Clear and on the following day they sailed east up along Bantry Bay. A brisk westerly wind drove them towards the town of Bantry at the head of the bay. The shore defences were pitiful and beyond them the road to Cork lay open. At this point, the second-in-command, General Grouchy, decided to not to land until Hoche turned up. Hoche never turned up, but the wind now turned around to the east and blew a gale that made a landing impossible. Tone's frustration was recorded in his journal, where he claimed that he could have tossed a biscuit ashore, a pardonable exaggeration. But it was no use: the east wind was relentless and dense fog made visibility impossible. Some ships began to drag their anchors and orders were given to cut their cables and make for the open sea again. By 17 January 1797, the expedition was back in Brest. As Tone noted mournfully in his journal: 'Well, England has not had such an escape since the Spanish Armada, and that expedition, like ours, was defeated by the weather.' The 'Protestant wind' of legend, that had frustrated the Armada and then blown William of Orange to Torbay a hundred years later, seemed to have done the trick again.

Tone was right about one thing. England had indeed got a tremendous fright. Likewise, the hopes of Irish revolutionaries had been lifted by the French presence. There were reports of huge numbers of Defenders under arms in Ulster and north Leinster. An Insurrection Act was quickly passed making it possible to proclaim troublesome areas and impose martial law. The Militia and the Yeomanry were augmented. Habeas corpus (the writ requiring that an accused should be produced in court so that the justification for their detention can be examined) had been suspended in October 1796 – even before the French expedition – in response to the chronic Orange-Defender disturbances in Ulster. Leaders of the United Irishmen in Belfast were charged with high treason and imprisoned.

On 13 March 1797, General Gerard Lake proclaimed martial law in Ulster. Lake was a capable officer but he was a dull brute who believed in summary justice. All persons in the proclaimed area not in the service of the crown were to surrender their arms. 'Nothing but terror will keep them in order,' he wrote on assuming his command and he was to prove as good as his word. Houses were searched and pillaged, acting on information from spies. Huge numbers of arms were recovered. What remained of the Belfast leadership of the United Irishmen was arrested. The Yeomanry were left off the leash and conducted a campaign of terror across the countryside. Houses were torched, men were flogged without mercy and nearly fifty United men were executed after proceedings that were no better than kangaroo courts.

Most of the early victims of this 'dragooning of Ulster' – Lake's own phrase – were Presbyterian United men. The most famous martyr was William Orr, a prominent farmer and owner of a bleach-green (a large, open area where linen could be laid out), who was hanged at Carrickfergus in October 1797 on trumped-up charges despite a recommendation of mercy from an already biased and packed jury. Orr became an icon in Presbyterian folk memory. Even long after the Presbyterians of Ulster had made their sometimes uneasy peace with the British state, he was remembered as the victim of a hideous injustice and a reminder of the stout independence of mind in that remarkable provincial community.

Presbyterians had furnished the provincial leadership of the United Irishmen, and without them the movement was three parts dead in Ulster. That, combined with the increasing viciousness of the Yeos in the countryside, changed the complexion of things. The Yeos, who between themselves and the Militia had about 70,000 men under arms by the start of 1798, simply went on a sectarian rampage. Orange houses and arms were left alone. Indeed, many members of the Yeomanry were also members of the Orange Order. All the fire was now directed at the Defenders. Troops were billeted on suspect houses, floggings and half-hangings continued without let-up, not to mention the practice known as shearing – cutting off a suspect's earlobes. The longest remembered torture was pitch-capping, in which a piece of thick paper soaked in pitch was fixed to a victim's head and set alight.

In late 1797, Lake found himself saddled with a new military superior. General Sir Ralph Abercromby arrived in Ireland as commander-in-chief. He was a thoughtful officer and he was horrified by what he found. The licence and indiscipline of the army, the Militia and the Yeomanry, fully encouraged by Lake, was anathema to him. He tried to restore discipline but the Irish authorities were in the grip of hysteria following the near miss at Bantry Bay; they were quite content with Lake's methods. Abercromby feared that Lake's *dragonnade* would foment rebellion rather than suppress it. He was to be proved right. But in the short term, he realized that he was getting nowhere. He resigned. Lake, no less, replaced him and promptly brought his reign of terror to north Leinster.

And then he took them ever further south. By March

1798, counties as far south as Wexford were being proclaimed
and subjected to all the horrors of Lake's methods. The
repression was most pronounced in areas like north Co.
Wexford where the United Irishmen were believed,
correctly, to be most numerous. The Castle's intelligence
was improving. It had a formidable network of spies, of
whom Leonard McNally was just one. Others included
Francis Higgins, the proprietor of the *Freeman's Journal*,
Dublin's leading newspaper, a man known universally as the
Sham Squire. He was an unscrupulous and shady opportun-
ist and he was the centre of an efficient spy network reporting
to the Castle authorities.

The network was successful. On 12 March 1798, it betrayed
the presence of the Leinster directory of the United Irishmen
who were meeting in the house of Oliver Bond, a prosperous
wool merchant. All of the Leinster leadership except for one or
two absentees were captured and arrested. The most important
of these absentees was Lord Edward FitzGerald, an exact
contemporary of Wolfe Tone. The remarkable thing about
Lord Edward was the fact that he was the younger son of the
Duke of Leinster, Ireland's senior peer. He was therefore the
scion of the oldest Hiberno–Norman family in the country.
He had served with distinction in the British army in the
American war and in Canada in the 1780s before returning to
Europe. He was in Paris in the early days of the Revolution
and he knew Thomas Paine. He married the daughter of
Philippe Égalité, the duc d'Orleans. His revolutionary fervour
did not diminish on his return to Ireland. As MP for Kildare,
he despaired of the Irish parliament reforming itself and instead
threw in his lot with the United Irishmen.

Although Lord Edward escaped capture in March, his luck
did not hold. One of the Sham Squire's agents was Francis
Magan, like Leonard McNally a barrister and a United man,
and it was he who was responsible for the betrayal of Lord
Edward. The Dublin town major, Henry Sirr, captured
FitzGerald in a house in Thomas Street on 19 May 1798. In the

fierce exchange of gunfire in a confined space, Lord Edward was hit and died of his wounds in Newgate on 4 June.

By then, however, the country was ablaze.

Despite the hysteria of the time, it must have seemed to the more rational elements in the Irish administration that the revolution-ary beast had been slain. Ulster was cowed and its Presbyterian elite, the most formidable regional leadership available to the United Irishmen, thoroughly broken up. Lake's *dragonnade* had resulted in vast seizures of arms. The Leinster directory's capture had also revealed their insurrectionary plans to the Castle. Lord Edward FitzGerald, their leading military light, was under arrest and dying. The French had lost interest in Ireland, with Napoleon taking an invasion force to Egypt.

And yet the insurrection happened.

On the night of 23–4 May 1798, mail coaches leaving Dublin were attacked and burned out. This was the prearranged signal for the rising. The United plan had been for the principal rising to take place in Dublin, with supporting rebellions in the prov-inces as a distraction. Dublin was key. But the United organization in the city was in tatters following the arrests in March and May. The city remained tense but peaceful. There were desultory risings in surrounding counties which were quickly snuffed out with exemplary violence. The orgy of pitch-cappings, half-hangings, summary executions, house burnings, floggings and other manifestations of Lake's preferred methods now accomplished exactly what they were intended to forestall, as Abercromby had feared.

Some of the worst violence was on the northern borders of Co. Wexford. This generally fertile county, at the south-east-ern corner of the island, had a higher-than-average Protestant population, about 25 per cent of the total. It provided the political leadership in the county, and had often split the two county seats in parliament between liberal and conservative interests. But as the 1790s wore on and tensions increased, the voters did what people are inclined to do in anxious times:

they rallied to the conservatives who won both county seats in the 1797 election. A collapse in grain prices hit the county hard. Wexford had a greater proportion of land under tillage than most Irish counties.

Into this combustible situation now came people from across the county border, bearing tales of army and Yeomanry atrocities. Moreover, the *dragonnade* now spread into the north of the county with all its attendant horrors. There also appeared the North Cork Militia under their Protestant officers complete with a travelling Orange lodge – to augment the three lodges already established in north Wexford – which did nothing to lower tensions. The terrified peasantry determined to resist. The county leadership of the United Irishmen, comprising a minority of liberal Protestants and a number of prosperous Catholic tenant farmers, provided an officer corps. Despite harassment from the authorities, they succeeded in effecting a reasonably efficient mobilization of men and materiel on the night of 26–7 May across the northern part of the county. Additional leadership was provided by a number of Catholic priests, of whom the most prominent was Father John Murphy of Boolavogue. His church had been burned by the Yeos.

A successful arms raid in the village of Camolin supplied the contents of the armoury at the mansion of Lord Mountnorris. The main body of rebels, about 2,000 strong, now assembled in the region of Oulart Hill, south of Camolin and east of Enniscorthy, the market town set in the centre of the county. Here, they learned that the North Cork Militia was approaching. Sensibly, they occupied the rising ground on the hillside. What followed was a national sensation.

It was a basic assumption among military men that a disciplined force, acting under orders, will always defeat an armed mob regardless of numbers. That thought must have been in the heads of the North Cork Militia at Oulart because they advanced against the rebel position uphill in open countryside. Their first volley of shots would have been the first time the rebels had ever heard such a thing. But the rebels held steady nonetheless, under the leadership of Fr John Murphy. They drew the troops into an enfilading counter-attack and then charged. It was the Militia who broke ranks and fled. It was a rout.

The rebels quickly occupied nearby Enniscorthy and then the county town of Wexford. Thousands of recruits now swelled the ranks, which may have grown as strong as 15,000 men. The Wexford republic was proclaimed. But like the dog that caught its own tail, what were they to do now? What had been planned as a provincial sideshow to the Dublin rising was now the main act. The United Irishmen had either to spread the rebellion or wait for its suppression. Sensibly, they looked west, with a view to capturing the strategic town of New Ross on the upper tidal reaches of the Barrow estuary. On the far side of the river lay the counties of Kilkenny and Waterford; upstream was Co. Carlow. New Ross would give them options as well as access to the sea and the possibility of relief or resupply by that route.

On 5 June, about 10,000 rebel troops besieged New Ross in what became the decisive battle of the rebellion. About 2,000 are thought to have had firearms; the rest were pikemen, but pikes could be formidable weapons in close-quarter street fighting. The town was defended by the regular garrison under Lieutenant-General Johnson, who had marched up from Waterford at the first hint of trouble, with General Eustace adding a smaller detachment of troops from Co. Carlow. In addition to these regular troops, the New Ross Yeomanry and the Clare and Dublin Militia were deployed. The result was a desperate see-saw battle that raged back and forth all day. Luke Gardiner MP, the sponsor of the Catholic Relief Acts twenty years earlier, met his death here leading crown troops against the rebels: his liberalism was situated firmly in the context of the kingdom of Ireland and could not possibly extend to embrace the ideal of republican independence prompted by the French Revolution.

The battle of New Ross resulted in total defeat for the rebels, who got fewer than 3,000 men away after the battle. They lost a huge amount of materiel, including all but one of their six artillery pieces.

Worst of all, they were now trapped in Co. Wexford.

Along the line of the defeated rebels' retreat, about 10 km (6 miles) east of the town, lay a place called Scullabogue. Here, at a farmyard barn, a group of prisoners – almost all of them loyalists and Protestants – were held in rebel hands. Some of the retreating survivors of the battle now called for the execution of these prisoners in reprisal for atrocities committed by crown troops during the battle. It is likely, in the confusion of a frantic street battle, that both sides committed atrocities. But the defeated rebels were in no mood for such even-handedness. They wanted blood. Hesitant at first, those guarding the prisoners then began to execute the male prisoners by shooting them on the lawn. They then took the rest, including women and children, and locked them in the barn, which they torched. None survived. Over a hundred people died at Scullabogue.

Whatever the motivation for this ghastly act, it had nothing to do with the civic and republican ideals of the United Irishmen. This was reminiscent of the Thirty Years War, not the Enlightenment. For Irish Protestants, especially in Ulster, it echoed the remembered horrors of 1641 and convinced many that Catholics could never be trusted, that they were all brutes under the skin and that liberal Protestant attempts at accommodation and support for the relief of Catholic disabilities was a fool's game.

The influence of French secular republicanism was new in Ireland, less than a decade old and disproportionately strong in Presbyterian Ulster, in towns and among the educated and literate. Sectarian divisions between Catholic and Protestant, on the other hand, not only went back 250 years to the Reformation: it had been the defining line of division in Irish public life for all that time. Even on the most generous reading of 1798, it is naive to suppose that civic republicanism somehow displaced sectarianism during the rebellion. Sectarianism had been there in full measure before 1798, especially among the rural poor. Then there was the context. Lake and his thugs had done more and worse on their side of the divide and had sown the wind. But whatever context provides an explanation for Scullabogue, the fact is that republicanism demanded a higher standard of itself. To fail that standard so blatantly was to reveal the continuing reality of a confessional solidarity that trumped the best hopes of the republic and that would manifest itself in the coming century in the emergence of a specifically Catholic nationalism.

The Wexford rebellion was in full retreat after New Ross. Wexford town was recaptured and the rebels' last stand was at Vinegar Hill, just outside Enniscorthy, on 21 June 1798. There were more atrocities on both sides. In all, about 30,000 people died in Wexford in the most bloody month in Irish history. The majority of them were non-combatants. One historian simply described the Wexford rebellion as 'a lethal mixture of idealism, sectarianism, agrarianism, revolutionary organization, state terrorism, mayhem and massacre'. That about sums it up.

Meanwhile, a remarkable rising had occurred in Ulster. Following arrival of the sensational news of the Wexford rebels' successes at Oulart and Enniscorthy, what was left of the Ulster leadership decided to make a stand. In counties Antrim and Down, Presbyterian United men under Henry Joy McCracken and Henry Munro took up arms. They had been goaded beyond endurance by Lake but even then had hesitated to rise, so weakened were they from his depredations. They were pitifully short of arms. They had a few minor successes but failed to hold Antrim town for more than a few hours. The Down rebels were defeated at Ballynahinch on 10 June. They never even threatened Belfast, the commercial capital of the province and, more significantly, its biggest garrison. Likewise, there was no rising in the west. The Protestant citadel of Derry city was undisturbed. The Ulster rebellion, like the United Ireland movement in the province, was confined to counties Antrim and Down.

These were the two counties with the greatest number of Presbyterians. Just as important, they had the fewest Roman Catholics. Where Catholics were present in greater numbers, as elsewhere in the province, radical republicanism was a luxury that Protestants generally felt they could not afford. Instead, Armagh rules – Orange Order and Defender atavisms – were more likely to obtain. The Ulster rebels were unrepresentative of Ulster Presbyterianism generally, let alone the wider Ulster Protestant community.

The French Revolution was profoundly anti-Catholic Church, which it regarded as a sink of reaction and superstition. In France itself, the bitterest revolutionary wars were civil wars, especially in the Vendée, where counter-revolutionary Catholic peasants rose in revolt against the new order. They were crushed with merciless savagery by Hoche, who had behaved no better than Lake. The peasants of the Vendée had rebelled in the names of throne and altar, and it seemed to all supporters of the Revolution that Catholicism was an enemy. Certainly, the papacy was bitterly opposed to the Revolution from the start: much of the passion of subsequent French history derived from the contest between republican secularism and reactionary clericalism.

All this made the principles of the French Revolution perhaps too congenial to Presbyterian Ulster, where its anti-Catholicism was easily compatible with ancient local sentiment. It certainly militated against the fullest embrace of the United Irish ideal of Protestant, Catholic and Dissenter joined in a common citizenship. The Ulster rebellion, when it finally came, was confined to the two counties with the fewest Catholics and therefore with the least sectarian tension: ironically, the minimal Catholic numbers created the oxygen for republican sentiment to thrive.

With the government victories at Vinegar Hill, Wexford and Ballynahinch, it seemed that the brief efflorescence of republican separatism in Ireland had been snuffed out. Not quite: there was a double coda. First, a small French expedition under

General Humbert arrived in the far west, in Co. Mayo, in August, picked up local support and lasted six weeks before the inevitable surrender. Finally, Wolfe Tone returned to Ireland as part of another small French fleet. Wearing the uniform of a French officer, he was arrested and taken to Dublin where he committed suicide.

And so it finally ended. With Tone's death on 19 November 1798, the most momentous year in Irish history closed. The 1790s have been described as the crucible in which modern Ireland was formed, a judgement that will find few dissenters. The fault lines that ran through that decade ran through all of nineteenth-century Ireland. Many are with us still. If, according to the twentieth-century Chinese party leader Zhou Enlai, it is too soon to judge the historical significance of the French Revolution, the same might be said of the tempest it created in Ireland.

14

UNION

The United Irish rebellions had been intended to deliver a non-sectarian Irish republic. Their actual outcome resulted in a union of the kingdoms of Britain and Ireland in a single state, and moreover one where profound sectarian antagonism was firmly embedded. The sectarian excesses in Wexford – however unrepresentative of the broad United leadership in the county – had nonetheless sent shock waves through Protestant Ireland and contributed to the failure of the Ulster rebellion to spread beyond two counties.

For years, there had been occasional talk of a union of the two kingdoms along the lines of the Scottish Act of Union of 1707. After 1798, it moved to become an urgent priority for London. The prime minister, William Pitt the Younger, and the Dublin administration were determined on it and duly set the wheels in motion. They had to resort to bribery, intimidation and patronage on a scale that shocked even their contemporaries – this in an age not squeamish about political corruption. That said, the administration worked hard to gain the support of Protestant public opinion in the country and there is solid evidence to support the view that a majority was in favour of the measure.

Opposition to the union was strongest among those elements

of the Ascendancy elite who did not want to see their autonomous powers surrendered to the imperial capital. Dublin,
which would lose its status as a parliamentary capital, was
opposed. Mercantile Belfast was generally supportive. The
Orange Order, on the other hand, was bitterly opposed. In
part, all this was the normal reluctance of any group of power
holders to yield it up to others. It was also grounded in the
suspicion that London would be softer on the Catholic question than a colonial parliament in Dublin. In this, the opponents
of the union were certainly correct, for the original proposal
for an Act of Union would have included the removal of most
remaining Catholic disabilities. In this it was a re-run of the
Relief Act of 1793, sponsored from London and forced down
the throat of a deeply reluctant Dublin parliament.

The principal Irish supporter of the union was John
FitzGibbon, Earl of Clare, lord chancellor of Ireland. The son
of a Catholic who had conformed to the established church, he
was a calculating, cynical careerist in a decade of heady idealism. 'Black Jack' FitzGibbon has had a bad historical press,
much of it deserved. But he was a cold-eyed realist and he
understood one big thing: that the Protestant interest in Ireland
was bound absolutely to the connection with Britain. Without
it, as he never ceased to warn, the dispossessed and resentful
Catholics – still smarting from the Cromwellian dispossessions
of the 1650s – would overthrow the existing order. He regarded
all forms of Protestant accommodation with Catholics as
suspect. He abominated the Presbyterians. And on the evidence
before him, he drew a conclusion contrary to that of Protestant
ultras who opposed the union: that the Irish Protestant interest
would be safer in a pan-Protestant state than as an elite minority in a sea of Catholics. It was a view that was largely justified
by events in the nineteenth century. It certainly drew the overwhelming support of later generations of Irish Protestants
until 1922.

Ultimately, opponents of the union had little to fall back on
other than scaremongering or appeals to the spirit of 1782. But

the spirit of 1782 had been overwhelmed by the spirit of 1798. Protestant Ireland had stared into the abyss. Now it implicitly accepted FitzGibbon's relentless logic.

The Act of Union of 1801 abolished the kingdom of Ireland as a separate entity. With it went the Irish parliament, that bastion resistant to the last against parliamentary reform. The United Kingdom was born and with it the Union Jack, uniting the crosses of Saints George, Andrew and Patrick. Instead of 300 members in the old Irish parliament, Ireland was now to send 100 MPs to Westminster. The Church of England and the Church of Ireland were united as one, a provision that was to become important seventy years later.

Repeal of the union would dominate Irish political life in the nineteenth century. It was to be the central demand of Irish nationalism, which would develop into an overwhelmingly Catholic project. It was ironic, therefore, that most Catholic opinion in 1800 welcomed the union. In the first place, it meant the end of the unreformed and corrupt parliament of the Protestant ascendancy and begetter of the Penal Laws. In the second place, it was to be accompanied by a measure of Catholic Emancipation. Locked in a deadly struggle with France, William Pitt recognized the need to avoid a disaffected population in Ireland. The relief measures now proposed would essentially grant Catholics full parliamentary rights in return for a government veto on Catholic episcopal appointments. The Catholic hierarchy conducted discussions with the London government in this broad context.

It would be easier to grant full political rights to Catholics in the overall Protestant context of a union parliament. In a purely Irish context, however, Catholic political rights would be a direct threat to Protestant hegemony. This was a variation on FitzGibbon's theme, although he was personally opposed to all concessions to Catholics. As things were to work themselves out, he was not alone.

The plan foundered on the inflexible opposition of the king. George III regarded such concessions as a violation of his coronation oath, which pledged to uphold the Protestant nature of the state. Like a lot of stupid people, it took a great deal to get an idea into the king's head but once there, there was no shifting it. The failure to couple Catholic Emancipation with the union was regarded as a betrayal by Irish Catholic opinion, one that blighted relations between Catholics and the new order from the start.

The new regime meant that Ireland was no longer a separate kingdom but an integral part of the British metropolitan state. In one respect, however, there was little change. The Irish administrative machinery remained not just a Protestant preserve, but increasingly an Orange one. The horrors of 1798 seized the imagination of many Irish Protestants, who did what people everywhere do when they feel threatened and vulnerable. They sought refuge in a more radical and defensive statement of their position. In the Protestant community, the ultras were able to say to the liberals: we told you so. And thus the ultras controlled the Castle in the early years of the union. The practical effect was to underscore the oppositional bitterness between Protestant and Catholic in Ireland. Liberal Protestants were pushed towards the margins of their own community. The prevailing temper of Irish Protestantism under the union grew ever more defensive. Many Irish Protestants took satisfaction from the fact that the defeat of the rebellion was mainly the work of the Militias and the Yeomanry, rather than the regular army. They therefore tended to remember 1798 as a victory over the enemy within, a providential deliverance which was all their own work. It was also rather too easy, as early Protestant historians of the rebellion demonstrated, to see 1798 as a re-run of 1641.

Meanwhile, in the first two decades of the new century, a sea change was occurring among the Catholics, which was to be the decisive social and intellectual shift in nineteenth-century Ireland. The idea of the modern Irish nation was being born.

The principles of republican government, independence and popular sovereignty had all been asserted in 1798. This was the

work of a political elite, many of them Protestant radicals
intoxicated by the revolutionary fervour coming from France.
This new ideal of a civic order, indifferent to religion, was
severely damaged by the sectarian outrages in Wexford and by
the chronic sectarian poison in the Ulster countryside. The last
aftershock of 1798, the failed insurrection of Robert Emmet in
Dublin in 1803, also resulted in unintended tragedy. It was
quickly snuffed out and was in fact little more than an affray,
but one which claimed the life of Lord Kilwarden, the Lord
Chief Justice, a notably liberal judge. The irony was that
Kilwarden's birth name was Arthur Wolfe. He was a member
of the family for whom Wolfe Tone had been named and he
himself had used his influence to help save Tone's life back in
1794 when Tone's intrigues with Jackson had been betrayed to
the government. After a speech from the dock that still reso-
nates in Irish history, Robert Emmet was hanged.

In place of civic republicanism, the older tradition of
Catholic self-consciousness reasserted itself. But now it took
new form. Ever since the Reformation, Catholics had felt
themselves to be a distinct community. In this they were little
different from many such communities across Europe. The
Habsburg Empire contained within its borders such diverse
ethnic and linguistic groups as Bohemian Czechs, Hungarians,
Slovenes, Poles, Croats and many others.

What changed in Ireland was what later changed in the
Habsburg lands. The ethnic sub-groups gradually asserted
their rights to national status, to a state of their own independent of the empire. Why the change? What was happening in the
Irish Catholic community in the early nineteenth century?

First, the revolutionary idea of popular sovereignty had
influenced even people who were otherwise hostile to the
French Revolution. Second, an embryonic national consciousness began to form. Gaelic Ireland – to take the larger element
in the Catholic community – had long had a cultural unity
while being divided politically. Only as Catholics began to
believe that what they had in common was paramount and that

what divided them was of less consequence did the community
begin to develop a national self-consciousness. The failure to
accompany the Act of Union with the specifically confessional
measure of Catholic Emancipation encouraged this emerging
sensibility. It meant that, from the beginning of the nineteenth
century, the nationalist demand and the demands of the Irish
Catholic community became yoked together.

This emerging nationalist consciousness was a startlingly
modern idea. In eighteenth-century Ireland, a Catholic in the
Glens of Antrim felt no sense of common political purpose
with a Catholic in Kerry or Clare. By the end of the 1820s, this
sense of communal affinity was developing among Irish
Catholics. By the 1880s, it was the most potent force in Irish
life. Why did it happen, and why did it happen when it did?

First, there is the intellectual revolution: the idea of popular
sovereignty that provided a template into which ideas that had
hitherto been diffuse could now cohere. In other words, the
key contribution of the French Revolution – the idea that
political power rose up from the sovereign people of the nation
rather than descending through a king from God – made the
sort of mobilization that occurred in early nineteenth-century
Ireland possible. Until that thought had embedded itself in the
consciousness of the politically active classes, themselves an
expanding group, the first, slow steps towards democracy
could not have been taken.

Second, there was the rise of a Catholic middle class, itself
the very epitome of a politically active group. All nations
require a leadership element to focus their emerging national
consciousness. In every European case – in Poland, Bohemia,
Hungary, Germany – the people who made the running were
always the same: lawyers, doctors, professors, younger sons of
minor gentry. These were educated people, ambitious but
usually frustrated by institutional or political impediment to
their advance. These impediments were invariably embedded
deep in the structures of the old regime. The opening of
Clongowes Wood College in 1814, the first Jesuit secondary

school established in Ireland since the Reformation, was a key moment in the development of this new nationalist class. It was followed by a wholesale expansion of secondary schooling for the Catholic elite in the succeeding decades.

Third, there was the gradual destruction of distance which helped to create a sense of national as distinct from local community. Better roads and coach services and canals were a beginning, but above all it was the coming of the railways that made this possible. Goods and services could now be distributed nationally. The railway created a national press, because it facilitated the countrywide distribution of newspapers published in Dublin. By the second half of the century, there was a national community in the sense that matters of common national interest had a means of common expression. There was a national conversation going on. The Catholics of Antrim were no longer remote from those of Kerry: they no longer shared just a common culture, but now had common political aspirations as well. And the first of those aspirations was fair play for the Catholic community, which began with the demand for Catholic Emancipation. Later, nationalism demanded the repeal of the union; later, after the Famine, it recast this demand in the form of the home rule movement; finally, it asserted itself in arms and formulated the demand for full independence from Britain.

The self-conscious community of Irish Catholics began its life in the first two decades of the nineteenth century, in the era of Orange administrative dominance. The sense of betrayal over Catholic Emancipation went deep. It was this cause that became the focus of Catholic aspiration. Moreover, it found a leader and organizer of genius. His name was Daniel O'Connell.

O'Connell was the scion of a minor Gaelic aristocratic family from Co. Kerry. His background was classically part of that hidden Ireland of the *ancien régime*. The O'Connells had survived and prospered in a modest way in their remote coastal fastness, not scrupling to trade in smuggled goods if necessary.

Like many sons of prosperous Catholics in eighteenth-century Ireland, the young Daniel was sent to the Jesuit schools in Saint-Omer and Douai to be educated. O'Connell arrived in France in 1791 and witnessed at first hand enough of the violence associated with the French Revolution to give him a lifelong aversion to political violence in general. He later studied law in London.

O'Connell was a key figure – perhaps even *the* key figure – in the modernization of Ireland, but in his educational formation he was very much a product of the *ancien régime*. He was never comfortable with French revolutionary principles. He inclined to see French-style republicanism as an anti-clerical minority tyranny. His achievement, on the other hand, was to entail the mobilization of an overtly confessional community – the Irish Catholics – at a time when that community was itself borrowing as much of the language and grammar of the French Revolution as it could comfortably absorb. The Irish Catholics had been a self-conscious community since the Reformation: after O'Connell it thought of itself as a nation.

He was one of the first generation of Catholics allowed to practise law under the terms of a Catholic Relief Act of 1793. He qualified in 1798, the year of rebellion. He was a member of a lawyers' reserve militia mobilized to defend Dublin against a threatened United Irish attack that never materialized. He went on to practise on the Munster circuit, made and spent fortunes and married happily.

He was drawn to political prominence from 1808 on by the veto controversy. The proponents of Catholic Emancipation assumed that – as at the time of the union – the Catholic hierarchy would concede to the British government a veto on Irish episcopal appointments as a quid pro quo for Emancipation. The demand for a veto of some sort had been there since the last quarter of the eighteenth century, as the Catholic Church had started to emerge from the wilderness years of the penal era with an institutional vigour that astonished and dismayed London. The proposed veto was intended to exercise at least some degree of negative control over the leadership of this potentially dangerous body. Moreover, it was the norm in many parts of Europe: the Protestant kings of Prussia exercised a veto over the appointment of bishops to the Catholic Church in Poland, for example.

The more radical, middle-class faction among Irish Catholic activists was unimpressed by Prussia or anywhere else. They were adamant in opposition to the veto. An older, more aristo-cratic leadership – both among the hierarchy and the laity – was open to the possibility but they were overborne. The contro-versy rumbled on all through the 1810s. The anti-vetoists represented, in part, a generational change, and, in part, a class one: what was significant was the exceptional vigour with which they argued for the absolutely free-standing autonomy of the Catholic community and its church. The community was not going to yield any power of review to England in respect of the one national institution that did not already answer to it. The veto question implicitly became a bell-wether for the emerging national question.

This was part of the great change that was quietly trans-forming Irish Catholicism. The aristocratic old order had been prepared to accommodate itself to the state, however reluc-tantly, in a typically *ancien régime* way. The radicals were not. The passions aroused by this issue split Irish Catholics bitterly and made any united political action on Emancipation impos-sible until the wounds had healed in the 1820s.

The Catholic Church had suffered the disabilities of the Penal Laws for most of the eighteenth century. It emerged into the new century in remarkably fine shape, considering the rigours of the old one. All the dioceses had bishops in resi-dence, there were numerous priests, the Irish church was in full communion with Rome and while many peasant practices persisted, which the clergy deplored as superstitious, there was a movement towards doctrinal and liturgical orthodoxy that advanced steadily as time went on.

The church was strongest where the community was strongest.

One of the striking things about the church in the early nineteenth century was its regional disparities. In the impoverished
west of Ireland, it still remained a pre-modern peasant body. But
in the south-east, in the rich river valleys and towns where the
Old English Catholic middle class had survived the bad days in
good order – trading, farming, maintaining family networks
through inter-marriage, educating their sons in Catholic countries abroad – the church was strong. The simplest way to
illustrate this is to look at the foundation dates of Catholic institutions. The cathedral in Waterford – a fine neoclassical building,
product of a self-confident, wealthy community, not at all the
impoverished, humiliated people of folk-memory – dates from
1793. The same year saw the opening of what is now Carlow
College and was then the first post-penal era institution of higher
learning for Catholics in the country. The adjacent cathedral was
begun in 1828, as was the parish church in Dungarvan, Co.
Waterford. In nearby Youghal, Co. Cork, the parish church was
built in 1796 in mock-Anglican style. Clongowes, as already
noted, opened in Co. Kildare in 1814. These are all very early
foundation dates: most of the institutional revival of Catholicism
in the rest of the island – especially in church building – came in
the second half of the nineteenth century.

The Catholic elite of the south-east, roughly east of a line
from Dublin to Cork, was a generation or two ahead of the rest
of the co-religionists in terms of its social cohesion, wealth and
influence. It is no coincidence that so many leading figures in
the nineteenth-century hierarchy come disproportionately
from this region. Paul Cullen, the first ever Irish cardinal, who
dominated the Irish church in the generation after the Famine,
was from Ballitore, Co. Kildare. His nephew, Patrick Francis
Moran, was cardinal archbishop of Sydney and a key figure in
the Irish Catholic diaspora of the late nineteenth century.
Cullen's predecessor as archbishop of Dublin, Daniel Murray,
was born near Arklow, Co. Wicklow. John Warren Doyle, the
formidable and influential bishop of Kildare and Leighlin in
the 1820s, was from New Ross, Co. Wexford.

Similarly, it is remarkable how many of O'Connell's political lieutenants in the campaign for Emancipation came from the south-east. Thomas Wyse from Co. Waterford, who married a Bonaparte, was one such. Another was Richard Lalor Sheil from Co. Kilkenny. Denys Scully was from Kilfeacle, Co. Tipperary. All were hugely influential in their time; all came from wealthy backgrounds; Sheil and Scully were lawyers.

Irish nationalism, or at least the version of it that was to dominate the history of the island for the next 150 years or so, first developed among the relatively privileged community of Catholics in the south east. Their project was overtly confessional, the relief of remaining religious disabilities through the winning of Catholic Emancipation. Beyond that, they looked for repeal of the union, confident in the superiority of Catholic numbers.

15

O'CONNELL

Part of the growing self-consciousness of the Irish Catholic community was a reaction to a Protestant evangelical revival in the early decades of the nineteenth century. This phenomenon could trace its roots back to the Methodist revival of the previous century, which saw John Wesley make twenty-one visits to Ireland between 1747 and his death in 1791. The aftershock of 1798 convinced many ardent Protestants of the need for a mass conversion of Catholics. In addition to the Methodists, who continued their founder's work, a number of other missionary bodies were founded early in the new century. They included the Hibernian Bible Society (1806) and the Irish Evangelical Society (1814). There were others, including societies whose members could preach in Gaelic and which therefore could penetrate the western seaboard counties, previously neglected. In aggregate, this enterprise came to be known as the Second Reformation.

Its long-term successes were few, given the degree of effort and energy expended on the cause. But contemporaneously, it galvanized the Catholic leadership. In particular, it prompted the institutional development of the church west of the Dublin-Cork line, where it had been weakest. The result was the steady advance of the Catholic Church in Ireland throughout the course of the nineteenth century, leaving it in a position of unchallenged moral and political authority in the post-Famine era.

That was at the elite level. At the level of the Catholic populace, a robust and visceral sectarianism found expression through continuing agrarian troubles, which easily embraced political grievances as well. Thus the phenomenon of the mythical 'Captain Rock', just one among many minatory figures conjured up in the imaginations of agrarian protesters and taken very seriously indeed by the landed interest against whom the Captain's depredations were directed. (The activities of 'Captain Swing', an equally mythical figure of the 1820s, had a similar effect on the southern counties of England at the height of popular protests against the introduction of threshing machines, continuing enclosure of commons and the death of the so-called moral economy based on communitarian values.) Captain Rock's activities, and those of many other agrarian protest movements, were given a specifically sectarian twist by the excitement surrounding the so-called Pastorini prophecies.

Signor Pastorini was the pseudonym of one Charles Walmesley, an eighteenth-century English Catholic bishop who published *A General History of the Christian Church* in 1771. In this work, he went beyond history into the realm of prophecy by a highly charged interpretation of the Apocalypse of St John. He predicted the triumph of Catholicism and the destruction of Protestantism – or at least of Anglicanism – by 1825. The prophecies were popular in a number of countries but they became a kind of craze in early nineteenth-century Ireland, especially as the supposed year of deliverance neared. The millennial expectations aroused by Pastorini overlapped with myths of deliverance already embedded in the agrarian societies, with their rhetoric of Jacobite nostalgia, to create a volatile compound.

The raising of Catholic consciousness, both at elite and popular levels, had immediate political consequences. Not least among these was a growing awareness of the size of the

Catholic vote which, allied to a continuing sense of grievance, exclusion and victimhood, posed a potentially fatal threat to the Protestant interest. The establishment of the Catholic Association in 1823 by Daniel O'Connell was the moment when these various currents coalesced in a remarkable movement of political mobilization. Indeed, it might be said that the Catholic Association – established as a vehicle for the promotion of elite causes – drew the sting of the populist millennial movement. It did this through a revolutionary initiative: the Catholic rent.

For a subscription of a penny a month, associate members could be admitted. Thus began the mass mobilization of the Irish poor in a political cause which quickly became focused on Catholic Emancipation, or the removal of residual Catholic disabilities. It was the first such mobilization of the masses in Europe or America, anticipating Andrew Jackson's populist Second Party System in the United States by at least four years. It was without any parallel in contemporary Europe.

The Catholic rent was collected after Sunday mass by priests, who quickly became the local officer corps of the association. Catholic clergy were members of the association *ex officio*. It made sense to mobilize them in this way, for the church provided the only nationwide – or near nationwide – institution in nationalist Ireland. (Once again, and unsurprisingly, the movement was strongest in Leinster and Munster and weakest in Connacht; Ulster, as we shall see, was another matter altogether.) It thus gave the Catholic Association a national structure at one remove. The priests – and the bishops – gave their willing allegiance in support of such conspicuously Catholic demands.

One element of the Catholic population that is easily overlooked is the large number of demobilized soldiers who had fought in the Napoleonic wars. Like all military personnel, they had inculcated habits of order and discipline. These traits fed into O'Connell's popular mobilization. It was not simply a case of O'Connell and his lieutenants, by some form of political sorcery assisted by the priests, taming an unruly mob. The church itself, with its growing institutional conformity in doctrine and practice – a process not complete until after the Famine but already well in hand – reinforced this growing pattern of social discipline. This discipline was to be tested, and to prove strong, in the tumultuous electoral contests to come.

Another development assisting the gradual development of social discipline was the establishment of a rudimentary national police force. The 'Peelers' were the work of the eponymous Robert Peel, the formidable chief secretary of Ireland from 1812 until 1818, and while they did not cover the whole island, they could be deployed at short notice in trouble spots. Critically, they were under central control, rather than at the whim of prejudiced local magistrates, for whom Peel had a sovereign contempt. The Peelers were significant in themselves, but their real importance lay in their breaking the local control of law and order. By putting in place a centrally controlled force, Peel laid the basis for the later (Royal) Irish Constabulary.

Notwithstanding all these developments, there was nothing inevitable about O'Connell's eventual triumph in 1829. The years following 1815 brought their difficulties as well as their opportunities for the Catholic cause. The end of the Napoleonic wars meant that pressures on London to mollify Catholic opinion in Ireland were eased. King George III was still alive and as stubborn as ever on the emancipation question. His son, George IV, a corpulent sot, eventually succeeded his father in 1820 but proved just as reactionary on the Catholic question. He visited Ireland in 1821 – the first English or British monarch ever to do so for a wholly peaceful purpose – and was so drunk on arrival that he could not be put ashore at Dún Laoghaire, to the south of Dublin, but had to be quietly landed at the little fishing harbour of Howth, on the northern end of the bay. A well-meaning Emancipation bill introduced at Westminster in the same year by the Irish lord chancellor, Lord Plunket, was defeated in the House of Lords. At any rate, O'Connell had refused to support it because it once more allowed for a government veto on episcopal appointments.

The quarrel between vetoists and anti-vetoists was only finally settled in the following years, a reconciliation that facilitated the establishment of the Catholic Association. Another Catholic Relief bill, sponsored by the radical Sir Francis Burdett, was introduced in 1825: it was conditional upon two so-called 'wings' or conditions. These were disenfranchisement of the forty-shilling freeholders (i.e. the poorest segment of the electorate) and state payment of the Catholic clergy. Astonishingly, O'Connell, who was in London giving evidence to a parliamentary select committee examining the state of Ireland, supported Burdett's bill – securities and all. Given his previous anti-veto antipathy to such securities, this was a dramatic change of position. It anticipated his eventual abandonment of the forty-shilling freeholders – after they had done much of the heavy lifting for him – in 1829. On this occasion, it made no difference: once again, the House of Lords did what it did best and voted down a reform measure that had the support of the Commons.

There were, therefore, powerful forces at the heart of the British state which were profoundly hostile to emancipation and to O'Connell's agitation in Ireland. The Catholic Association was banned but O'Connell simply reconstituted it as the New Catholic Association in 1826 and carried on as before. The breakthrough came in the Waterford election of 1826. The Tory candidate was Lord George Thomas Beresford, son of the Marquis of Waterford, brother of the Anglican archbishop of Armagh and scion of the family interest that had dominated Waterford politics for generations. As with other Ascendancy grandees, he took the votes of the forty-shilling freeholders entirely for granted. After all, they were his father's tenants who dare not face the consequences, which might well include eviction, of defying their landlord's political wishes, and would not previously have dreamed of doing so in an age of deference. Opposing him was a young liberal landlord,

Henry Villiers-Stuart, sponsored by local Catholic Association activists. Villiers-Stuart won. Astonishingly, the forty-shilling freeholders faced down the Beresfords and attended instead to the urgings of Catholic leaders – including their priests.

This seismic result was then echoed in a number of other constituencies, with a repeat of the same sectarian polarities as in Waterford. The culmination of this political revolution – for that was what it was, replacing deference to Ascendancy interests with Catholic communal solidarity – came in the Co. Clare election of 1828.

Early in that year, the Duke of Wellington formed a government which was ostensibly opposed to emancipation. However, the government leader in the Commons was the formidable Peel, whose knowledge of Ireland from his years as chief secretary left him fearing the need to yield some reform under the pressure of O'Connell's campaign and the electoral defection of the Irish forty-shilling freeholders. His serpentine political mind was a world removed from the ultra simplicities of the Duke. The by-election in Clare effectively gave Peel his pretext to conduct an orderly retreat on the issue.

The by-election was caused by the appointment of the sitting MP, William Vesey-FitzGerald (ironically a liberal Protestant and a supporter of Catholic Emancipation) to a government post in London. Under contemporary parliamentary rules, such an appointee had to offer himself once again for re-election. Vesey-FitzGerald's re-election should therefore have been a routine matter, a mere going through the motions. But the cat was thrown among the pigeons when O'Connell himself stood, although he would be barred from entering parliament.

The Clare by-election was one of the foundation moments of modern Irish nationalism. The contest was drenched in the most uncompromising sectarian rhetoric: O'Connell knew his market. Although his rival was a supporter of the Catholic cause and the son of a popular landlord who had himself been an opponent of the Act of Union, O'Connell played the two cards that were to sustain popular Irish nationalism for more than a century to come: faith and fatherland. He represented himself to the electors of Clare as one whose 'forefathers were for centuries the chieftains of the land and the friends of her people'. Describing Vesey-FitzGerald as 'the sworn libeller of the Catholic faith' – this because he had taken the oath of allegiance, anti-Catholic bits included, as all MPs were obliged to do – he drew the contrast with himself: 'one who has devoted his early life to your cause, who has consumed his manhood in a struggle for your liberties'. In effect, as one of O'Connell's biographers notes, his 'energies were directed to prising the peasant vote from the proprietors by the lever of religion'.

It was an uncompromising display of Catholic power. Every parish priest in Co. Clare bar one worked on O'Connell's campaign. In the course of the poll itself, conducted in Ennis, the county town, by open roll-call vote over a number of days, one priest helpfully explained to the crowds that an elector who had voted against O'Connell had just dropped dead! Another exhorted the voters to support O'Connell in terms that left nothing unsaid:

> You have heard the tones of the tempter and charmer [Vesey-FitzGerald], whose confederates have through all ages joined the descendants of the Dane, the Norman, and the Saxon, in burning your churches, in levelling your altars, in slaughtering your clergy, in stamping out your religion. Let every renegade to his God and his country follow Vesey Fitzgerald, and every true Catholic Irishman follow me.

This self-dramatizing farrago of victimhood through the ages might raise a supercilious smile in sophisticated drawing rooms. It hit a powerful nerve in Co. Clare in 1828; a version of it continued to serve Catholic Ireland as a rough epitome of its history well into the twentieth century; there are many in modern Ireland who might argue with the tone but not with the substance. The Irish nation was forming itself in uncompromisingly Catholic terms. It was going to be hard for Protestants not to recoil from this new nation. If Vesey-FitzGerald's face did not fit, what Protestant face would? Ireland had moved a long way in a generation from the blithe idealism of the United Irishmen.

O'Connell won. He polled 2,057 to Vesey-FitzGerald's 982. The Tory government was now in a bind. O'Connell was the duly elected member for Co. Clare with over two-thirds of the vote. But he was unable to take his seat, if only because of the anti-Catholic clauses in the oath of allegiance. Peel was horrified by O'Connell's 'tens of thousands of disciplined fanatics' and prudently concluded that it was worth facing down King George IV and the Tory ultras in order to mollify O'Connell's 'hereditary bondsmen'. Faced with outright electoral revolt in Ireland, and the implicit threat of something worse, the government capitulated. Catholic Emancipation was granted: Catholics could now sit in parliament, being required to take only a revised and inoffensive oath; hold office; and become judges. The price extracted to save some of the government's face was the raising of the franchise threshold in Ireland from 40 shillings (£2) to £10. Thus the 40-shilling freeholders, who won Catholic Emancipation, were disenfranchised for their pains – at least for the moment.

It was O'Connell's greatest hour. He was fifty-four years old and beyond question the dominant figure in Irish life. To his contemporaries, he was a mixture of hero and enigma. He had titanic energy and organizing ability; a sulphurous temper; torrential eloquence; vast reservoirs of charm. He was a genuine liberal in many respects, as his parliamentary career was to prove – he was philo-Semitic, a free-trader and an anti-slaver at a time when these were litmus tests of liberalism – yet he led a movement that was nakedly confessional. His political organization was based on the Catholic parishes and with the parishes came the priests. O'Connell stands accused of introducing the priests into Irish politics. He might have replied that he simply used the most practical means to hand and that, after all, the confessional rivalry between Protestant and Catholic was the decisive line of division in Irish life.

It was. The problem for O'Connell was that Ireland was not all Catholic. The three provinces of Leinster, Munster and Connacht were overwhelmingly so. But the northern province, Ulster, was not.

Ulster had a Protestant majority. It was not a united community. Tensions between members of the established Church of Ireland (Anglican), mainly of English descent, and the Presbyterians of Scots descent were very marked. The liberal impulse in Presbyterianism, with its instinct for democracy, had found expression in 1798. Although much chastened thereafter, it took a long time for this liberal Presbyterian tradition to die. But by 1830, it was increasingly under challenge.

Presbyterianism, with its highly literate congregations, was a fertile ground for theological disputation. In the first half of the nineteenth century, conservative and orthodox subscribers to the Westminster Confession of Faith – the foundation document of the Church of Scotland – gradually marginalized the so-called non-subscribers within Ulster. In broad political terms, it was a victory for conservatives and evangelicals over those of a more liberal, accommodating temper.

The one thing that united all Ulster Protestants, whether in the Church of Ireland or of any shade of Presbyterian, was suspicion and dislike of Catholics. The antagonism ran long and deep, right back to original Plantation days, and it had never abated. It was no coincidence that the swing to conservatism in Presbyterianism coincided with the growing advance of Catholic interests under O'Connell.

As part of his campaign to organize nationally, O'Connell looked towards Ulster. Like Connacht, but for different reasons, it was not nearly as promising territory as the southern and eastern provinces. There was no self-confident Catholic middle class around which a mass movement could form and which would provide leadership for it. Moreover, there was a Protestant majority, many of whom were enthusiastic Orange partisans. The point was made with some vigour in September 1828.

O'Connell approved an initiative by one of his more maverick allies, 'Honest' Jack Lawless, a Belfast journalist, to try to extend the reach of the Catholic Association to Ulster. This initiative was known by the revealing title of 'the invasion of Ulster', Honest Jack's own formulation. He led a large crowd north but was repulsed by a formidable gathering of Orangemen in Ballybay, Co. Monaghan. It was the first town on the southern reaches of Ulster where Protestants felt confident enough to muster in serious numbers. Lawless wisely backed off. Humiliatingly, that was as far as things went for the 'invasion' force: in the face of the first concentrated Ulster Protestant resistance to a nationalist initiative, all they could do was to retreat.

It was a portent. Resistance – bringing weight of numbers to bear in concentrated form – became the essence of the Ulster Protestant position as the nineteenth century wore on. There were lots of Ulster Protestants; they were concentrated in a small area; they were not going anywhere and there was no shifting them.

By the 1830s, the broad pattern of modern Irish history was in place. The Catholic community had realized its collective self-image and embarked on its political project. It gradually absorbed the key French Revolutionary idea of popular sovereignty, but located it in the context of a much older indigenous tradition. What began as an agitation to relieve Catholic disabilities gradually developed first into a campaign for Irish autonomy within the United Kingdom and later into a demand for outright independence. But Ulster, with its local Protestant majority, was outside this process and antagonistic to it.

The advance of the Irish nationalist project is interesting. It was not unique in Europe but its methods were. The contrast with Polish nationalism makes the point nicely. The Poles had seen their country dismembered in the three partitions of the late eighteenth century and divided between Russia, Prussia and the Habsburgs. Their nineteenth-century nationalist movement found itself facing three states with no tradition of representative government. So the leadership of Polish nationalism embarked on what they called 'organic work': educating the people in their history and folklore; artists and writers producing didactic work on Polish themes; economic development; movements for social cohesion.

The kind of people who led this organic work were from the same sort of social background as O'Connell's lieutenants in Ireland: people like Thomas Wyse, Richard Lalor Sheil and Denys Scully. But where the Poles directed their energies to what might broadly be called cultural and economic development, the Irish chose politics.

They did so because the country of which they were a part, the United Kingdom, had one of the longest continuous traditions of representative government in Europe. Britain was no democracy – not yet – but it did possess representative institutions, of which the most important was the House of Commons. It meant that Irish nationalism had a representative forum in which to express itself from the start. From 1829 to 1914, the House of Commons in London was the focus of all constitutional nationalist effort.

In Poland, organic work represented the only nationalist alternative to insurrection. In Ireland, it was politics. From the beginning, Irish nationalism was about numbers and representation; it was about incremental change and the practical politics of the here and now; it was populist. Thus the emphasis on organization and mobilization, on ward politics, and the impatience with theory. Irish populist politics first developed under O'Connell. It was perfected later in the century under Charles Stewart Parnell. It has been exported wherever the Irish diaspora has gone in numbers and has given the world, among other things, Tammany Hall and much of the Democratic Party in the United States; a significant element of the Labour Party and trade union movement in Britain; and a substantial part of the Labor Party and trade union movement in Australia.

All this made Irish nationalism unusual in a European context. In Ireland, politics came first and culture followed. In comparable continental countries, it tended to be the other way around. This may explain why, in the 1920s and 1930s, so many of the new states in Europe turned towards various forms of authoritarian government, while Ireland – despite the bitterness of the Civil War divide – did not. Politics had become second nature to Irish nationalists. With its internal logic of compromise, the political process provided the normal means of settling great public issues. Only on the confessional issue did Irish nationalism echo Poland, where an ardent Roman Catholicism became the mobilizing bulwark of national senti-ment in opposition to Lutheran Imperial Germany and Orthodox (and later Communist) Imperial Russia. Similarly, Irish nationalism became the political project of Irish Roman Catholic in opposition to Protestant Britain. Tragically, it also aligned Irish nationalism in opposition to Protestant Ulster.

After Emancipation, O'Connell became one of the most famous men in Europe albeit his Irish career in these years ended in bathos and anti-climax. He was unique in contempo-rary terms in combining liberalism with Catholicism, at a time when political Catholicism on the continent was associated with Metternich's system of authoritarian reaction and a desire for the restoration of the *ancien régime*. He was a hero to names as great as Goethe, Montalembert, Balzac and de Tocqueville. In the House of Commons in 1844, the historian Thomas Macaulay – never one to coin a phrase when a para-graph was to hand – acknowledged O'Connell's celebrity:

> Go where you will on the continent: visit any coffee house; dine at any public table; embark on board of any steamboat; enter any diligence, any railway carriage; from the moment that your accent shows you to be an Englishman, the very first question

asked by your companions, be they what they may, physicians, advocates, merchants, manufacturers, or what we should call yeomen, is certain to be 'What will be done with Mr O'Connell?' Look over any file of French journals; and you will see a space he occupies in the eyes of the French people.

O'Connell entered parliament in London in February 1830 and gradually formed a loose group of supporters around him. This was not a party in any modern sense, with all the discipline and regimentation that term implies. Until the fall of Wellington and Peel in 1832, he had little parliamentary leverage. The accession of the Whigs to power in that year improved the position. O'Connell felt much closer to the Whigs, with their generally more liberal inclinations, than he possibly could to the royalist and reactionary Tories – especially given the latter's Orange allies in Ireland.

O'Connell reached an understanding with the Whigs which brought some immediate benefits. The long-running sore of the tithe question was settled. Tithes were a tax – notionally one-tenth of earnings – levied either in cash or kind for the upkeep of the clergy of the established Church of Ireland, whose congregations constituted barely 10 per cent of the entire Irish population. Tithes had always been resented and had been the proximate cause of sporadic campaigns of agrarian violence ever since the 1760s. These campaigns had escalated in the early 1830s, resulting in serious violence in the countryside. In general, attempts to enforce payment – or worse to distrain (seize) goods for non-payment – met with fierce resistance. The settlement of this issue removed one of the most potent sources of social unrest in Ireland.

Resistance to payment had been sporadic among Catholics since the 1760s. But in the period of heightened expectation following Catholic Emancipation, the sense of grievance turned to outright revolt. By the 1830s, almost two-thirds of the total income of the Church of Ireland came from tithes. Given this level of dependence, it was not an issue easily resolved. At the same time, it was a chronic source of grievance among people not in communion with the Church of Ireland, upon whom fell the main burden of payment. Moreover, from 1735 until 1823 pasturage was excluded from the scheme, which meant that the best land was exempt. Given the reality of land-holding patterns, this meant that wealthy members of the Church of Ireland paid less than their due proportion for the upkeep of their own church, while the principal burden fell on poorer Catholics and – in Ulster – Presbyterians.

The 'Tithe War' started in Graiguenamanagh, Co. Kilkenny, in October 1830 when the cattle of the parish priest, Fr Martin Doyle – a relation of the formidable Bishop James Warren Doyle of Kildare and Leighlin – were distrained for non-payment. A campaign of non-payment first spread throughout South Leinster and Munster: once again, this critical region was in the vanguard of modernization. Eventually twenty-two of the thirty-two counties in Ireland were involved. Although formally a campaign of passive resistance, it inevitably turned violent.

The use of police and troops to distrain goods and livestock resulted in serious clashes. Fourteen people were killed at Newtownbarry (now Bunclody), Co. Wexford, in 1831 when distrained cattle were sold off to settle unpaid tithes. In all, over 43,000 decrees were issued against defaulters, while Lord Gort claimed in 1832 that the anti-tithe campaign had resulted to date in 242 homicides; 1,179 robberies; 401 burglaries; 568 burnings; 280 cattle maimings; 161 assaults; 203 riots; and 723 attacks on houses. The withdrawal of police and the Yeomanry from tithe enforcement duties in 1833 took much of the heat out of the situation, but by now the total arrears were more than £1 million. In effect, London gifted this sum to the Church of Ireland – an open acknowledgement that the traditional tithe system was no longer viable.

The tithe question was not settled by legislation until 1838, when O'Connell – who had kept his distance from the agitation while benefiting politically from it (he was not the last Irish nationalist to master this trick) – formed a proposal which would mean the state taking over responsibility for clerical payments, while a local tax would be levied in support of the newly formed Irish Constabulary. The proposal was broadly adopted by the government and, although much watered down in the House of Lords, was carried. The net effect was to convert the tithes into a rent charge, making them invisible. The hated tithe proctors, who had conducted the assessments and collected the tithes, disappeared from the land. With them went the visible reality of the problem itself.

Other reforms effected by the O'Connell–Whig alliance included the modernization of the archaic system of municipal government by widening the franchise. Among other things, it allowed O'Connell to become the first Catholic lord mayor of Dublin for 150 years. A Poor Law enacted in 1838 provided a minimal structure of poor relief in what was still a desperately poor country. The English Poor Law system was extended to Ireland, ignoring the report of a Commission of Enquiry that had recommended a system for Ireland different from that of England and tailored more to the specific requirements of the country. The report's recommendations had included subsidized emigration for the very poorest as a way of relieving the ever-growing pressure on land caused by the rising population. In bypassing the report in this regard at least, the new Poor Law unwittingly ensured that within a decade famine would accomplish what legislation had avoided. O'Connell opposed the Poor Law Act, as much out of opportunism as conviction.

In the 1830s, the Irish administration was increasingly staffed by Catholics and liberal Protestants, weakening the Orange grip on Dublin Castle. The under-secretary (head of the Irish civil service), Thomas Drummond, famously reminded Irish landlords that 'property has its duties as well as its rights', not the sort of sentiment normally expected from the Castle. The establishment of the Irish Constabulary (the 'Royal' prefix came later, for services rendered in helping to put down the Fenian insurrection of 1867) and the Dublin Metropolitan Police in 1836 put Irish law enforcement on a modern footing.

With the possible exception of the coming of the railways nothing in Ireland in the 1830s was more important for the future than developments in education. Many schools had been established in Ireland in the seventeenth and eighteenth centuries. Most were Protestant, but from the 1770s onwards the institutional revival of Catholic education began in earnest. In particular, new teaching orders of nuns were founded: the Presentation Order founded by Nano Nagle in Cork in 1776; the Irish Sisters of Charity founded by Mary Aikenhead in Dublin in 1815; the Sisters of Mercy founded by Catherine McAuley also in Dublin in 1831. The distribution of convents followed a now familiar pattern: clustered disproportionately in Munster and Leinster and much scarcer, at least until later in the century, in the north and west.

No single teaching order had a greater influence on nineteenth-century Ireland than the Christian Brothers. Once more, it was a product of the south-east quadrant, that early powerhouse of the institutional Catholic revival and by extension the crucible of Irish nationalism. Its founder, Edmund Ignatius Rice, had been born in Callan, Co. Kilkenny, and had made a fortune in trade in Waterford as a young man. It was in that city that he opened the first Christian Brothers' school in 1802. The Christian Brothers became the educators of the sons of the Catholic poor, leaving the well-to-do to the Jesuits and others. They developed a disciplined and efficient approach to education. They were unsentimental and utilitarian: they regarded liberal humanism as a luxury their charges could ill afford, and something moreover which was offensive to their assertively Catholic, nationalist and – as time went on – Gaelic ethos.

Between all these different groups – and adding in the small private, fee-paying academies known as 'hedge schools' – there was an astonishing number of schools in Ireland by 1830: more than 10,000. It was at this point that the government decided to establish a centralized national system. Under an act of 1831, an inter-denominational system of national primary schools was established. By the end of the nineteenth century, it had over a million pupils in almost 9,000 schools. But by then, the original inter-denominational ideal had long since been abandoned under pressure from the various churches, all of which wanted educational control of their own flocks. Denominational control of education was to persist all through the twentieth century, surviving the upheavals of revolution, independence and partition. It was carried into secondary education, as that system developed from the 1870s on, and even into the third-level sector. Trinity College Dublin was effectively a Protestant redoubt until the second half of the twentieth century. Its rival institution in the capital, founded in 1854, took the unambiguous name of the Catholic University; it was the remote ancestor of University College Dublin, now the largest third-level institution in Ireland.

The first Irish railway, the Dublin & Kingstown, opened in December 1834. Within twenty years Dublin was connected to Belfast, Cork and Galway and there were a host of minor lines, radiating from these centres, either planned or already in place. The expansion of the Irish railway system continued up to the 1920s, when road transport began to supplant it.

The railways were crucial in the process of consolidating national consciousness. The journey from Dublin to Cork, which had taken two days by coach, was reduced to seven hours in 1849 and four hours by 1887. It was the greatest advance in mobility in human history and it led to all sorts of unanticipated consequences. As mentioned, it made possible the creation of a genuinely national press, by providing a distribution mechanism from Dublin. Thus, people at either end of the island could read the same newspaper on the same day. Likewise, it made the distribution of everything from tinned foods to beer easier and helped to create a national retail economy. It offered opportunities for leisure travel to tens of thousands to whom it was previously denied: the great Victorian 'watering places' – such seaside resorts as Bray, Tramore and Clifden – all owe their origins to the railway.

The railways annihilated distance, one of the characteristic features of the modern world. They helped to develop a genuine national community. The new kind of nationalism ushered in by the French Revolution created the ideal of the nation state. But the railways gave it a physical reality. It is one thing to imagine the national community; it is another to realize it by travel. Before the railway, people in Co. Antrim had more contact with Argyll than with Kerry. Tyrone did not know Cork. Wexford and Donegal might have been in different countries. The railways connected people in a way that gave physical expression to their underlying cultural unity. Dublin's position as the nodal point in the railway system consolidated its role as the national capital rather than just a colonial outpost.

The first reliable Irish census took place in 1841. It showed a population of just over eight million people, the only time such a figure has been achieved. Prior to this date, all estimates of population are no more than best guesses, lacking the statistical rigour of a modern census. That said, it is likely that prior to 1760 the total Irish population was less than two-and-a half million.

The astonishing rise in the Irish population in the century before the Famine was remarked on by contemporaries. It was accounted for by a number of factors: the widespread introduction of the easily cultivated and nutritious potato, which replaced grain as the staple diet of the poor; economic expansion, especially in agriculture, which raced ahead in the years of the Revolutionary Wars as Ireland helped to provision the British army; early marriages with high fertility rates; lower infant mortality; and endless subdivision of tiny holdings.

The vast majority of Irish people were poor. However, this bald statement requires some qualification. There were considerable regional diversities. The rich limestone lands of the south and east supported a vigorous commercial agriculture in grain and cattle. Ireland remained a net exporter of food: it is estimated that about two million people in Britain were fed with produce imported from Ireland. In the first half of the

1840s, just before the Famine, there were about 5,000 livestock
fairs held across the country each year. On the other hand, the
poorer regions were wretched. In Connacht, the poorest province, 64 per cent of all farms were five acres or less. This was a
subsistence economy with a vengeance. In one of the Connacht
counties, Mayo, there were 475 people for each square mile of
arable land. In general, the pattern of small holdings, rural
overcrowding, severe poverty and lack of capital was more
pronounced as one went further north and west.

The reliance on a single crop, the potato, had obvious risks
in the event of crop failure or – the more common hazard – a
smaller harvest than expected, which would mean some lean
months in the coming year. The advantage of potatoes,
however, was their exceptional nutritional value. The diet of
the pre-Famine Irish poor, buttermilk and potatoes, was
monotonous but healthy. Visitors commented with surprise
on the physique of the Irish rural poor, comparing it favoura-
bly with that of their equivalents in richer countries. Other
advantages included the ease with which potatoes could be
cultivated – too easily, said the critics – and their ability to
flourish on marginal land otherwise unsuitable for tillage.

There is no doubt that the potato monoculture in the poorer
parts of Ireland discouraged the introduction of commercial
agriculture. The few improving landlords who tried this met
with fierce resistance. Commercial agriculture meant, among
other things, the enclosure of land previously worked in
common. The so-called rundale system of cooperative farming,
in which long strips of land were farmed by extended families,
was wonderfully fair in ensuring that no family member had a
monopoly on the best land. Everyone got more or less the
same share of good and bad land. This was socially cohesive
and economically insane: it was a guarantee of low yields and
offered no incentive to innovate or improve.

The great exception to this general picture was Ulster. Not
only was reliance on the potato less than in the other three
provinces, there was a thriving flax and linen industry in place

since the late eighteenth century. Agriculture was more varied than elsewhere, and the domestic employment offered by linen weaving supplemented farm incomes. Moreover, the finishing and marketing of linen products was concentrated in Belfast, where it was the largest source of early industrial employment. Nor was Ulster exceptionalism something new. As early as the 1750s, John Wesley, the founder of Methodism, had reported that 'no sooner did we enter Ulster than we observed the difference. The ground was cultivated just as in England and the cottages not only neat but with doors, chimneys and windows.'

In the 1830s, the first stirrings of the Industrial Revolution were already visible in Belfast. The fact that industry roared ahead in Belfast and much of Ulster during the nineteenth century and failed to do so in the three southern provinces was one of the most significant developments in the story of modern Ireland.

In a changing world, no change is more fundamental than that of language. The death of languages is a melancholy feature of modernity: the standard speech of metropolitan elites overwhelms regional dialects and local patois. As modern states form themselves, the metropolitan language of commerce, law, administration and journalism exercises a powerful hold. An ambitious provincial, anxious to make a career in business, law or the civil service, must learn the language of power. The metropolitan explosion of newspapers and books in nineteenth-century Europe reinforced the tendency. In the twentieth century, radio, television and the internet accelerated it further. Regional speech – both patois and minority languages – suffered accordingly. Ireland has been no exception to this process.

English had obviously been the language of the Ascendancy in the eighteenth century. But the vast majority of the Irish population in 1800 spoke Irish, either as the sole vernacular or bilingually. By the mid 1830s, it was estimated that about 50 per cent of the population spoke the old language. The 1851 census gave a figure of one-and-a-half million people – less than a quarter of the whole population – who spoke only Irish. This precipitous decline obviously reflects the devastating effects of the Famine. It was a decline that has continued unabated to the present day. The Famine merely accelerated a pre-existing pattern.

Daniel O'Connell's first language had been Irish. As an adult, he was a champion of Catholic rights, the effective developer of what became the mainstream nationalist tradition, but he was indifferent to the Irish language to the point of hostility. He was able to mobilize mass opinion in Ireland first on a specifically Catholic issue and secondly on a national one – the demand for the repeal of the union – without ever touching on the cultural question of the decline of Irish. O'Connell effectively yoked Catholicism and nationalism together: the injection of language revival as a vital part of the nationalist project did not happen for another fifty years.

O'Connell's indifference to Irish was rooted in a utilitarian view of language itself. In 1833, admitting that the use of Irish was diminishing among the peasantry, he observed that 'the superior utility of the English tongue, as the medium of all modern communication, is so great, that I can witness without a sigh the gradual disuse of Irish'. This might be the voice of any ambitious provincial in Europe in the age before the idea of cultural nationalism established its dominance.

The anglicization of Ireland is perhaps the key cultural development of the entire nineteenth century. Ironically, anglicization marched hand-in-hand with nationalism. It was driven forward, as national movements tend to be, by an educated elite whose members were most likely to be anglophone. The Catholic middle class, which provided the officer corps of nationalism from O'Connell's time onwards, moved in an explicitly anglophone world: it was no accident that the southeast of the island, that forcing house of modernity, was also the most anglicized part. Provincial newspapers, hugely influential in the spread of nationalist ideas, were published in English.

The growing number of Catholic secondary fee-paying schools – aimed at the children of the middle class – increasingly modelled themselves on the English public schools. Education in the liberal professions, especially the law and medicine, was not just in English but closely adhered to English models. There was a great irony in all this: just as Ireland was moving farther from England politically, it was drawing closer to it culturally. By the mid-century, the immense prestige of an England approaching the apogee of her power – the workshop of the world, rich beyond the dreams of earlier generations – had a powerful gravitational pull for all within its orbit.

The Whigs fell from power in 1841, to be replaced by the Tories under Peel. Clearly, that was the end of a programme of worthy reforms in Ireland. O'Connell could now turn to the larger constitutional issue. He launched a campaign for the repeal of the union of 1801 and the restoration of a parliament in Dublin. O'Connell went for broke. He revived the methods that had stood him in such good stead in the Emancipation campaign: a national organization, again leaning heavily on Catholic parish structures, complemented by fundraising and propaganda. To this potent brew he added a new element, the so-called 'monster meeting'.

Monster meetings were enormous public gatherings designed to show the formidable powers of organization and control that O'Connell exercised over the people. They aimed to intimidate the government by sheer weight of numbers and by the implicit threat of public disorder on a massive scale. The meetings were organized at historic sites like Tara, Co. Meath, and were always addressed by O'Connell.

Three things contributed to the failure of the repeal agitation. First, the Catholic hierarchy, although sympathetic, did not feel that repeal was as urgent a measure as Emancipation had been and did not throw its weight behind it to the same degree. Second, there was no body of sympathetic opinion in England as there had been in the earlier campaign. Third, Peel exploited this knowledge to take a stand against O'Connell. When a monster meeting was announced for the Dublin suburb of Clontarf – site of a famous battle against the Vikings in 1014 – the government banned it. Fearing violence, which he loathed, O'Connell backed down and abandoned the meeting.

O'Connell briefly ended up in prison for his pains, although the conditions of his confinement were luxurious by the standards endured by most contemporary prisoners. More importantly, Clontarf was his Waterloo. This extraordinary man – brilliant, charismatic, vulgar, idealistic and cynical by turn – was finally a burnt-out case. He had been, as much as Parnell was to be forty years later, the 'uncrowned king of Ireland'.

Well, almost. For by then an internal opposition had developed. It was called Young Ireland. It was in part a generational challenge to O'Connell. Its leading figures were disaffected young bourgeois who were repelled by the open sectarianism of O'Connell's rhetoric. The name of their group echoed those of the contemporaneous Young Italy and Young Germany, each grounded in a similar social membership. These movements were a post-Romantic appeal to the spirit of cultural nationalism, emphasizing the importance of ethnicity and language. The leader of Young Italy, Giuseppe Mazzini, was also a promoter of popular democracy, something which linked him to O'Connell, although ironically he dismissed Irish nationalism on the grounds that Ireland was too small a unit to sustain a separate existence.

The emphasis on culture and language in Young Ireland's philosophy marked it off from O'Connell's utilitarianism and its vitality and freshness contrasted vividly with his declining fortunes as the 1840s wore on.

On 15 October 1842, the first edition of the *Nation* newspaper appeared in Dublin. The founders were Charles Gavan Duffy, a self-educated journalist; John Blake Dillon, a barrister; and Thomas Davis, barrister and minor poet. All were provincials from middle-class backgrounds: Dillon and Duffy were the sons of shopkeepers, Davis of an army surgeon.

The *Nation* was an astonishing success, at one point in the 1840s claiming a readership of almost 250,000. It was a radical nationalist paper. Although it supported O'Connell's repeal campaign, its emphasis was different to his. The group clustered around the *Nation* introduced a different strain of nationalist thought to Ireland. It defined the nation less in legal terms – popular sovereignty and the will of the people – than in cultural. It was literary – Davis was the pre-eminent popular poet of his day and some of his poems are still popular in ballad form – and it wished to promote a distinctively national literature. It was the first national movement to propose a revival of the Irish language. It emphasized the iconography of modern Irish nationalism: the harps and shamrocks, round towers and Irish wolfhounds, and introduced the tricolour flag. One of the Young Irelanders, Thomas Francis Meagher, brought the green, white and orange flag back from Paris in 1848, an obvious imitation of the revolutionary *tricolore*.

Young Ireland was a repeal ginger group but relations between them and O'Connell were tense. O'Connell's utilitarianism had led him to accept, however reluctantly, a confessional context for his campaigns. His was a substantially Catholic movement. Young Ireland, with its emphasis on culture, proposed a more inclusive definition of nationality. It was rooted in different soil to the non-sectarianism of the United Irishmen in the 1790s but the fruits were very similar. O'Connell emphasized the practical politics of Catholic numbers; Young Ireland's focus was the idealist politics of a nation in which common citizenship would override religious differences.

In 1845, the British government established three universities in Ireland, the so-called Queen's Colleges, at Belfast, Cork and Galway. They were founded on a strictly non-sectarian basis. No state funding was provided for the support of chairs of theology, although private endowments were not forbidden. The campaign for a Catholic university had been a major demand from O'Connell and the British hoped that the Queen's Colleges would satisfy the demand. Not so. O'Connell and the bishops denounced the 'godless colleges' and redoubled their campaign for a specifically Catholic institution in which the church, not the state, would hold the reins.

Young Ireland welcomed the Queen's Colleges as a major step forward. They recoiled from a confessionalism that effectively coupled Irish identity with Catholicism. Davis himself was a Protestant. There was a terrible irony here: O'Connell's populism was democratic; Young Ireland's idealism was not. It was an elite subset of nationalism with shallow roots among the people, for all the popularity of the *Nation*.

This fault-line in Irish nationalism would reappear. In the meantime, Davis died tragically young in 1845. O'Connell's prestige was diminished since the climbdown at Clontarf. By early 1847, overwhelmed by the disaster of the Famine, he stood for the last time in the House of Commons, barely audible and trembling in the grasp of the illness that would kill him before the summer was out, begging alms from his enemy for a country that could no longer save itself. For by now Ireland was in the grip of the Great Famine.

He begged the help of parliament, failing which he predicted that a quarter of the population of Ireland would be lost. He was right. Death and emigration saw to that.

16

FAMINE

In June 1845, a new and mysterious potato blight appeared in Belgium. By September, it had made its way to Ireland. It resulted in the loss of about one-third of the Irish potato harvest that year. It was a crisis but not a disaster. The blight had appeared late in the year and much of the crop was already harvested when it struck. Even so, the failure of the staple crop on such a scale created a major social problem. It was not unprecedented. There had been partial failures of the crop in every decade of the nineteenth century. The difference was – although no one knew it at the time – that this was a new, virulent and utterly mysterious kind of blight.

The Tory government of Sir Robert Peel responded promptly. Peel had been chief secretary of Ireland from 1812 to 1818 and had provided £250,000 for the relief of distress during food shortages in 1817, in the course of which about 50,000 people had died.

In November 1845, Peel's government spent £100,000 on buying and distributing Indian corn from the United States. It set up a commission to study the causes of the blight and instituted a series of public works which provided subsistence wages for the poor. Peel was a free-trader but not an ideologue. Government assistance of this kind was contrary to the principles of free trade, which believed that the self-regulating internal logic of the economic system could only be distorted by government interference. Nonetheless, Peel's government *did* intervene strongly and promptly in the face of such an urgent crisis.

In the summer of 1846, however, the Tory government fell. Ironically, its defeat came as a result of its own success in forcing through the repeal of the Corn Laws. These laws, the great symbolic target of all free-traders for a generation, had placed restrictions on the importation of grain into the United Kingdom and had had the effect of acting as a kind of hidden subsidy to large landed interests.

The new Whig government was led by Lord John Russell. It was much more doctrinaire in its espousal of free-trade principles and instinctively less likely than Peel had been to bend or otherwise trim them in the face of circumstance. This had serious consequences in Ireland, for there was a wholesale failure of the potato crop in the summer of 1846. The blight reappeared earlier that year, before any harvesting could begin. This was the real beginning of the Great Famine.

The distress of the previous year had clearly left parts of the population in a poor position to cope with the shattering effects of total potato failure. The response of the Whig government in London was to reduce grain importation into Ireland and to attempt to run down public works schemes. Despite this, almost 500,000 desperate people were employed in such public works by the end of 1846 and nearly half as many again three months later. Contrary to its own instincts, the government established soup kitchens to feed the people in 1847. But its heart was not in it and they were closed down again at the end of that disastrous year.

Why did the government respond in such a cold-blooded way?

It was an article of faith in Westminster that Ireland was a social and economic mess. Its landlords were feckless and reactionary, not given to the sort of modernizing improvements that had transformed English agriculture. The tenants were seen as a slothful human mass kept in a permanent state of backward subsistence by their reliance on the potato. The doctrinaire free-traders wanted a wholesale shakeout of Irish agriculture: enclosure, modernization, assisted passage schemes for supernumerary tenants, and so on. Because none of this was happening or likely to happen, Ireland was regarded by the free-trading Whigs as a chronic invalid.

In their eyes, the Famine was the inevitable consequence of this situation and an opportunity to remedy it. To many Whigs who were also devoutly evangelical Protestants, the Famine could be seen as the wrath of a righteous Providence. No major figure in the British administration made this connection more blatantly than Charles Edward Trevelyan, the head of the Treasury and a devout evangelical. Although a civil servant and therefore, in theory, subject always to political direction, in practice he effectively made policy for Ireland, a country which he had never visited and of whose particular circumstances and differences he had no knowledge. This did not deter him from writing a book entitled *The Irish Crisis*, in which he set out the providential interpretation of the Famine in stark prose. The calamity was 'the direct stroke of an all-wise and all-merciful Providence . . . which laid bare the deep and inveterate root of social evil . . . [It] was the sharp but effectual remedy by which the cure is likely to be effected.'

The government's strategic aim was to minimize its own direct involvement in Famine relief and make Ireland responsible for bearing the cost. The cost of local relief was to be borne by Irish landlords and the Poor Law system was expected to be the means whereby relief was given. This strategy was grounded in an assertion that a local crisis should be treated locally and should not become a burden on national finances. This assertion dovetailed neatly with the core value of free trade, that government interference in the economic mechanism was harmful and damaging in itself. There was no doubt that free trade had made Britain rich. But now it was making Ireland starve.

After the failure of 1846, people were reduced to eating seed potatoes. Ironically, the crop did not fail in 1847 but yields were low because so little had been sown. Black '47 entered the folk memory. People were not simply dying of starvation but also of the illnesses induced by starvation, especially typhus and relapsing fever. Vast hordes of sick and dying wandered the countryside, throwing themselves on to the workhouses established under the Poor Law system, which proved utterly inadequate to the task. The Poor Law was suddenly shouldering a burden it had never been intended to bear.

By now, press reports were appearing in London which gave a vivid picture of the distress. *The Times* sent the Dublin-born William Howard Russell later to become the most famous war correspondent of the age – to the west of Ireland. His accounts of what he saw horrified him and his readers. The *Illustrated London News* carried images of starving people and Famine funerals in West Cork that are still shocking today. This resulted in a redoubling of private charitable relief and the opening of Famine funds. Private charities had been a significant force in the relief of distress since 1845, the Quakers in particular playing a heroic role.

The rise in mortality and distress in 1847 was overwhelming. The scaling down of public works left the poorest people destitute, so that many had no money to buy such grain as was available for purchase. The rudimentary public health system buckled under the strain. An economic recession in Britain itself meant business failures and unemployment in the industrial north of England, diverting some sympathy and relief nearer to home and away from Ireland.

Famine relief was primarily seen by the government as a local charge upon the Irish landlords and the Poor Law system. But the worse things got, the less local agencies could cope. The more landlords were stretched, the tougher the line they took with tenants unable to keep up their rental payments. Evictions increased, throwing ever more wretched, destitute and starving families on to the roads. Naturally, the main burden of this disaster fell upon the poor.

This process was accelerated in turn by a piece of legislation known forever after as the Quarter-Acre Clause. The Poor Law Extension Act 1847 stated that 'occupiers of more than a quarter-acre of land are not to be deemed destitute, nor to be relieved out of the poor rates'. Thus starving peasants were faced with the need to surrender their tiny holdings in order to qualify for poor relief. Naturally, those who did so never recovered them. This piece of social engineering had the effect of consolidating the size of farms, a necessary and desirable reform in general terms but an extraordinary one to introduce in the circumstances. Its author was a Co. Galway landlord called Sir William Gregory. His wife Augusta Persse, many years his junior, would later achieve fame as Lady Gregory, *éminence grise* of the Irish Literary Revival. It is worth noting that a majority of O'Connell's MPs supported the Quarter-Acre Clause: utilitarian and free-trade assumptions were not confined to British Whigs and Tories.

Then the potato crop failed again in 1848. It was another catastrophic failure, as in 1846. The government made further poor relief dependent on the collection of arrears in the Poor Law rates. Nearly £1 million was duly collected but at the cost of growing agrarian unrest. Emigration beckoned for many. Landlords faced ruin. There were further minor failures of the potato crop up until 1852, although the worst of the devastation was over by 1849.

The 1851 census told the story simply. It recorded a population of just over 6.5 million people. The corresponding figure ten years earlier had been just under 8.2 million. The population of Ireland had been reduced by 20 per cent in a decade, over 1.5 million people. Of these, at least half died; the rest emigrated. Emigration became a way of life from then on, causing the population to decline to less than 4.4 million in 1911. In seventy years, the span of a single life, the population of Ireland was almost cut in half.

*   *   *

The Famine was a natural ecological disaster. The government's response turned the disaster into a catastrophe. It applied an economic theory that may have made sense in the medium and long term but which had the immediate effect of exacerbating the distress. It held to its free-trade beliefs with religious certainty – this in an age when religious belief informed every aspect of life. Indeed, the contrast between Protestant material success and Catholic poverty had a melodramatic hold on many English minds. The Irish system of landholding and agriculture was indeed antique. It was overdue for reform, and the Famine was in that sense providential: the wrath of the Protestant god directed at the feckless and the lazy.

Almost a million people died in the process. Millions more emigrated, many taking with them a hatred of Britain for letting Ireland starve. Whether that was a fair or an unfair judgement, it was an understandable one. The last great subsistence crisis in Europe occurred in a part of the richest country in the world and its effects were made more severe than they otherwise might have been by the deliberate actions of that country's government. The government was hypnotized by its ideology, sincerely so, but at the cost of its humanity.

There were winners and losers. The most obvious losers were the pre-Famine landless poor, who bore the heaviest casualties. Those who emigrated were in general marginally more prosperous. They had enough to get themselves to ports and to pay their passage. But they too lost the only life they knew and were driven into exile. Many landlords were ruined. Two pieces of legislation called the Encumbered Estates Acts established procedures for the disposal of their estates. The new owners were usually less sentimental about traditional rural obligations than their predecessors had been.

In the long term, the union of Great Britain and Ireland was a loser. The Famine fatally weakened the moral legitimacy of British rule in Ireland. In the eyes of Irish nationalists, the constitutional assertion that Ireland was a fully integrated part of the metropolitan British state seemed more and more a fiction. Britain treated Ireland not as an equal part of the United Kingdom but as a troublesome colony.

The Famine radicalized nationalists. It coincided with Europe's 'year of revolutions', 1848. Just as the United Irishmen of the 1790s had been inspired by the French Revolution of 1789, so now the radical Young Irelanders – John Mitchel, William Smith O'Brien and others – were inspired by the Paris revolution that established the Second Republic in February 1848. They and others had formed themselves into the Irish Confederation in 1847 on the occasion of their final break with the Repealers.

The movement was riddled with government informers and spies. Mitchel was arrested in May and convicted on a charge of treason-felony. He was transported for fourteen years, first to Bermuda and later to Van Diemen's Land (Tasmania). He escaped to the United States in 1853. There, he wrote *Jail Journal*, a bitterly anglophobe polemic that later became one of the sacred texts of Irish nationalism. He practised journalism in Knoxville, Tennessee, where he settled. Tennessee was a Confederate state in the American Civil War and Mitchel supported the right of the Confederacy to secede, just as he had supported the right of Ireland to secede from the United Kingdom. He lost two sons fighting for the South in the Civil War.

The remaining Irish Confederation leaders were effectively harried out of Dublin by government pressure. They tried to raise troops for a possible autumn rising in Tipperary and Kilkenny. They held a meeting at Ballingarry, Co. Tipperary, in July 1848 to discuss the way forward. A majority was for avoiding armed action, at least for the moment. A minority, led by O'Brien, was in favour. The issue was forced by a company of police which entered the village and took up a position in the house of Mrs McCormack, a widow. Some of O'Brien's more enthusiastic supporters attacked this position. Two insurgents were killed before the arrival of police reinforcements brought the affray to an end.

It was derided as the Battle of the Widow McCormack's Cabbage Patch. But it was also remembered as the rising of 1848. However inflated that claim might have been, it was typical of the Young Ireland achievement. They were propagandists rather than men of action. Their legacy was the creation of a myth – or at least a part of a myth. While mainstream nationalism would eventually revive itself along a broadly O'Connellite model – constitutional politics and the support of the church – the memory of 1848, like that of 1798, was a reminder of other possibilities. Young Ireland, like the United Irishmen, became part of an internal opposition within Irish nationalism.

The biggest winners of all in the fallout from the Famine were the wealthier tenants, although this was by no means obvious at the time. In the midst of the most appalling starvation and destitution, they maintained their social position. Not all tenants were poor. On the contrary, a comfortable tenant class and their merchant cousins in the towns survived the Famine very well. Once again, it is instructive to look at the foundation dates of Catholic institutions in order to appreciate how economically vigorous parts of the Catholic community remained in the Famine years. Kilkenny's Cathedral of the Assumption was begun in 1843; building continued until 1857. The parish church of St Mary's in Clonmel, Co. Tipperary, is dated to 1837–50. St Aidan's Cathedral, Enniscorthy, Co. Wexford (1843–8) was designed by A. W. N. Pugin, no less. He also designed the Loreto convent in nearby Gorey.

All these examples are within the rich south-eastern quadrant, where there were communities of Catholics wealthy enough to endow and erect such impressive structures at a time when the country was being engulfed in a demographic cataclysm. Nor was the process any longer the exclusive preserve of the southeast. The Catholic cathedral of St Patrick in Armagh was begun in 1840; the Franciscan church in Galway dates from 1849; the cathedral of SS Peter and Paul in Ennis, Co. Clare, was consecrated in 1843; that of St Mary's in Killarney (by Pugin again) in 1855 after thirteen years of building.

While the real explosion in Catholic institutional building does not happen until the second half of the nineteenth century, what is significant is the degree to which the process is already well established before and during the Famine. The people who paid for all this – the Catholic provincial middle class – were the group that profited most from the Famine.

The landlords and the whole ascendancy world were weakened. The rural poor were decimated. The social engineering desired by the doctrinaire free-traders was well under way. Farm sizes grew. Subdivision of holdings was ended. Enclosures proceeded and the system of communal agriculture was finally abandoned in the west in favour of individual holdings. Marriages were postponed until tenancies could be inherited; younger children had to shift for themselves, often by emigrating. There was a deeply unsentimental social calculus in post-Famine Ireland. Among tenants, the watchword was 'never again', even though (or perhaps because) theirs was the class that emerged least scathed from the Famine. In a sense, the dirty work that enabled them to become the dominant social force in Ireland from the 1880s on had been done for them. And it could all be blamed on the British.

The Catholics who did well out of the Famine were the backbone of the land movement, of Parnell's electorate, of the Catholic laity and clergy, of the Gaelic Athletic Association, and of all subsequent nationalist agitation. It was their class that was celebrated and sentimentalized in Charles Kickham's *Knocknagow* and other novels of the virtuous rural life. It was their grandchildren, by and large, who inherited the independent Irish state in 1922.

17

CULLEN

The Famine changed Ireland irrevocably. It ushered in the age of the farmer. Farmers became the key social group from the 1850s onwards. First as tenants, later as owner–occupiers, their material interests became associated with those of the nation itself, a situation that persisted until the economic changes of the 1960s shifted the balance of power towards the urban middle class.

The land question was the key question after the Famine. In time, land and the national question became one. In their own eyes, farmers were the real Irish nation. Agriculture was simply the most important economic activity in the country and much of the economic life of provincial Ireland depended on the prosperity of farmers. In the towns, industries such as brewing and distilling drew their raw materials from the countryside.

As farm sizes increased, the basic shape of modern Irish agriculture emerged. The key change was the shift from tillage to pasture. A great deal of the tillage economy of the pre-Famine period had been of the subsistence kind. That ended, as almost all Irish agriculture went on to a commercial footing. Large farms emerged, particularly in those flat eastern counties near Dublin which were best suited for pasture. These holdings, often referred to as 'ranches', were to be the source of

ongoing resentment from smallholders. In part, this was due to
the no-nonsense commercialism of the ranchers.

The ranchers were an interesting group. Many were
Catholics and nationalists, shopkeepers and other town-dwellers who had accumulated some capital and were in a position
either to rent or buy the large holdings for grazing. There was
huge social prestige attached to the ownership or control of
land. The ranchers were a new rural elite. Their position within
the broader nationalist consensus was anomalous. On the one
hand, they often provided the kind of social leadership and
financial support on which nationalist movements depended;
on the other, they drew the fire of smallholders who asserted
the superiority of tillage as the backbone of self-sufficient
family farms. There was plenty of potential in all this for class
war in the countryside – and it did break out from time to time,
with cattle drives and other actions directed against the ranchers – but in general it was kept under control. Unity in the
nationalist community overbore every other consideration,
especially until the hated landlord system was dismantled in
the early twentieth century.

Post-Famine Ireland was never classless. On the contrary,
small social differences were often keenly felt in a manner typical of a provincial small-town and rural society. Both the rural
and urban working classes – the landless agricultural labourers
and the unskilled slum-dwellers in the cities – were held in
something between disdain and contempt by the prevailing
petit bourgeois culture. Yet the imperative demands of national
solidarity never permitted the development of fully blown
class politics.

In the aftermath of the Famine, nationalist Ireland was
exhausted and demoralized. As politics atrophied, the Catholic
Church filled the void. It was a church which was reinventing
itself. The pre-Famine church had a broadly Gallican thrust.
This meant an emphasis on the autonomy of local bishops in
matters of a civil and temporal nature. Spiritual matters were,

of course, subject to full papal authority. Gallican ideas contrasted with ultramontanism, the view which stressed the central authority of Rome in all matters affecting Catholics.

In 1850, Paul Cullen was appointed archbishop of Armagh. Three years later, he was translated to Dublin and in 1866 he became the first Irish cardinal. He had been born in Co. Kildare in 1803 and ordained in Rome in 1829. In 1832, he was appointed rector of the Irish college in Rome. His entire formation as a cleric had therefore taken place in the shadow of the Vatican. He was recognized from the first as a person of exceptional ability: hard-working, rigorous, disciplined and intellectually accomplished. Cullen was an ultramontane by conviction and temperament alike.

He was Rome's man in Ireland and he left an imprint on the Irish church that was not seriously shaken until the clerical sex scandals of the 1990s. The Catholic Church became the undisputed centre of moral authority in nationalist Ireland. No politician could ignore it.

The process of weakening the Gallican element began with the first major initiative of Cullen's episcopacy. In 1850, on instructions from Rome, he summoned a national synod of the church at Thurles, Co. Tipperary. It was the first Irish national synod since the twelfth century and the first formal meeting of all the bishops of Ireland since the seventeenth. The synod predictably redoubled the church's condemnation of the 'godless colleges' and resolved on the establishment of a Catholic university. It also adopted decrees designed to tighten discipline in the Irish church; to ensure that matters in dispute were referred to Rome for decision, thus weakening discretionary power at diocesan level; and to introduce sodalities and devotions for the laity uniformly throughout the country. The whole thrust of the Synod of Thurles was to centralize and standardize as far as possible and to introduce 'Roman' practices at the expense of traditional forms of local piety, many of which the ultramontanes regarded as little better than superstition.

Much has been made of the so-called devotional revolution in the Irish church. This was the process whereby Catholicism progressively abandoned traditional folk practices: patterns (gatherings at traditional shrines); wakes; and stations (masses celebrated in private houses). The new emphasis was to be on uniform devotions conducted under formal clerical supervision in churches. Strict Sunday observance; regular attendance at confession and communion as decreed in canon law; the widespread introduction of continental devotions such as those to the Sacred Heart and later to the Immaculate Conception; benedictions; processions carefully marshalled and disciplined by the clergy; sodalities, confraternities; public retreats and missions: all these features were characteristic of the devotional revolution. Some were already in place before Cullen's time, and as we saw the process made its own contribution to the discipline of O'Connell's political agitations. But Cullen gave them all his enthusiastic and urgent support, quickening the pace of change.

As with politics, the devotional revolution was most developed in the south-east of the island, less so (until Cullen's time) as one went north and west. The growth of church building in the second half of the century, and the assertive and dominating presence of so many fine churches, reflected the new centrality of the parish church in the lives of the faithful. In a sense, it represented the industrialization of Irish Catholicism. The churches were like spiritual factories, where people now had to travel to worship at set times and in a disciplined manner ordained by their clerical overseers.

After the failure of 1848, the remaining Young Irelanders scattered. Some, like John Mitchel, were transported. Others, like John Blake Dillon, escaped abroad before taking advantage of an amnesty in 1855 to return without ever again being a major force in politics. Charles Gavan Duffy was a Westminster MP for three years but gave it up in disgust and emigrated to Australia. He lived a long life, became prime minister of Victoria in 1871 and accepted a knighthood two years later before ending his days in retirement in the south of France.

The source of Gavan Duffy's disgust was an abortive attempt to organize Irish nationalists at Westminster. It started in the wake of the Famine, when two organizations were established – one on Ulster, the other in Leinster – to secure the rights of tenants at a time when they were under increasing threat of eviction from landlords. In the three southern provinces, tenants had neither customary nor statutory protection from their landlords' whims. However, the so-called Ulster Custom held in most of the north. It was never universal either in application or definition, but essentially it meant that a departing tenant could dispose of his tenancy to the highest bidder, subject to the landlord's approval of the newcomer. It usually included compensation to the value of any improvements that the departing tenant had made.

The Ulster Tenant Right Association was established in 1847, mainly to protect Presbyterian tenants from Anglican landlords. It aimed to make the Ulster Custom (free sale, as it called it) statutory. In a remarkable development, the Ulster and Leinster associations merged in 1850 to form the Irish Tenant League, a genuinely non-sectarian and national association. By now the Ulster Custom had become more elastically defined, which definition formed the so-called Three Fs – free sale, fair rent (to be set by an independent tribunal) and fixity of tenure (no eviction if rents properly paid). The Three Fs became the core demand of all agrarian tenant groups for the next generation.

The glad, confident morning of the Irish Tenant League did not last long. It took little to detach the Catholic south from the Protestant north. The revival of the Catholic Church in Britain had led to an attempt to restore the old pre-Reformation dioceses. This provoked a Protestant reaction and the government rushed through legislation forbidding the Catholics from using any of the traditional territorial names for their restored dioceses: these names were retained exclusively for the established church (the Church of England). Irish Liberal MPs, most of them supporters of the Irish Tenant

League but also dependent on Catholic votes, formed an Independent Irish Party in protest against the legislation. Ignoring Gavan Duffy's advice to have nothing to do with the new party, the Tenant League threw its support behind it. In the 1852 election, forty-eight MPs were returned in the party's interest, all of them pledged to independent opposition. Significantly, however, not one of them was from Ulster: the overt association between the party and a Catholic agitation was simply too rich for the Protestant blood. The so-called 'League of North and South' may have been a chimera, but it had been a benign one. There was never to be another one.

The party itself was a fiasco. Known variously as the Irish Brigade and the Pope's Brass Band, it was completely compromised when two of its leading figures, William Keogh and John Sadleir, accepted government office in defiance of their election pledges. Moreover, it made the serious error of picking a quarrel with the Catholic Church in the person of Cullen, not a man to be crossed. Sadleir came to a bad end: a director of the Tipperary Joint-Stock Bank, he was £200,000 overdrawn on his own account when he committed suicide in London, whereupon the bank was discovered to be insolvent. Depositors lost almost £400,000. Keogh, after a career as a notably reactionary judge, eventually died by his own hand as well.

It was these squalid transactions that drove Gavan Duffy into despairing exile. But the buffoonery of the Pope's Brass Band gave parliamentary politics generally a bad name. It all seemed a leaden age after the heroics of O'Connell and the cataclysm of the Famine. Gavan Duffy was not alone in feeling a sense of disgust. It was shared by many, especially by others who had been involved in Young Ireland. And some of them had an alternative.

No subset of Young Ireland was of greater importance for the future than the Fenians. The Fenian Brotherhood or Irish Republican Brotherhood (IRB) was founded jointly in Dublin and New York in 1858. The Dublin founder was James Stephens, a 1848 veteran who had fled to Paris where he had involved himself in various revolutionary secret societies. From them, he acquired the organizational principles he put in place in Ireland. The basic Fenian structure was this: a local leader, known as a centre, was chosen. Each centre chose nine captains who chose nine sergeants who chose nine men. Information was passed to each rank on a need-to-know basis only. Within a few years, Stephens had tramped the country and established a national network based on this structure.

The New York organization was principally the work of John O'Mahony, another 1848 veteran. The introduction of Irish-America into the equation was a critical development: no subsequent nationalist movement has been indifferent to the enormous potential of the transatlantic diaspora.

The Fenians believed in the force of arms. They were a secret, militant, revolutionary society dedicated to the violent overthrow of British rule in Ireland and the establishment in its place of an independent Irish republic. They were uninterested in politics, with its trimming and prevarication. They borrowed their methods from the tradition of European left-wing secret societies. Which brought them head to head with the Catholic Church.

The ultramontane Catholicism of Pope Pius IX was bitterly opposed to revolutionary secret societies. The church had been an uncompromising enemy of revolutionary France and a strong supporter of the reactionary regimes established by Metternich after the final defeat of Napoleon. These regimes had been overturned in 1848 and Pius himself had had to flee from Rome for two years.

In these circumstances, it was inevitable that the Catholic Church in Ireland would regard the Fenians as part of an international conspiracy against the legitimate order. Cullen was no friend of the British state but he was determined to ensure that Irish opposition to it was firmly under church control. He exercised effective control over loose alliances of Irish MPs at Westminster in the 1850s and 1860s, but these groups were never effective and never caught the public imagination.

The Fenians did. Stephens was a talented organizer and numbers swelled. In particular, Fenianism appealed to lower middle-class young men in the towns. This was a group significantly lower on the social scale than most of the Young Irelanders had been. In this sense, Fenianism played its own part in the democratization of Irish nationalism.

Success inevitably meant police penetration, despite the cell structure. In 1865, Stephens and the leadership of the Fenians were arrested in a pre-emptive strike by the government. They had indeed been planning a rising for that year, hoping to exploit the services of Irish-American soldiers demobilized at the end of the American Civil War. The loss of momentum in 1865 was fatal and that generation of Fenians never recovered from it. Stephens dithered on his release from prison. He sailed to New York and became fatally embroiled in the poisonous internal politics of the Irish-Americans. Stephens was eventually deposed and a small group of American Fenians sailed to Ireland. In March 1867, they tripped off a feeble rising that was hardly more heroic as a feat of arms than 1848. But the aftermath was significant. First, the 1867 rising entered the apostolic succession of Irish rebellions. Second, Fenian prisoners became a focus of political agitation. Third, two of these prisoners were the subject of a rescue bid. A police van in Manchester containing the two was attacked and the men released but a policeman was killed in the process. Three men, William Allen, Michael Larkin and William O'Brien, were hanged for this deed. These were the 'Manchester Martyrs' and their executions galvanized nationalist Ireland. The song 'God Save Ireland' was written in their memory and became the unofficial national anthem for the next two generations.

The Clerkenwell bomb was the last and most dramatic action of the Fenian campaign. A leading Irish-American Fenian, Ricard O'Sullivan Burke, was arrested in London in November 1867. Burke was the Fenians' leading arms agent in Britain. He had been involved in the rising in Ireland earlier in the year and had been the principal organizer of the Manchester prison van rescue that had resulted in the execution of the Manchester Martyrs. He had been betrayed by an informer. He was charged with treason-felony and lodged in Clerkenwell House of Detention.

His fellow Fenians were determined to spring him. On the afternoon of Friday 13 December, a barrel of dynamite was placed against the wall of the prison. When it exploded, it demolished an 18 m (60 ft) section of the wall together with all the houses on the opposite side of the street. Clerkenwell was a densely packed working-class area. Seventeen people died; one woman went mad; forty women gave birth prematurely. At least one hundred-and-twenty were badly injured. And it was all for nothing. The plan had been betrayed to the prison authorities. Burke was in a double-locked cell and the exercise yard, where he was supposed to have been, was deserted.

The destruction of life and property on such a scale shocked and outraged British public opinion. The new prime minister, William Ewart Gladstone, reacted more thoughtfully: he began to cast around for a series of reforms that would bind Ireland more closely to the British state by addressing legitimate grievances.

Gladstone's first legislative measure was the disestablishment of the Church of Ireland. Although the largest Protestant denomination in the country, it still accounted for barely 12 per cent of the total population. It had been the established church since Henry VIII's break with Rome in the 1530s and its position as the official state church had been confirmed by the Act of Union, which united it to the Church of England. Disestablishment therefore unravelled a key provision of the union settlement. The logic of this was not lost on unionists, for if one provision could be set aside what was to stop the whole thing being subverted? Cullen can only have smiled grimly at the sight of the established church's ritual humiliation. As a nationalist – albeit one of an anti-Fenian stripe – he welcomed this weakening of the union structure. As a Catholic – far more important to him – he rejoiced. He was not alone among the Catholic hierarchy in seeing this moment as the end of the Protestant ascendancy. A further small but telling moment came in 1873 with the removal of all religious tests for graduation from Trinity College Dublin, previously the intellectual centre of an exclusive Irish Anglicanism.

Following disestablishment, Gladstone next turned to tackle an issue that went to the very heart of Irish discontent: land. In the aftermath of the Famine, the Encumbered Estates Acts provided a mechanism whereby debt-ridden estates could be sold off free of encumbrances. The effect was not just to transfer land from bankrupt to solvent landlords but to introduce the idea that the road to solving the Irish land problem ran through Westminster.

Before the Famine, relations between landlord and tenant were regarded as a simple matter of contract law, an agreement between two contracting parties. The relative strengths of the parties were deemed irrelevant. Government interference through legislation in what was regarded a free transaction between individuals was thought unnecessary and oppressive. The Encumbered Estates Acts changed all that. Parliament was now a player, since the law of contract had proved unequal to the task.

There were to be eighteen Irish land acts passed between 1870 and 1903, all intended to equalize the relationship between landlord and tenant by positive discrimination in favour of the latter. Gladstone's act of 1870 was the start of this process. It gave legal force to certain customary practices, in particular the Ulster Custom. A departing tenant now had the right to be compensated for improvements made by him and also to sell his interest to the highest bidder subject to the landlord's approval of the purchaser. These customary rights, which had been generally confined to the northern province, were now extended to the whole country by force of law.

18

INDUSTRY

There was another kind of revolution in Ireland at the mid nineteenth century. The Industrial Revolution hardly affected the three southern provinces but it transformed Ulster. The term itself refers to a complex series of economic advances that began in Britain from the 1780s onwards and spread gradually and unevenly through Western Europe in the nineteenth century. The key developments were the harnessing of steam power, the accelerated development of coal and iron mining, and the move from domestic piece work by individual crafts-men to factory production by armies of semi-skilled and unskilled workers. This development meant the growth of industrial cities and a surge of population from the countryside to the towns.

The Industrial Revolution had originated in Britain, where it was mainly focused in the midlands, north and west. Ireland, with its lack of iron and coal, seemed unpromising territory. But the exception proved to be in eastern Ulster, where the centralization of the linen bleaching industry in Belfast marked the first stage in the industrialization of the province and the beginning of Belfast's phenomenal nineteenth-century expansion. Its population in 1808 was about 25,000; in 1901, it was almost 350,000.

Ulster began to acquire the sinews of commerce. Three major joint-stock banks were established in the province in the 1820s and 1830s – the Northern, Belfast and Ulster banks. All had their head offices in Belfast, not Dublin. Moreover, branches of British insurance companies were present in the city, providing the means of alleviating the hazards of uncertain trading conditions. Ulster industry, especially linen and cotton, had prospered during the Napoleonic wars. There was an irony here, because the wars had brought benefits to the southern provinces as well but on the agricultural front. The southern provinces fed the army; the northern one clothed it. After the inevitable post-war recession, the Industrial Revolution in Ulster really took off in the 1820s.

In 1828, the York Street linen mill was established. An enormous premises by the industrial standards of the times, it became the focus of Belfast's pre-eminence as a centre of the international linen trade. By 1850, there were sixty-two such mills in Belfast alone. The need to import coal and flax – because the industry had expanded beyond the ability of local resources to supply the mills – meant the development of Belfast port. Already, it was the busiest port in Ireland, handling a volume of trade that exceeded £8 million in 1838. In 1849, a new deep-water channel was completed in Belfast port, allowing deep draught shipping access to the quays even at low water. Queen Victoria visited Belfast the following year and the channel was renamed in her honour. From this, there grew the shipbuilding industry which was the city's pride in the late Victorian and Edwardian eras.

In 1858 Edward Harland bought a small shipyard in Queen's Island in Belfast Lough. The island was artificial: it has been formed from the spoil and sludge dredged up to build the Victoria channel. Three years later, he went into partnership with Gustav Wilhelm Wolff. Harland & Wolff was to become one of the giants of British shipbuilding: it built the most famous ship ever to sail and sink, the *Titanic*, in 1912. Wolff's uncle, Gustav Schwabe, was already a major figure in the shipping business in Liverpool. When he established his White Star Line in 1869, he placed all his orders for ocean-going ships with Harland & Wolff, thus setting the company on the road to riches. Its revolutionary designs produced ships that combined elegance and speed as well as technical innovation. A smaller yard, that of Workman Clark ('the wee yard'), was established on the Lagan in 1880 where it flourished until the Great War before finally closing in 1935.

Railways came early to Ulster: the first prospectus of the Ulster Railway – which in time became the northern end of the Dublin–Belfast line – dates from 1835. Shares in the company were first issued the following year and were fetching prices eight to ten times their nominal value. Ulster was not immune to the first railway mania. The first section of line, between Belfast and Lisburn, opened to the public in 1839. Other lines, radiating west and north of the city, followed in the 1840s. The effect was to draw more and more of the trade of rural Ulster towards Belfast port, thus accelerating its growth. Indeed, Ulster railways pioneers regarded this, rather than the link to Dublin, as their first priority.

The magnificent Antrim Coast Road, to this day the only true corniche – a road cut into a cliff – in Ireland, opened in the early 1840s, a magnificent feat of civil engineering. It properly connected the Glens of Antrim to the rest of Ireland for the first time: hitherto, the Glens had easier access to the west of Scotland than with the rest of the island to their back. William Makepeace Thackeray travelled the road shortly after its opening, writing in *The Irish Sketch-Book*: 'The Antrim Coast Road . . . besides being one of the most noble and gallant works of art that is to be seen in any country, is likewise a route highly picturesque and romantic; the sea spreading wide before the spectator's eyes upon one side of the route, the tall cliffs of limestone rising abruptly above him on the other.' Nor was it just linen and ships, roads and railways. The Belfast region produced other textiles, tobacco products, engineering and other commodities typical of the

new industrial age. In effect, Ulster became part of the economy of north-west Britain. Its economic fortunes could
hardly have made a greater contrast with the agricultural
provinces to the south, reeling from the effects of the Famine.
The leaders of industry in Ulster were almost all Protestants:
their identification with their co-religionists in Britain was
augmented by common economic and material interests.
Ulster was becoming more different, not less.

Behind the impressive modernity of industrial Ulster, however,
there loomed the long shadow of sectarian hatred. Industrialization
meant migration from country to town and the migrants brought
their ancient enmities with them. As early as 1850, Belfast in
particular was a city segregated by confessional allegiance, especially in working-class areas. There were serious inter-communal
riots in 1857, 1864, 1872 and 1886, a tradition that deepened in the
twentieth century and is still virulently present in the city today.

The nineteenth century was an age of faith. Religion was
central to life and to people's belief systems in a way that is
almost beyond the understanding of even the most devout
modern believer. Religious differences were sharply felt,
doctrinal and theological rivalries keenly contested. This was
true of Europe in general. In Ireland, such differences were
sharpened by the overlay of inherited ethnic and class polarities. But Ulster was a special case. Nowhere else in Ireland was
the balance of populations so volatile and unstable or the
burden of the past so oppressive. Ulster was not only running
a course different to that of the other three provinces; it was
doing so in the face of internal divisions that had their roots in
the seventeenth century and that were being renewed and
strengthened in every generation.

The riot in 1886 was in response to the threat of the first
Home Rule bill (discussed below). More people died in these
disturbances than in Robert Emmet's rising, the rising of 1848
and the Fenian rising of 1867 combined, although you might
be forgiven for thinking otherwise. The pattern was clear.

Catholics from the countryside, come to work in the shipyards and mills, clustered together among their co-religionists in recognizable enclaves. Likewise, the Protestant poor preferred to stay with their own kind. Inevitably, the interfaces between the two confessions were potential – and at regular intervals, actual – flashpoints.

Until the Industrial Revolution, Belfast had been an overwhelmingly Presbyterian town and one of a generally liberal temper. The inundation of the new proletariat changed that. But it was not the only force working for change. A critical transformation had occurred in Ulster Presbyterianism itself. A theological dispute between two parties within the church – dubbed Old Light and New Light – grew ever more intense in the first half of the nineteenth century. In general, New Light had dominated the church in the eighteenth century and had been associated with the liberalism that had found political expression in Presbyterian support for the United Irishmen. From 1800 on, however, the Old Light tendency renewed itself. It stressed a more traditional, inflexible Calvinism: inevitably, this entailed a less accommodating attitude towards Catholicism.

Its advance can be gauged from a comment in the 'Ordnance Survey Memoir' for Connor, Co. Antrim, in 1835, which noted that the district had been a hotbed of rebellion in 1798. 'However, since that time, their politics have changed, and now they seem indifferent and careless on the subject.' The Old Light finally triumphed by 1840, marginalizing its opponents. In that year, it established the General Assembly of the Presbyterian Church in Ireland – still the governing body of the church – along orthodox and traditional lines.

This conservative Presbyterianism got a further shot in the arm in 1859 during the dramatic events known as the Ulster Revival. This was an outbreak of populist piety or religious hysteria – take your pick according to preference – in eastern Ulster. It affected all Protestant denominations. As with all such manifestations, it emphasized conversion, personal rebirth and salvation, visions and every form of irrational excess.

At a time when Irish Catholicism was renewing itself dramatically under Cullen – emphasizing those doctrines and devotional practices that were most remote from Protestantism – the Protestant churches, and especially the Presbyterians of Ulster, were engaged in an equal and opposite exercise. The churches, and their congregations, were moving further apart.

The intellectual leader of Old Light Presbyterianism was Revd Henry Cooke, a trenchant opponent of O'Connell and Repeal. On the only occasion on which O'Connell ever visited Belfast – a significant fact in itself – Cooke challenged him to a debate, which O'Connell uncharacteristically refused. Cooke laid much of the groundwork for the later unanimity of support among Ulster Protestants for the union. His co-religionist Revd Hugh Hanna, known as 'Roaring Hanna' because of his incendiary anti-Catholic street preaching, did nothing to dampen sectarian tensions, nor did Revd Thomas Drew, whose sermon to Orangemen on 12 July 1857 referred, among other things, to 'the arrogant pretences of Popes and the outrageous dogmata of their blood-stained religion'. This was the prelude to ten days of sectarian rioting in which the Orangemen were enthusiastically assisted by the Belfast police.

It is not just an exercise in even-handedness to point out that Catholics could be just as absolutist in their claims as Protestants. The famous Dominican preacher, Fr Tom Burke – who had delivered the panegyric at the dedication to the O'Connell monument in Glasnevin cemetery, Dublin, in 1869 – put things very bluntly in addressing an American audience three years later: 'Take an Irishman, wherever he is found, all over the earth, and any casual observer will at once come to the conclusion, "Oh he is an Irishman, he is a Catholic". The two go together.'

Burke's confident assertion was in no sense unrepresentative, nor was Burke himself a foaming incendiary, although not one to avoid religious controversy. He was a former Rector of the Irish College in Rome and a theological advisor to the Irish bishops at the Vatican Council of 1869–70. The point was that

Catholics and Protestants lived in parallel mental and imaginative worlds. The universalism of one inevitably excluded the other, making 'the other side' ever more invisible and, in times of controversy or stress, less human.

Just as Catholicism and Protestantism increasingly emphasized their differences and asserted their particularities with growing vehemence, so their concomitant political demands were stated ever more shrilly. Asserting the virtues of the tribe was now the order of the day. In the three southern provinces, with its overwhelmingly Catholic population, this prepared the way for enormous political and agrarian reforms. But in the Ulster cockpit, with its unstable sectarian geography, it was lethal.

19

PARNELL

On 1 September 1870 the Home Government Association was launched in Dublin by Isaac Butt, a barrister and former MP. Its basic demand was for some form of devolved autonomy for Ireland or, in the brilliantly vague term in which it couched the demand, home rule.

The term was deliberately elastic. In the early days, in Butt's formulation, it amounted to a call for devolved domestic parliaments for Ireland, Scotland and England (but not for Wales). Westminster would remain sovereign and would deal with foreign and imperial matters.

Part of home rule's early appeal lay with some members of the Church of Ireland who felt betrayed by disestablishment and who thought that a Dublin parliament could be a better safeguard for Protestant interests. Butt himself was a Protestant.

As the 1870s wore on, the home rule movement took on a more overtly nationalist hue. Constitutional nationalists and ex-Fenians were drawn to it; it also attracted the support of parish clergy, although not yet of the hierarchy. In the 1874 general election that ousted Gladstone and installed Benjamin Disraeli, candidates pledged to home rule won fifty-nine seats. But they did not constitute a party in any modern sense. Butt was a gentlemanly but ineffective leader; he lost the support of many of his original Protestant adherents without gaining the confidence of the Catholic hierarchy; and the Fenian and neo-Fenian element among his MPs were effectively out of his control. From 1876 on, they began disruptive filibustering tactics in Westminster.

This unseemly challenge to the decorum of the House of Commons eventually forced a change in its rule with the introduction of the 'guillotine' to foreclose debates. It also threw up an alternative to Butt. His name was Charles Stewart Parnell. He was from an old Co. Wicklow landed family and had been MP for Co. Meath since 1875. He ousted Butt as party leader of the Home Rule League in 1880.

The previous year, he had acquired an even more important position when he became president of the Land League. This organization had been founded in October 1879 mainly due to the energy and drive of Michael Davitt, the son of an evicted tenant farmer from Co. Mayo. An ex-Fenian with a conviction for gun-running, Davitt was dedicated to the wholesale overthrow of the landlord system.

The founding of the Land League coincided with an agricultural depression and a consequent reduction in agricultural earnings. The threat of eviction loomed for tenants unable to pay their rent. Memories of the Famine only a generation old stiffened the determination to resist. Irish-American money provided the means to organize. A loose administrative structure meant that the best organized and most ruthless could dominate the organization, and that meant Fenians and other advanced nationalists. The demand was simple: peasant proprietorship.

Parnell therefore found himself at the head of an organization whose essential demand was revolutionary. In the summer of 1879, he already had good contacts with Fenians on both sides of the Atlantic and had their confidence. In 1879, a deal was agreed between the Supreme Council of the IRB – the Irish Republican Brotherhood, the formal name for the Fenians – and Parnell's supporters in the Home Rule League. This was the so-called New Departure.

The New Departure meant the organizational and financial support of Fenianism for parliamentary action in return for the prosecution of new policies. First, there was to be a totally independent Irish party at Westminster without ties to any national British party and dedicated to Irish self-government. Butt's federal idea was to be scrapped. Second, the land agitation was to be brought to parliament in the form of a demand for legislation to create a peasant proprietorship.

By the autumn of 1880, the land war was in full swing. Across the country – except, significantly, in most of Ulster – agrarian protesters who previously had merely sought rent abatements in view of the recession were now demanding the abolition of the entire landlord system. Evictions were resisted by violence; where they occurred, revenge was taken on landlords either by attacks on themselves or their livestock; murders, burnings and boycotting increased.

The land war escalated into a wholesale attack on the landlords not just for what they were but for what they represented: the British connection. They were portrayed as a British garrison holding Ireland for the crown against the will of the people. The stakes were raised to the point where the social authority of the ascendancy was fatally wounded. The absolute communal solidarity of the tenants, under the leadership of the Land League, was now the key agent of social control. To take up a farm from which another had been evicted was to guarantee being boycotted (the word originated in the land war: the eponym was Captain Charles Boycott, a land agent in Co. Mayo). Land League courts effectively supplanted crown courts in many parts of rural Ireland, foreshadowing the Sinn Féin courts of 1919–21.

Gladstone returned to power in 1880 and embarked on a dual policy of coercion and conciliation. The use of special police powers to curb the excesses of the Land League was combined with a substantial concession to them. Gladstone's second Land Act – that of 1881 – conceded the 'Three Fs': the right of free sale by an outgoing tenant; fixity of tenure to replace ordinary tenancies; and a fixed rent to be determined by land courts. Parnell at first opposed the act on the grounds that it was not radical enough. The government lodged him in Kilmainham prison in Dublin whereupon rural crime escalated out of control. He was released as part of the 'Kilmainham Treaty', whereby he undertook to accept the act – with some cosmetic improvements – in return for using his influence to quell the agitation. The Kilmainham Treaty was an acknowledgement by the government that Parnell was, in the famous phrase, the uncrowned king of Ireland.

Even the hideous Phoenix Park murders of May 1882, less than a month after the Kilmainham Treaty, did not shake the new Gladstone–Parnell alliance. A group called the Invincibles – Fenian ultras – set upon Lord Frederick Cavendish, the new chief secretary of Ireland, and Thomas Burke, the under-secretary, as they were walking in Phoenix Park in Dublin. Using surgical knives, they killed them both. Public opinion on both sides of the water was horrified. Parnell, fearing that his whole strategy was compromised, offered his resignation of the party leadership to Gladstone (but not to his own party). Gladstone declined it.

The government outlawed the Land League, but the movement was already split between those who were happy with the new act and the radicals. Besides, Parnell was quite happy to see the end of the League, for in his eyes it had served its purpose. As might be expected of a landlord, he was not an agrarian radical. He had ridden the tiger to a position of influence such as no one had had in Ireland since O'Connell. Its work was done and he was happy to dispense with it.

Besides, the Irish-American Fenian ultras spent much of the 1880s involved in a sporadic campaign of dynamite bombing in England. A 'skirmishing fund' was established to finance this activity, which in concept and method anticipated the Irish Republican Army (IRA) campaigns of a century later. The Tower of London, Underground stations, Scotland Yard and even the chamber of the House of Commons itself were all targeted before the campaign was suppressed by the police in 1887. Among the many Fenians sentenced for their parts in this campaign was Thomas J. Clarke, destined to be the first signatory of the proclamation of the republic in 1916. The dynamite campaign was yet another reason for Parnell to distance himself from Fenian extremists while keeping mainstream Fenians safely on board the party ship.

He turned to the cause that really held his interest: home rule.

In October 1882, the organization that succeeded the Land League was formed. Called the National League, it was firmly under Parnell's control; its purpose was to harness for home rule the mass support that had secured the 1881 Land Act and to act as a constituency organization for the Nationalist party, as we may now begin to call the home rule MPs.

The National League controlled the constituencies and the candidates chosen. Each candidate had to pledge to support and vote with the Nationalist party at Westminster, failing which he undertook to resign. Everything was centralized. Local particularism – never very subterranean in Ireland – was suppressed. At the apex of the entire structure was Parnell, the Chief. This structure was borrowed from Irish-American municipal politics, where ruthless discipline had delivered big-city administrations into Irish hands. The American Fenians who had insisted on an independent, pledge-bound party at Westminster as one of the terms of the New Departure knew what they were doing. Tammany Hall came to the banks of the Thames.

The other key factor in the rise of the Nationalist party was its alliance with the Catholic Church. This is one of those phenomena that seem perfectly natural in hindsight, but which were much more problematic in practice. First of all, Parnell was a Protestant. Second, he had close associations – to put it no stronger – with the Fenians, whom the church abominated as a revolutionary secret society after the French fashion.

Third, he had exploited and profited from the Land League agitation, of which the church was deeply suspicious because of its subversion of the civic order.

On the other hand, it was clear that the Nationalists were an overwhelmingly Catholic party. Even in Butt's day a significant number of them had been loud champions of Catholic causes, most crucially that of denominational education. It was also clear that the National League was vastly more disciplined than the Land League had been. Dr Thomas Croke, the nationalist archbishop of Cashel, was an early supporter of Parnell. Others followed. The crucial alliance was forged in 1884, when the hierarchy agreed to throw the moral and organizational weight of the church behind the party; in return the party undertook to promote Catholic educational concerns in parliament.

Denominational education was a central concern of the church throughout the nineteenth century. The bishops founded a Catholic University in Dublin in 1854, with no less a person than Cardinal Newman as its first rector. It was the forerunner of University College Dublin, now the country's biggest university. The hierarchy was determined to resist state interference in Catholic education at every level. The agreement between Parnell and the bishops meant that the party would act as a parliamentary watchdog in this matter.

The education question had acquired a greater importance since the Intermediate Education (Ireland) Act of 1878, which formalized the expansion of secondary education in the country. The system was centralized and state examinations were held. The state, through a newly established Education Board, assumed responsibility for financing the system. The emphasis was on a humanities-based academic curriculum. From the 1880s onwards, this growing secondary system provided a ready supply of clerks, junior civil servants and – in the case of an elite minority – university undergraduates. In short, it laid the basis for the expansion of the Irish Catholic middle class. Like all open educational systems it generated a quiet revolution of rising expectations, the full effects of which would not be felt until 1916–22. Technical or vocational education – directed at working-class pupils – was less developed and followed only as a kind of afterthought at the turn of the century.

The general election of 1885 was the first to be fought under a greatly widened franchise introduced by act of parliament the previous year. In effect, the Representation of the People Act extended the vote to all male heads of households except for a few statistically insignificant exceptions. Further legislation abolished most of the traditional borough constituencies – notoriously prone to corruption – and introduced a uniform constituency system. Ireland now had an electoral roll that was transformed at a stroke, rising from 226,000 to 738,000 persons. Unsurprisingly, the beneficiaries of this meritocratic extension of the vote were the populist parties on both the nationalist and unionist sides.

When the election results were declared, the Nationalists had won eighty-six seats and found themselves holding the balance of power in the House of Commons. After a brief tactical flirtation with the Conservatives, Parnell renewed the Liberal alliance. It was a telling moment. Parnell had always insisted on the absolute independence of the party. Now political realities were dictating otherwise. Henceforth, it was to be the Liberals or nothing. The price he extracted was the introduction of the first Irish Home Rule Bill by Gladstone in 1886. It split the Liberal party and was defeated. The Liberals fell from power, not to return – except for a brief interlude in the early 1890s – for twenty years.

From the perspective of 1886, however, that was part of an unseen and unknown future. To contemporaries, Parnell had staged a stunning coup. A bill to create an Irish parliament to deal with domestic affairs had been sponsored on the floor of the House of Commons by the prime minister. Its defeat was less significant than the fact that it had happened at all. What had been unthinkable ten years earlier was now a central fact of political life. Like all great politicians, Parnell made the weather. The 'Irish Question' was on the British agenda. It would remain there in one form or another until the 'solution' of 1920–2. Its aftershocks are there to the present day.

Of the eighty-six seats secured by the Nationalists in the 1885 election, seventeen were in Ulster. This represented a simple majority of the province's thirty-three seats. The other sixteen were all Conservatives. Ulster Liberalism was destroyed at the polls. Tenants on either side of the sectarian divide who had previously voted Liberal now chose the Conservatives (if Protestant) to defend the union or Nationalist (if Catholic) to subvert it. Politics in the province took on the reductive form it has had ever since: for or against the union.

Combined with Gladstone's conversion to home rule, this was the moment of truth for Ulster Protestants. They mobilized a pan-Protestant movement in defence of the union. They feared that what they regarded as the backward, agricultural, Catholic south would overwhelm the progressive, industrial, Protestant north. Confessional and material self-interest dovetailed neatly.

Ulster Conservatives now moved closer to the Orange Order, with its tradition of cross-class popular mobilization. Borrowing freely from nationalist techniques, they organized a series of mass meetings across the province culminating in a mass rally in the Ulster Hall in Belfast on 22 February 1886. The principal speaker was Lord Randolph Churchill, the dazzlingly unstable younger son of the Duke of Marlborough and father of Winston. Churchill's formula, 'Ulster will fight, and Ulster will be right' became a rallying cry for Ulster Protestants.

The defeat of the Home Rule bill two months later seemed like a deliverance. The return of the Conservatives under Lord Salisbury removed the immediate danger but the crisis had changed the political landscape in Ulster forever.

The tensions surrounding the home rule crisis tripped off the worst sectarian rioting that Belfast had yet seen. From June

to September, the riots went on sporadically leaving an official
death count of thirty-one, although unofficial estimates
suggested the figure was nearer fifty. Belfast was, more than
ever before, a city divided absolutely along sectarian lines. In
this, it reflected the wider Ulster reality which was determined
by the delicate confessional demography of the province.

The franchise extension that proved so important in the elections of 1885 was in many ways just the reflection of a
developing public opinion, a widening of the public sphere. As
mentioned, the transport revolution effected by the ever-
expanding railway system had united different parts of the
island in a manner previously unthinkable and provided the
distribution system for national newspapers, which acquired a
growing importance. The two most venerable Irish papers, the
Belfast Newsletter and the *Freeman's Journal*, dating from
1737 and 1763 respectively, could now expand beyond their
traditional readership bases in Belfast and Dublin. The
Freeman, in particular, became the most important voice of
nationalist Ireland, so much so that during the Parnell split of
1890–91 both sides tried hard to seize control of it. A national
newspaper furnished its community with a common agenda, a
common rhetoric and grammar, a common pulpit for the
dissemination of political and social views. It was a force for
national integration as distinct from local particularism. As
such, the expansion of the national press in the second half of
the nineteenth century was a key development.

It reflected the growing literacy rate in Ireland. The 1841
census estimated that fewer than half of those aged five or more
could read. By the census of 1911, the figure had risen to 88 per
cent. The wholesale destruction of the poorest classes in the
Famine, whether through death or emigration, together with
the steady expansion of the education system, had accounted
for this impressive increase. The newspapers therefore had a
viable customer base as well as an efficient distribution system.
The *Irish Times* was founded in 1859, mainly as the voice of

southern unionism. From 1905 on the *Freeman* was increasingly challenged by the new *Irish Independent*, destined to
become the leading organ of lower middle-class nationalism in
the twentieth century. The *Cork Examiner* dated from 1841:
technically it was classed as a national newspaper, although it
was never strong outside its regional base in Munster.

The development of a national press was paralleled by the
equally impressive and important growth of local newspapers,
most of them unapologetically partisan in their politics. The
Munster Express, published in Waterford, dates from 1859. The
first edition of the *Leinster Leader* announced itself in 1881 as
the voice of the nationalist community in Co. Kildare. The
Limerick Leader (1889) declared itself to be 'a faithful organ of
the National Party'. In all, it was estimated that the number of
provincial papers increased from 68 in 1850 to more than 120 by
the 1880s. The number of overtly nationalist newspapers
published outside Dublin grew from zero in 1861 to 34 in 1891.
Newspaper proprietors and editors were important and influential figures within the overall nationalist movement.

As with nationalism, so with unionism. The *Belfast
Telegraph* dates from 1870. Two of the most important local
Ulster papers that championed the unionist cause both date
from the 1820s; the *Impartial Reporter* (surely one of the least
apposite titles in the history of journalism) in the marchland of
Co. Fermanagh and the *Londonderry Sentinel*. These early
foundation dates reflect the high literacy rates of Ulster
Protestants (especially Presbyterians) as well as anxiety at the
growth of O'Connellism. Their effect among unionists was
similar to that of their nationalist equivalents: they provided a
forum for news and debate, and therefore furnished the means
to create an integrated political community.

To Parnell and the Nationalists, the defeat of the Home Rule
bill seemed just a temporary setback. The immense prestige of
Gladstone lay behind the cause; Parnell's reputation had never
stood higher; it seemed only a matter of time before the natural

pendulum of British politics would restore the Liberals to power and home rule to the political agenda.

In 1889 *The Times* falsely accused Parnell of conspiring with the Invincibles in the Phoenix Park Murders of 1882 and of approving the deaths of Cavendish and Burke. The whole thing was based on the forgeries of a journalist called Richard Pigott. A commission of inquiry exposed the fraud, leaving Parnell's public position stronger than ever. On his return to the Commons, he got a standing ovation from all sides. He was just forty-three years of age, at the height of his powers, adored in nationalist Ireland, respected at Westminster, the undisputed leader of a nation-in-waiting. It was this that made his fall so shocking.

For many years, Parnell had lived with Katharine O'Shea, the estranged wife of Captain William O'Shea, MP. O'Shea had squandered an inheritance and proved an incompetent businessman before entering politics in 1880. He lost his seat in 1885. He knew of the affair between Parnell and his wife and tolerated it. He could not afford to sue for divorce, since he was dependent for financial support on an elderly aunt of Katharine's who would have been scandalized by such a course. She eventually died, at which point Willie O'Shea's inhibitions deserted him. He sued for divorce, citing his wife's adultery and naming Parnell as co-respondent.

Amazingly, nationalist solidarity held. The Catholic bishops clearly disapproved of the behaviour of the Protestant adulterer but stayed their hand. The parliamentary party prepared to re-elect Parnell as leader. It was at this point that elements in the Liberal party withdrew their support for Parnell. The nonconformist conscience was being exercised.

There was a strong element of Christian moral earnestness in some Liberals' support for home rule: Gladstone himself was animated by it. Now these Liberals were telling Gladstone that Parnell's continued leadership of the Nationalist party would subvert the Liberal alliance. He was in their eyes a morally unfit person. Gladstone was now faced with either sacrificing Parnell or losing the leadership of Liberalism. He presented the Nationalists with a hideous dilemma. They could have Parnell or the Liberal alliance but not both.

The party split on 15 December 1890. The majority chose the Liberals. Parnell attempted to reconstruct his political fortunes in a series of three bitterly fought by-election campaigns in Ireland over the following year, all of which he lost. The church, determined not to be out-moralized by a crowd of English Protestants, turned against him. The split was a savage business, with passions inflamed beyond reason on both sides. It darkened Irish nationalist life for a generation.

Parnell's frenzied by-election campaigns killed him. Never robust, he was drenched to the skin while addressing a meeting in Creggs, Co. Roscommon, and caught a chill which developed into pneumonia. He dragged himself back to Brighton in England, where he lived with Katharine, and died there on 6 October 1891. His remains were returned to Dublin where his funeral attracted over 100,000 mourners. He is buried in the most impressive grave in Ireland, in Glasnevin cemetery under a single boulder of Wicklow granite bearing the simple legend PARNELL.

20

CULTURE

Parnell was dead. The party was split between the anti-Parnellite majority and the Parnellite minority. The 1890s was a wretched decade for Irish nationalist politics. The Nationalists eventually reunited in 1900 under the leadership of John Redmond, who had headed the Parnellite faction. The assumption of the leadership by someone from the smaller group was a conscious attempt to bind the wounds. But while the party gradually recovered its sense of purpose, it never regained the iron unity and discipline of Parnell's day.

In the meantime, the Conservative governments of Lord Salisbury resumed their policy of 'killing home rule with kindness'. This meant social and economic reforms and initiatives designed to prove that good government was better than self-government. The policy had first been articulated under an earlier Tory government in the late 1880s and early 1890s. The then chief secretary, Arthur Balfour, had established the Congested Districts Board in 1891 to assist in development schemes for the poorer parts of the country – mainly along the Atlantic seaboard. The initiatives included infrastructural developments: many of the country's quaint narrow-gauge railways were financed by the board. Harbours were constructed. Cottage crafts and education in modern agricultural methods were encouraged.

The Local Government Act of 1898 modernized an antique system, sweeping away grand juries and Poor Law boards and establishing democratically elected county councils and urban councils. This had the important effect of making numbers count at local level, replacing unionists with nationalists in most cases. Many stalwarts of the Irish revolution first cut their political teeth in these local assemblies.

The most momentous piece of legislation came in 1903, when the chief secretary, George Wyndham, introduced the Land Act that has ever since borne his name. The Conservatives had long been of the view that a move to tenant purchase was the solution to the land question, which had flared up intermittently ever since the suppression of the Land League. The so-called Plan of Campaign, an agitation that had lasted from 1886 to 1891, had simply been the most vivid example. The Plan aimed to reduce rents by withholding them and banking the funds with trustees instead. It was mainly concentrated in the south and west and while it demonstrated that the 1881 Land Act was no final solution to the land problem, it never developed the potency of the earlier Land League. Instead, it proved a drain on the funds of the National League, much to Parnell's chagrin. He opposed the Plan, although interestingly he could not stop it outright. It was sponsored by some of his brightest and most energetic MPs, including Tim Healy, Tim Harrington, William O'Brien and John Dillon. It was no coincidence that all four were anti-Parnellites when the split came. Parnell's fabled hauteur did not always sit well with intelligent and ambitious subordinates.

Wyndham's 1903 act, therefore, was the product of an unsolved problem. It provided government funds to buy out the Irish landlords and transfer the land to the former tenants who now became independent proprietors. Thus the independent family farm came to pass. The act resulted from a conference at which all interests had been represented, so it was a consensual piece of legislation. The main principles of the act had been hammered out at this conference of landlords and tenants, in which the former were the guiding spirits. This was a remarkable achievement, considering the mayhem in the countryside a mere twenty years earlier. But it was also a tacit admission from the landlords that the game was finally up. Ever since the economic devastation left by the Famine, through the disestablishment legislation and the Land Wars of the 1880s, which finally announced the collapse of tenant deference, the tide had been going out on the old Ascendancy.

The purchasers were given long-term loans by the government. The repayments, over thirty-five years, generally annualized at a lower figure than the old rents. From the landlords' point of view, payments were in cash rather than bonds and the government offered a 12 per cent premium for estates that were sold in their entirety.

No piece of legislation in any parliament has had such a transforming effect on a country. It was the moment of triumph for the former tenants, who were now established not just as proprietors but soon would be the most significant social group in the country. Now they were an interest, no longer a cause: one of the ironies of their triumph is that the Nationalist party no longer had its core issue to rally and unite it. The land question was effectively settled. In being settled, the Cromwellian land settlement of the 1650s was finally undone.

Although few realized it at the time, the Fenian moment was at hand. The paralysis of parliamentary nationalism offered an opening to a group that had been overshadowed by Parnell for a decade. The Fenians had represented a kind of internal opposition within the larger nationalist tent. They were a radical ginger group. As a movement with particularly strong transatlantic connections, they had access to money and expertise. Their membership was drawn disproportionately from lower middle-class town-dwellers of the south and east, so that they were an identifiable social sub-group in a nationalist movement that was still overwhelmingly rural and whose great populist integrating cause was land reform. Indeed, the Fenians were chary of the whole land agitation, partly because they were townies and partly because many of them were themselves property owners in a small way and sensitive to the rights of property. Ideologically, they distrusted the land agitation as a distraction from what they regarded as the only clear goal appropriate to nationalist ambition: separation from Britain.

Nonetheless, they had survived the fiasco of 1867 and still had enough vigour to mount the London dynamite campaign of the 1880s. Despite their doubts about the Land League, they had played an important role in its success: as we saw, American Fenians were crucial in securing the New Departure of 1879 that effectively set the Land League in motion. Fenianism was as much a mood, a temperamental disposition, as anything else. Its adherents were usually better educated than the general run of the population. Many possessed tough, assertive personalities. They had good organizational skills and were to be found at the radical cutting edge of most nationalist movements. They insinuated themselves into Parnell's movement – although Parnell had the measure of them after 1882 – and were prominent in agitations such as the Plan of Campaign. Police reports identified them as shopkeepers and publicans, commercial travellers, auctioneers, journalists and such like. In short, they were men of modest substance and some education. They had ambitions. They had ideas. They dreamed dreams. They were an ideal revolutionary class. And from the 1890s on, they were everywhere.

Every significant cultural and social movement in nationalist Ireland after the fall of Parnell had its Fenian presence. Indeed, as we see below, the Gaelic Athletic Association was almost an exclusively Fenian enterprise. The great irony was that the activity which the Fenians despised and at which they appeared to be no use – politics – was eventually where they were to have their greatest triumph. But all that lay in the future. In the meantime, there was organic work to be done and myths to be made.

In 1893, the Gaelic League was formed. The founder was Eoin Mac Néill, a historian of early and medieval Ireland. The first president was Douglas Hyde, the son of a Church of Ireland rector from Co. Roscommon. A scholar and linguist, he had delivered a lecture in 1892 under the title 'The Necessity for De-anglicising the Irish People', in which he called for an arrest in the decline of the Irish language and deplored the advance of what he regarded as a vulgar, English commercial culture.

The new organization established itself quickly. It had as its aim the revival of Irish as the common vernacular. It conducted language classes. It published stories, plays and a newspaper, *An Claidheamh Soluis* (The Sword of Light). It opposed a campaign led by John Pentland Mahaffy, the Provost of Trinity College Dublin, to have the Irish language removed from the Intermediate school syllabus. It established language teacher training colleges. By 1908, there were 600 branches of the League around the country.

The Gaelic League successfully revived the Young Irelanders' idea that cultural and linguistic autonomy was a good thing, and was part of a greater national revival. Hyde naively thought that the language was a non-political issue on which people of all religious and social backgrounds could meet without rancour. The League was indeed non-political for the first twenty-two years of its life. But its implied purpose was clear: the re-Gaelicization of Ireland. In some ways, it was a very Victorian phenomenon, appealing to the same kind of medieval nostalgia that animated the Pre-Raphaelites and the Arts and Crafts Movement in England. It was also implicitly reactionary. The Gaelic League was part of an anti-modern, anti-urban reaction that saw virtue in rural simplicity, in contrast to the morally dubious and anglicized cities. This was a phenomenon by no means confined to Ireland. It is to be found in some degree in all sorts of oppositional and revolutionary movements in the twentieth century from the Nazis to the Khmer Rouge. At least Ireland was spared such excesses, and suffered nothing worse at the hands of this sensibility than the literary censorship and Éamon de Valera's social fantasies.

By injecting a strong cultural element into the national mix, the Gaelic League was part of a larger movement that developed from the 1890s onwards. What is commonly called the Irish Literary Revival was the work of a remarkable generation of writers and intellectuals. It is often represented as a reaction to the sordid politics of the Parnell split and a search for a more honourable and positive means of expressing national sentiment. Certainly, W. B. Yeats thought so. Many years later, when making his acceptance speech in Stockholm upon winning the Nobel Prize for Literature he declared unambiguously: 'The modern literature of Ireland, and indeed all that stir of thought which prepared for the Anglo-Irish war, began when Parnell fell from power in 1891. A disillusioned and embittered Ireland turned away from parliamentary politics; an event was conceived and the race began, as I think, to be troubled by that event's long gestation.'

The literary revival – indeed the whole cultural revival of which it was the most distinguished part – drew inspiration from the Young Ireland poets associated with the *Nation* as well as from the work of antiquarians and Celtic scholars in Ireland and on the continent. Like all such movements, it required a central figure. It found it in Yeats.

Yeats was not simply a poet of genius but also a very considerable man of action. He had started publishing in the late 1880s and continued in the following decade. His influential *Celtic Twilight* collection appeared in 1893 and gave the entire movement a name that stuck. Yeats was fascinated by mysticism and eastern religion and managed to translate both to a Celtic locale. He shared this enthusiasm with many leading figures in the movement, most notably the remarkable George Russell (whose pseudonym was AE).

It was also, to a remarkable degree for a movement of its kind, Protestant. Yeats, Russell and Lady Gregory, the patron and *éminence grise* of the movement, were all Protestants. So were J. M. Synge and Sean O'Casey, its two great dramatists, as were many of its minor figures. It has been speculated that they represented an enlightened Protestant vanguard, aware that the game was up for the old order with the disestablishment of the Church of Ireland and the end of the estate system, and anxious to find a role and make a stamp on the new Ireland.

The Gaelic League and the literary revival overlapped in places and shared a common sensibility. Both were anti-utilitarian and romantic. This brought both movements, but especially the literary revival, on to a collision course with the very utilitarian Catholic middle class. This group was the backbone of actual, living nationalist society. It had little interest in mystic speculation, although its national pride was flattered by the dramatic representation of Irish heroic myths. Yeats's play, *Cathleen Ní Houlihan*, first performed in Dublin in 1902, was a thinly disguised call to arms against England and famously gave the poet qualms of conscience in later years.

Yeats was many things, including a Fenian sympathizer (perhaps even an actual Fenian for a while) but was consistent in his distaste for the middle class. His thoroughly reactionary dream of a union of aristocrats and peasants against the philistine bourgeoisie left no place for the very people who were inheriting the new nationalist world that was forming all about him. The farmers, shopkeepers, clerks and suchlike who had been the backbone of Parnell's party had other voices to articulate their concerns and prejudices: voices like those of the brilliantly waspish lawyer and parliamentarian Tim Healy – the most eloquently vituperative of the anti-Parnellites – and D. P. Moran, a journalist with a supreme talent for abuse. His journal, the *Leader*, founded in 1900, was a scabrously entertaining cocktail of lower-middle class nationalist prejudice against Protestants, intellectuals, the English, the rich, Jews, nationalists like Arthur Griffith of whom Moran did not approve, and anything and anyone that caught the editor's ire. Moran was a bottomless pit of acid. His work was not that far removed in sentiment and tone from journals such as *La Libre Parole* in France – fiercely anti-Dreyfusard and anti-Semitic – and other similar continental papers that appealed to petit bourgeois paranoia and anti-Semitism.

Yeats's world and Moran's collided in 1907 when Synge's *The Playboy of the Western World* opened at the Abbey in Dublin. Yeats and Lady Gregory had founded the theatre three years earlier: it was one of the monumental achievements of the revival. Patriotic plays were one thing. The gritty realism of Synge was another. The *Playboy* is set in Co. Mayo and the peasant cast is presented, in part at least, as ignorant, credulous and superstitious. This was deeply offensive to a nationalist audience, which saw only stage-Irish caricature. They also shared the prissy puritanism of the age, so that when a reference was made to a 'shift' – a lady's undergarment or slip – it was the trigger for an already shocked and tense audience to riot.

The *Playboy* riot was not simply a contest between art and philistinism, although this was naturally the myth that Yeats made of it. It was a collision of different mental worlds. Ironically, both were attempting a transformative definition of Irishness and its place in the world. For the utilitarian middle class, virtue meant material progress, piety, respectability and movement towards home rule. Indeed, if you subtract the political element, the nationalist middle class had aspirations very similar to their counterparts in the rest of the United Kingdom. After the trauma of the Famine, less than a lifetime before, the advance in material fortunes was a source of pride. Synge's peasants seemed like some sort of pre-Famine horror, drawn by a condescending Protestant in a theatre run by the widow of Sir William Gregory – he of the Famine's Quarter-Acre Clause.

For Yeats and Synge, the autonomy of great art and its fidelity to reality were the supreme virtues. Part of the problem for the audience was precisely that Synge was not drawing stage-Irish characters: they were all too real. Synge had spent many nights in western cottages, listening and noting the vocabulary, syntax and utterances of western peasants. It was his fidelity in reproducing their speech – these people who were now a social embarrassment to the new bourgeoisie – that was troubling.

Set in the context of a powerful psychological drama, a truly stirring work of art, the tension proved too great.

That tension was caused by a gap between politics and culture in nationalist Ireland that nothing could bridge in the early twentieth century. Nationalist politics had focused on the material, most obviously on the land question. Its organizational methods were borrowed from Tammany Hall and were not for the squeamish. It was hand in glove with the Catholic clergy. It was careful and calculating. The cultural revival occurred after O'Connell and Parnell had set the material template for nationalism. It now attempted to overlay a cultural template and to furnish nationalism with myths and symbols. In this, it had considerable success but its sensibility was always at an oblique angle to the utilitarianism of the political and social mainstream. Unlike many other European national movements, where the culture came first and the politics second, in Ireland it was the other way round. In the end, as Yeats would discover, the politics would crush the culture, demanding of it a role subservient to the wishes and prejudices of the new dominant class. Nationalism cannibalized the cultural revival for those titbits it could digest. It rejected the rest.

If the Gaelic League attempted to stay non-political, the other key cultural organization of the period from the Parnell split to the Easter Rising in 1916 had no such inhibitions. On the contrary, the Gaelic Athletic Association (GAA) was a Fenian vehicle from the start. It has also been the most successful popular association in modern Irish history.

It was founded in Thurles, Co. Tipperary, in 1884. Its purpose was to preserve and promote the ancient game of hurling. In addition, it developed a code of football which went on to become the most popular spectator sport in twentieth-century Ireland. For the Fenians, it offered a perfect recruiting vehicle and its politics reflected Fenian radicalism right from the beginning. It was aggressively Parnellite at the time of the split and thereafter was to be found on the left of the nationalist movement on every occasion. It was republican in politics; hugely supportive of the Irish language and of Gaelic culture in general; tacitly Catholic, although not clerical, in its assumptions; and ferociously opposed to the symbols of British rule, not least the police. It imposed a ban on its members playing 'foreign games' – defined as soccer, rugby, hockey and cricket – which lasted until 1971.

In part, it was a reaction against the exclusiveness of other sports. Rugby was focused on elite private schools; cricket had a long association with both army and ascendancy; athletics was administered by a Trinity College elite which discouraged, to put it no more strongly, the participation of the wrong sort of chaps. The GAA was perfect for the people whose faces did not fit. To be fair, this point can easily be exaggerated: there is much local evidence from the late 1880s, when things were still fluid, that GAA clubs were founded by athletes who cheerfully played cricket and association football (soccer). The exclusiveness was not all one way: the ban on foreign games was also a form of exclusion, a kind of recreational tariff wall willed by the Fenian element in the GAA for political–cultural reasons.

At any rate, the GAA became the great popular mobilizing force in Irish recreational life. And it did so in a context that applauded exclusion, that insisted on the separateness of Gaelic games and the social life that revolved around them. Matches were played on Sundays, the only free day in the working week, which guaranteed that sabbatarian Protestants were unlikely to participate. The GAA soon spread to every Catholic parish in the country, with a local club often named for a saint or a patriot: thus Naomh (Saint) this-or-that, plus various Emmets, Tones, Sarsfields and so on. There were few named for O'Connell, whose aversion to violence made him *persona non grata* in Fenian eyes. This was ironic, given that its organizational structure so clearly mirrored O'Connell's own.

The GAA, the most Fenian and anglophobe of all nationalist organizations, was also of its time. The codification of sports

– a mid-Victorian phenomenon – meant the establishment of uniform rules for a game from a multitude of regional variants. The antecedents of soccer and rugby were local rough-and-tumbles with local rules. Cricket had a number of regional antecedents like stoolball (which could have as easily evolved into baseball as into cricket). Eventually, cricket was codified on the rules of the game as played in Kent, Surrey and Hampshire. The West Country and Yorkshire variations now had to accommodate themselves to the new national standard. In baseball, the New York game displaced rival versions such as town ball and the so-called Massachusetts game. All this was a product of the railway revolution, which made national championships possible for the first time, and therefore led to a requirement for a uniform set of rules.

The codification of hurling followed a similar path. The game had been particularly popular in three areas in pre-Famine times: in south Leinster and east Munster; on either side of the middle reaches of the Shannon where east Galway looks across to south Offaly and north-west Tipperary; and in the inaccessible fastnesses of the Glens of Antrim. The Famine dealt what was nearly a death blow to the game in the first two areas: indeed, cricket waxed strong in these areas in the post-Famine years. It was the need to revive hurling that inspired the founders of the GAA.

And revive it they did. But in codifying the game they faced a problem. The form of hurling played in the Glens of Antrim was significantly different to the southern game. Unsurprisingly, given the ancient association between Antrim and the west of Scotland (the Mull of Kintyre is plainly visible from the Antrim coast on a fine day), the game played there was closer to Scottish shinty. The two games, while clearly related, have very obvious differences.

Modern hurling was codified along the lines of the south Leinster game. Antrim had to adjust accordingly if it was to participate at national level. This interesting little exercise in internal imperialism was typical of how most sports were codified. The GAA may have been exclusive and different, but it obeyed the logic of all national sporting associations engaged in similar exercises.

The 1890s was the decade in which culture displaced politics in Ireland, at least for the time being. The material conditions for the triumph of Irish nationalism had been progressively consolidated in the course of the nineteenth century. Now it was time to develop enabling tribal myths. It was in these years, from the fall of Parnell to the outbreak of the Great War, that so many forces coalesced to furnish the tribe with a flattering narrative. Wyndham's Land Act created an independent yeomanry. The GAA epitomized simple athleticism and courage, bringing to physical life the myth of rural virtue conjured up in *Knocknagow*, the sprawling sentimental novel from the pen of the Fenian Charles Kickham. The cultural revival proposed the rural poor of the western seaboard – especially the Irish-speaking remnant – as a vision of authenticity towards which the rest of the nation should aspire. For the first two-thirds of the twentieth century, the *beau idéal* of Irishness was the Irish-speaking western small-holder: it was this vision of sober, Jeffersonian rectitude that Éamon de Valera famously celebrated in 1943 when he spoke of 'that Ireland which we dreamed of'.

It was, indeed, a dream but one possessed of great vitality and imaginative force. It was always in collision with material and instrumental reality, which gave it a certain kind of intellectual weightlessness, but myths can be as important as realities in the making of nations and states. Nowhere was the delusional aspect of the cultural revival more complete than in the matter of the Irish language – aspiration and sociology were in violent collision as the vernacular numbers dropped in every generation. Yet the revival of Irish has been a central feature of Irish public policy throughout the twentieth century and into the twenty-first. It remains a compulsory school subject in the Republic and, despite occasional low-level grousing, still commands overwhelming sentimental affection. It is still thought of as 'our language' when plainly the quotidian evidence is that it is not.

If the material conditions for nationalism had been established, so had those for partition. The unforgiving sectarian geography of Ulster was made plain in the 1885 election – the first fought under a franchise sufficiently wide to be truly representative and democratic. It has been confirmed in every test of public opinion in Ulster for more than a century. The more strident and insistent has been the nationalist demand, the more unyielding and sullen has been the unionist resistance. Look at a map showing the distribution of Protestants and Catholics in Ulster in 1911: the point where Catholic numbers weaken and Protestants begin to appear in strength is roughly where the line of partition was drawn in 1920. And within what became Northern Ireland, there was already a clear east-west divide between the Protestant heartland in the east (only counties Derry, Antrim and Down had Protestant majorities) and the local Catholic majority west of the River Bann.

The Irish *fin de siècle* was therefore the time when the twin forces that would dominate the island in the coming century took definitive form: the full realization of the nationalist self-image and the boundary of the unionist redoubt.

21

REDMOND

The political flux following the Parnell split produced a situation in which radical and maverick groups flourished. The one that endured was Sinn Féin, founded in 1905. In Irish, Sinn Féin means 'ourselves', not 'ourselves alone' as it is sometimes mistranslated. The point is worth emphasizing, because the mistranslation suggests a degree of separatist purity which the early Sinn Féin simply did not possess. Its emphasis was on economic and cultural self-reliance. Its leading figure, Arthur Griffith, was not himself a republican. He espoused a dual monarchy along the line of the Austro-Hungarian settlement of 1867. It is not hard to see how an emphasis on national self-reliance was easily compatible with separatism and republicanism, but Sinn Féin prior to 1916 was by no means wedded to either doctrine. It was, however, close enough in sympathy to those who were republicans to fool the British, who dubbed the 1916 rising the 'Sinn Féin rebellion'. As we shall see, Sinn Féin had nothing to do with 1916, but the name stuck nonetheless.

It is important not to exaggerate the importance of the early Sinn Féin. It was simply the most prominent of a number of radical nationalist groups, both in the political and cultural spheres. The later centrality of Sinn Féin should not blind us to its marginality in the first decade of the twentieth century. Especially after the return of the Liberals to power in Westminster in 1905, the Nationalist party's fortunes began to improve. There was, however, one key difference between Parnell's party and Redmond's. Parnell embraced the Fenians and contained them within the party structure. Redmond never had them securely on board. Until 1912 or so, this did not seem to matter. After 1916, it was fatal to Redmond's fortunes.

The Liberal governments of Henry Campbell-Bannerman and Herbert Asquith were not anxious to embrace the home rule cause which had so fatally fractured their party in Gladstone's day. Nonetheless, they thought that some ameliorative measure short of home rule might draw the sting of continuing nationalist campaigns and in the process allay unionist anxieties. The Irish Council Bill of 1907 was the result of this line of thought. It proposed the devolution of administrative functions overseen by a council of 106 members, 82 of whom would be nominated by London. Eight significant departments, including education and the Congested Districts Board, would be thus devolved. The bill pleased nobody (well, almost nobody: Patrick Pearse, later to become the iconic leader of the 1916 rising, was prepared to accept it) and it was withdrawn. Most nationalists felt it did not go far enough. Crucially the Catholic Church authorities were suspicious of a proposal that might disturb their de facto control of the educational system.

The two elections of 1910 each produced a hung parliament and, sure enough, the Liberal leader Asquith could only form a government with Redmond's support. Home rule was now back on the agenda whether the prime minister liked it or not. In April 1912, the third Home Rule Bill was introduced in the House of Commons. After ferocious Conservative opposition, it was not carried until January 1913. Predictably, it was then defeated in the Lords. However, the Parliament Act of 1911 had removed the Lords' veto, replacing it with a delaying power of two years. This meant that home rule would become a reality in 1914. The 1912 bill was Redmond's apotheosis. Parnell's dream, it seemed, was about to come true. Except, of course, that it never did.

In March 1905, the Ulster Unionist Council (UUC) was formed in Belfast. Northern unionists had been alarmed at the conciliatory manner of their southern counterparts during the negotiations that preceded the Land Act of 1903. The differences between southern and northern unionism were clear. In the south, the remnants of the old Ascendancy were reduced in fortune, land and prestige. In the north, a self-confident commercial aristocracy had been created by the Industrial Revolution.

The formation of the UUC announced the end of intra-Protestant rivalry and the creation of a communal solidarity that reflected that on the nationalist, Catholic side. Given the fractious nature of Protestantism, with its emphasis on individual conscience and judgement, this was a more difficult task than it seemed. Indeed, the kind of organizational unity represented by the UUC was easiest to sustain in times of crisis. When the crisis passed or abated, the underlying tensions resurfaced.

The real crisis for Ulster unionism came with the introduction of the third Home Rule Bill. With the power of the Lords now emasculated, it meant that victory in the Commons would be enough to force the measure through. The bill was anathema to all unionists.

The unionists had four advantages in their opposition to home rule: first, they were passionate about it and prepared to go to any extreme to win; second, they had a local majority in their Ulster heartland; third, they had the enthusiastic support of the Conservative party in Britain; finally, they had two leaders of real ability.

Edward Carson became leader of the UUC in 1910. Born in Dublin, he was a barrister in London, where his most celebrated performance had been in the destruction of Oscar Wilde at his trial in 1895. Carson was a commanding and rather mercurial figure, who brought immense prestige and good Conservative connections to the Ulster cause. In fact, the cause for him was that of Irish unionism throughout the whole island, although the focus was essentially on Ulster. He was in the O'Connell–Parnell mould of Irish leader, urging radicalism and mass mobilization to squeeze concessions from London. For that, he needed a mass movement. James Craig, a hatchet-faced millionaire typical of the new money plutocracy, gave it to him.

A series of meetings and rallies and an effective publicity campaign ensured that public opinion in Protestant Ulster was thoroughly mobilized. The campaign culminated in Ulster Day, 28 September 1912, with the signing of Ulster's Solemn League and Covenant by almost a quarter of a million men. This document or pledge was a conscious echo of the Solemn League and Covenant of 1643, in which Scots Presbyterians and English parliamentarians had united against the government of King Charles I. The historical parallel of united opposition to overweening authority was irresistible. The whole exercise was a brilliant *coup de théâtre*.

It became clear to the government that some concession would have to be made to Ulster opinion, as the popular campaign grew ever more shrill. But any concession to unionism would be resisted by Redmond and the Nationalist party. Indeed, part of the problem that now arose from trying to reconcile the irreconcilable was the steady erosion of Redmond's (and by extension, the party's) authority among nationalists, as they were seen to give ground on the original 1912 proposals in order to placate the unionists and the British.

Although the bill did eventually complete its parliamentary course, by then the whole focus had shifted from parliament. In January 1913, just as the Home Rule Bill was moving from the Commons to the Lords, the Ulster Volunteer Force (UVF) was formed by the UUC. It was a local militia designed to resist the implementation of home rule when it passed into law. It had the support of leading Conservatives in England, many of whom sent cash. Top military men offered their assistance. The UVF soon comprised 100,000 men and drilled quite openly: drilling was legal only if approved by two magistrates and was conducted for a legal purpose. The magistrates were seldom a problem, being sympathetic, while the government turned a blind eye to the blatant illegality. The Conservative opposition was in effect giving its support to a treasonable conspiracy in support of what it imagined to be the constitution.

The extent of the government's problem were seen in March 1914. Fearing that the UVF might raid arms depots, it instructed the commander-in-chief of the army in Ireland, General Arthur Paget, to prepare plans to frustrate any such attempt. Paget foolishly let it be known that officers with Ulster connections would not be obliged to take part in the action, but this merely prompted fifty-six other officers at the Curragh Military Camp in Co. Kildare to resign their commissions rather than move against Ulster. The shambles is sometimes called the Curragh Incident rather than the more traditional Curragh Mutiny, but the stronger term seems the fairer one, since the net effect was that the British government could no longer rely on the British army to act as an instrument of its will. For the first time since 1688, barrack-room politics had proved decisive.

In fact, the UVF had no need to raid arms depots, because in the following month they successfully landed 25,000 rifles and a million rounds of ammunition at three east Ulster ports, of which the Larne shipment was the biggest. The ease with which this was done and the fact that it was organized by the UUC, whose head was Edward Carson, a former solicitor-general of England, and whose principal organizer, James Craig, was a Conservative MP, demonstrated that unionism was prepared to stop at nothing in its defiance of parliament.

A last-ditch attempt to find some compromise between nationalist demands and unionist resistance came in July 1914, at the Buckingham Palace Conference, at which all parties were represented. But there was no magic formula. Irresistible force had met immovable object. There was no solution.

Then the Great War broke out. The Irish question was

parked. Home Rule was enacted in September 1914 but its provisions were suspended until the war was over. By then, the whole world was changed and Ireland with it. Home rule was dead.

In November 1913, a group of advanced nationalists in Dublin formed the Irish Volunteers in conscious imitation of the UVF. The principal founder, Eoin Mac Néill, who had been a founder of the Gaelic League twenty years earlier, became its first commander-in-chief. Redmond was alarmed at the thought of a nationalist militia outside his control and quickly moved to tame it. He succeeded – or thought he had – by having his nominees take over the executive committee. But the Volunteers also proved of interest to the Fenians, who after many years of drift had been revived by Thomas J. Clarke, a veteran of the dynamite campaign of the 1880s who had served fifteen years in prison. From now on it is best to use the Fenians' alternative name, the IRB (Irish Republican Brotherhood) because that was the term most commonly used by contemporaries.

Redmond's lack of real control was evident in the Howth gun-running of July 1914, when arms for the Irish Volunteers were landed in broad daylight at Howth, on the northern arm of Dublin Bay. This was a nationalist response to the Larne gun-running and, like it, was a publicity stunt. However, whereas Larne went off smoothly thanks to the collusion of the authorities, Howth ended in tragedy. Troops tried with little success to dispossess the Volunteers of their arms; the word of this failure spread, much to the merriment of the citizenry; and when a crowd of people in the city centre later taunted some British troops, things reached the point where the troops fired on the unarmed crowd, killing three of them. The contrast with Larne could hardly have been greater.

A month later, the outbreak of the Great War presented Redmond with a dilemma. Home rule was about to become law and now the United Kingdom, of which Ireland was and would remain a part of under home rule, was at war. Redmond committed the Volunteers to the British war effort, thus splitting the movement. About 160,000 followed his call and reconstituted themselves as the National Volunteers. Many Irishmen went to fight on all fronts in the war. They fought honourably according to their lights and those of their political leaders. About 30,000 died. The survivors would return to a country transformed, one where their courage in the face of the Great War's horrors often counted for next to nothing.

The minority who dissented from Redmond's decision included Mac Néill and the other original founders. They numbered about 12,000 and retained the name Irish Volunteers. But gradually it was not the formal leadership of the Volunteers who made the running, but a secret Fenian cabal. The IRB formed a military council of its own and infiltrated the inner command structure of the Irish Volunteers. Clarke and his young lieutenants like Sean MacDermott were set on a military action against British rule, a determination to assert the Irish republic in arms, before the end of the Great War. The IRB were therefore a minority of a minority, the most militant, doctrinaire and unyielding republican separatists in the nationalist tradition.

Their plans for a rising were laid in secret, unknown to Mac Néill and the Volunteer leadership. The only other group in their confidence was the tiny Irish Citizen Army. This was a trade union militia founded some weeks before the Volunteers themselves. Their original purpose had been to protect members of the Irish Transport & General Workers' Union (ITGWU) from the brutal attentions of the Dublin Metropolitan Police during the Lockout of 1913.

The Lockout – the greatest labour dispute in Irish history – arose from a collision of wills between William Martin Murphy, business tycoon and former Nationalist party MP, and James Larkin, the messianic labour leader who had mobilized the unskilled labourers of the Dublin slums. Living conditions for the lower working class of Dublin were among the worst in Europe, crowded in enormous numbers into rotting tenements in what had once been elegant Georgian townhouses now gone to ruin and filth. Murphy, the most powerful employer in the city, locked out workers in his transport company for refusing to give up their membership of the ITGWU, led by Larkin. The dispute spread across the city with other lockouts and sympathetic strikes and at its height about 25,000 men were out. The dispute dragged on into early 1914, by which time the workers were effectively starved back on the employers' terms. But in the meantime, the Irish Citizen Army had come into being.

Its leader was James Connolly, who replaced Larkin as head of the ITGWU at the end of the Lockout. Connolly was both socialist and Irish nationalist, an unusual combination. Most nationalists, even the advanced types in Sinn Féin or the Volunteers, were either cool about labour or downright hostile to it. The hostility reflected the petit bourgeois origins of many nationalists and also their concern to build up indigenous Irish commerce and industry: trade unions, in their eyes, were divisive nationally and destructive economically.

Connolly, on the other hand, was unusual in his context. Most socialists were instinctive internationalists, viewing nationalism as a reactionary form of manipulation by ruling classes. Any appeal to class solidarity was bound to offend calls for national solidarity. So Connolly's combination of socialist and nationalist conviction required a considerable amount of intellectual gymnastics to justify it.

The net effect was, however, that he found himself possessed of his own small militia in the form of the Citizen Army. He was a fine organizer, a practical man of action and a dedicated revolutionary. He wanted to ally himself with the Volunteers but feared that the leadership was too timid. In fact, there were three broad elements in the Irish Volunteers. The first, the non-IRB element under Mac Néill, were separatists who were prepared to resist the introduction of conscription in Ireland. The second were the mainstream IRB members, who were anxious for a rising and sought to build public opinion in support of such a course. Finally, there were the radicals on the military council who wanted a rising as soon as possible without waiting for public opinion.

It was to this group that Connolly attached himself, largely through his growing friendship with Patrick Pearse, the most public of them. A well-known teacher and journalist and a brilliant orator, Pearse had delivered a spell-binding oration at the graveside of the old Fenian, Jeremiah O'Donovan Rossa, in August 1915 which ended with the peroration about the British rulers of Ireland: 'The fools, the fools, the fools! – they have left us our Fenian dead, and while Ireland holds these graves, Ireland unfree shall never be at peace.'

There were soon to be more dead and more graves.

22

RISING

The rising of 1916 was planned in secret by the military council of the IRB and the Irish Citizen Army. IRB members not on the military council were kept in the dark, not to mention the mainstream leadership of the Irish Volunteers. In effect, the military council used the structure of the Volunteers to trip off a rebellion that they alone wanted at that time. Theirs was an authentic, unadulterated version of Fenian ideology: the use of military force to achieve an independent Irish republic.

The principal IRB planners were Thomas Clarke and Sean MacDermott, assisted in the latter stages by James Connolly. Pearse was to be the public voice of the rising: he drafted the proclamation of the republic, although with a significant contribution from Connolly. The vital business of procuring arms was entrusted to Sir Roger Casement.

Casement was originally from Co. Antrim, born into a prosperous Protestant family. He entered the British colonial service in 1892, apparently a perfectly conventional young man of his time and place. He was anything but: he was homosexual; a naturalist who acquired an international reputation; and a humanitarian. In 1904, he wrote a report that exposed the horrific treatment of indigenous workers in the Belgian Congo. In 1912, he published a similar report on the workers' conditions along the Putumayo River in Peru. Both reports created a sensation in Europe, exposing the dirty underbelly of imperialism. In the same year, Casement retired from the colonial service with a knighthood, but also with a distaste for imperialism in general that was now focused on his homeland.

He had become a committed Irish nationalist. He joined the Volunteers and spent the first part of the Great War in Berlin, trying to persuade Irish prisoners-of-war to form an Irish brigade to fight in a rising. He had little success. But his German contacts proved valuable in arms procurement. And so, in April 1916, Casement watched as a cargo ship, the *Aud*, was loaded with arms to be landed in Ireland for use in the military council's rising now planned for Easter Sunday. There were 20,000 rifles, a million rounds of ammunition and ten machine guns, mostly captured from the Russians at the battle of Tannenberg in 1914. The *Aud* set sail, followed closely by a submarine in which Casement travelled. They were bound for Tralee Bay in Co. Kerry.

The *Aud* got there first but was intercepted by the Royal Navy. Its captain scuttled the ship and the military council's longed-for arms shipment went to Davy Jones's locker. The submarine bearing Casement and his companions arrived later; they were put ashore, but Casement was captured. It was Good Friday, two days before the rising was due to be launched.

The British authorities in Dublin Castle had known that something was up but were not sure what. Now they felt that they could relax. They were almost as surprised by the turn of events as the Volunteer leadership. Realizing the extent of the deception used to get things to this point, Mac Néill ordered that all Volunteer movements and exercises over the Easter weekend were to be halted. The order was couriered to the provinces and also carried in the *Sunday Independent* newspaper.

The military council resolved to go ahead anyway. Despite all the confusion, they were determined on a gesture. The Easter Rising was the politics of theatre.

On Easter Monday morning, a group of 150 men occupied the General Post Office (GPO) in Sackville (now O'Connell) Street in Dublin. On the steps, Patrick Pearse stepped forward to read the proclamation of the republic, one of the most quoted documents in Irish history, to a bemused audience of citizens. A further six rebel garrisons were established at other positions around the city centre. The British, taken utterly by surprise, mobilized troops from the Curragh camp, about 55 km (35 miles) away, and moved them to Dublin. They began to throw a cordon around the city centre, trapping the various rebel garrisons within. On the Wednesday, they sailed the gunboat *Helga* up the river and used her guns to flatten Liberty Hall – Connolly's trade union headquarters. Troops entered Trinity College and the Shelbourne Hotel, giving them respectively a clear line of fire towards the GPO in Sackville Street and the garrison in the Royal College of Surgeons on the west side of St Stephen's Green.

In general, the rebel tactics were naive to non-existent. They fortified certain public buildings and dug in, inviting the inevitable British counter-attack. The rebels, with their tiny numbers, fought well. An outpost of the Boland's Mills garrison, on the south-eastern flank, ambushed reinforcements shipped in from Britain as they marched into the city, inflicting the heaviest crown casualties of Easter Week. It was a ferocious fight conducted by seven young rebels but it left over two hundred crown troops dead. But despite episodes such as this, there could only be one military outcome. No one was in any doubt on that score.

The main counter-attack on the GPO took place on Friday and Saturday, culminating in the evacuation of the building. The final surrender came at 2.30 p.m. on the Saturday. The rebels were rounded up and imprisoned. A military court was established to try them and by the time it had finished its work, fifteen leaders of the rising – including all seven signatories of the proclamation – had been shot. Connolly was the last of them. Wounded in the rising, he was tied to a chair and executed. The final coda came with the hanging of Roger Casement in August on a charge of treason.

At first, public opinion was indifferent or hostile to the rising. Gradually, anger set in as the gruesome series of executions continued. The British made martyrs of the leaders. The novelist James Stephens, who kept a diary of Easter Week, noted contemporaneously: 'The truth is that Ireland is not cowed. She is excited a little . . . She was not with the revolution, but in a few months she will be, and her heart which was withering will be warmed by the knowledge that men thought her worth dying for.'

Stephens was right. The Easter Rising transformed Ireland. The British called it the Sinn Féin rebellion, although Sinn Féin had nothing to do with it. Nonetheless, it was the Sinn Féin party which now became the focus of all those who celebrated the rising and were weary of Redmond. The party reconstituted itself in 1917. The founder, Arthur Griffith, stood aside to allow the leadership to pass to the most senior surviving garrison commander from the rising, Éamon de Valera.

The whole shape of Irish nationalism was changing. In part, it was a generational change. The leaders of the Nationalist party had all been young men in the 1880s. Now they seemed older than their years to a younger generation for whom the heroics of Easter Week were infinitely more glamorous than the parliamentary temporizing of ageing men. The Great War had blocked the emigration routes and bottled up a lot of young people in Ireland who might otherwise have found an outlet for their energies in the United States. For the new generation that had no personal memories of Parnell, Sinn Féin seemed fresh, vital and unapologetic.

Every political change, no matter how profound, requires a focus. The drift to Sinn Féin found its focus in the debate on conscription. Ireland was the only part of the United Kingdom in which conscription had not been imposed at the start of the war, an omission that spoke volumes in itself. The horrifying losses on the Somme in 1916 and at Passchendaele in 1917 tempted London to reconsider. At first, the prime minister, David Lloyd George, was not convinced of the effectiveness of extending conscription to Ireland, noting that it would produce relatively insignificant numbers of troops while robbing Irish agriculture – vital to the war effort – of labour. But continued losses forced the issue. In April 1918, the Military Services Act became law.

The Nationalists immediately withdrew from Westminster and returned to Ireland. There they made common cause with just about every element in nationalist civil society in opposition to conscription. It left the party in an awkward position, for it was implicitly conceding Sinn Féin's point that Westminster was a waste of time. If nationalist voters were asked to support abstention, why not vote for the real abstentionists?

The key to the success of the anti-conscription campaign was the unambiguous manner in which it united all shades of nationalism, especially – and most importantly – the Catholic Church. A pledge to oppose conscription was signed by nearly two million people throughout the country on 21 April: it had been drafted by Éamon de Valera, the Sinn Féin leader. There was a general strike on 23 April. There were demonstrations. It became clear to the government that any attempt to enforce the conscription law would result in massive civil disobedience and violence. Instead it funked the issue. By the time the war ended in November, conscription was a dead letter.

Conscription destroyed the Nationalist party. It had a fight on its hands with Sinn Féin up to that point, but it had not done too badly. True, it had lost three by-elections to the younger party in 1917 and early 1918, most famously in Clare where de Valera took Daniel O'Connell's old seat to launch a political career that would lead him to dominate his country at the mid-century. But as late as February 1918, the Nationalists had held South Armagh in a by-election against a strong Sinn Féin candidate and when John Redmond died in March, his seat in Waterford was held for the party by his son. In April, just two weeks before the introduction of conscription, the party held its seat in the East Tyrone by-election. There were special circumstances in all three Nationalist victories: the party was better organized in Ulster than elsewhere and in better shape to fight elections. In Waterford, there was a large sympathy vote.

Once conscription became the burning issue, however, the old party was doomed. When the war ended, Lloyd George called a general election for December 1918. Sinn Féin annihilated the home rulers to become the undisputed voice of nationalist Ireland. Pledged not to take their seats at Westminster, they constituted themselves as Dáil Éireann, the assembly of Ireland, meeting for the first time on 21 January 1919. On the same day, two unarmed policemen were shot dead in an ambush in Co. Tipperary in what was the first action of the Irish war of independence.

This war was prosecuted by the Irish Republican Army (IRA), as the Volunteers now styled themselves. Their relationship to Sinn Féin was ambiguous, although sharing a common separatist sensibility. There was no sense in which they were firmly under civilian control and direction, although this claim was advanced and was a useful fiction. The war of independence was a series of sporadic regional guerrilla conflicts, depending on the initiative of vigorous and committed local commanders. It was an ambush war, directed in the first place at the isolated barracks of the Royal Irish Constabulary (RIC). By forcing the RIC from large parts of the countryside, the IRA weakened the local eyes and ears of British rule in rural Ireland.

The British responded with a mixture of regular troops and auxiliaries, the infamous Black and Tans. It was a dirty war. The Black and Tans were ill-disciplined and often drunk. Many were rootless veterans of the western front, brutalized by their experiences. They were terrifying when they ran amok, as they did in Cork city centre and in the little town of Balbriggan, just north of Dublin, both of which they burned to the ground.

The IRA had a number of successful ambush battles against crown troops, especially in Co. Cork: the actions at Crossbarry and Kilmichael were particularly celebrated. Equally, however, the Cork campaign took a sectarian turn and a number of atrocities were committed against local Protestants. The new republic carried some antique baggage.

The military campaign was paralleled by a civil one. Sinn Féin established the rudiments of an alternative civil administration to the British, complete with a department of finance to raise loans, a very successful alternative court system to adjudicate local disputes and a vigorous propaganda arm. The key figure was Michael Collins.

Not yet thirty, this extraordinary force of nature was simultaneously minister of finance in the alternative administration, where he successfully administered the raising of Dáil loans both in Ireland and the United States, and director of intelligence of the IRA, in which role he ruthlessly infiltrated and damaged the British security system in Dublin Castle. Collins was prepared to play very dirty indeed, as he showed on the morning of Bloody Sunday, 21 November 1920, when his men executed eleven British agents in their beds in cold blood. In retaliation, a party of auxiliaries killed twelve people in Croke Park, the Dublin headquarters of the GAA, when they fired into the crowd during a football game that afternoon.

The war was fought to a stalemate by the summer of 1921. By then, the island had been partitioned. The Government of Ireland Act 1920 – successor to the ill-fated Home Rule Act of 1914 that never saw the light of day – bowed to the inevitable. Ulster could not be coerced into a nationalist state. So the 1920 act created two parliaments, one for the six most Protestant counties of Ulster, and one for the rest of the country. The northern parliament began to function and lasted until 1972. The southern parliament was stillborn, bypassed by the Dáil.

The birth of Northern Ireland was accompanied by an orgy of sectarian violence in the years 1920–22. The war of independence spread north and became entangled with the trauma of partition. The IRA attacked police and army as in the south; Protestant mobs drove Catholic workers from the Belfast shipyards; the IRA retaliated by burning businesses and big houses in rural Ulster to try to take the pressure off their beleaguered co-religionists in Belfast; the UVF was re-formed as the Ulster Special Constabulary – the notorious B Specials – a viciously partisan Protestant militia. Sixty-one people died in Belfast alone in the single month of March 1922.

In essence, the sectarian civil war that had been postponed by the outbreak of the Great War had now broken out in the Ulster cockpit. Inevitably, given the local superiority of Protestant numbers and the fact that they now controlled the levers of the state, the Protestants were able to bring a greater terror to bear than the Catholics. There were atrocities committed on both sides: it was not all one-way traffic. But the Protestant traffic was more lethal. Moreover, it polluted its own community, as well as terrorizing the Catholic one, by permitting the agents of the newly partitioned statelet literally to get away with murder.

The IRA's war of independence ended with a truce in July 1921. Negotiations between the Sinn Féin leadership and the British began in October and culminated in a treaty proposal on 6 December. It gave southern Ireland effective independence, along the same lines as Canada, but retained the oath of allegiance to the crown and therefore stopped short of a republic. The principal Irish negotiators were Griffith and Collins. De Valera, the political leader of Irish nationalism and the most subtle negotiating intellect, stayed at home. This was ostensibly to prepare the people for the inevitable compromise solution to come.

This made it all the more surprising that de Valera himself was one of the first to repudiate the terms of the treaty. After the heady five years of republican expectation since the rising, there was bound to be some degree of disappointment. Nonetheless, the Dáil approved the treaty by a narrow margin. There followed an uneasy few months before dissidents in the

IRA occupied the Four Courts in Dublin. Collins, by now chairman of the provisional government in charge of Southern Ireland until the Irish Free State set up under the terms of the treaty could take over, was pressurized by London into rooting them out. This he did, in June 1922, using field guns borrowed from the British.

This action tripped off the Civil War. It was bitter, as all these things are, but the provisional government held all the big cards. There was little resistance outside Munster and by April 1923 it was over. But it claimed the lives of Griffith – from a stroke – and Collins, from a sniper's bullet in his native Co. Cork. In the meantime, the Irish Free State had been born in December 1922. The last British troops left, as did the last British officials. The union flag came down and the tricolour flag first introduced by the Young Irelanders seventy-four years earlier now flew on all public buildings.

There were now two states in Ireland. In the south, the Irish Free State was effectively an independent country. It was overwhelmingly Catholic. In the six counties of the north east, Northern Ireland was an autonomous province within the United Kingdom. It had a population that was roughly two-thirds Protestant, but with a Catholic minority inflexibly opposed to the very existence of the state.

23

PARTITION

After the end of the Civil War, the Irish Free State got down to business. Its governing party, Cumann na nGaedheal, comprised those in Sinn Féin who supported the treaty settlement. Its leader, now that Griffith and Collins were dead, was W. T. Cosgrave, an uncharismatic man who had fought in 1916. The dominant figure in the first five years of the government was the brilliant but authoritarian Kevin O'Higgins, the minister for home affairs. Eoin Mac Néill was minister for education. Four other ministers had, like Cosgrave, fought in 1916.

The opposition – the political opponents of the treaty – retained the name Sinn Féin. They refused to take their seats in the Dáil and remained outside formal politics until 1927. In effect, this gave the Cumann na nGaedheal a clear parliamentary run. They could concentrate on government to the relative neglect of constituency politics, an emphasis that was to prove electorally fatal to them in the longer term.

The principal achievement of Cosgrave's government during its ten years in office was the establishment of the institutions of the new state. It fought the Civil War ruthlessly to a definitive conclusion. In the midst of that war, it established the police force of the new state – the Garda Síochana (Guardians of the Peace) – as an unarmed body. This was a remarkable change from British days. Henceforth, policing was to be consensual rather than coercive. The success of this courageous initiative underlined the basic legitimacy of the new state, even in the immediate aftermath of the Civil War. There is no doubt that a majority of people in the Free State accepted the treaty settlement, although with varying degrees of enthusiasm.

Economically, the Free State was orthodox and conservative, reflecting its dependence on the powerful civil servants who headed the Department of Finance. The one major economic initiative undertaken by the government was the establishment in 1927 of the Electricity Supply Board and the building of a big hydroelectric generating station on the River Shannon at Ardnacrusha, near Limerick. This was a departure from economic orthodoxy, which was otherwise all pervasive. It established what was a nationalized company in all but name as a monopoly supplier of electricity throughout the state.

A boundary commission set up under the terms of the treaty produced no change in the border. This failure – dashing the confident expectations of many nationalists in both north and south – reduced the government's prestige and ended the political career of the hapless Eoin Mac Néill, who had been the Free State's representative on the commission.

Cumann na nGaedheal consciously embraced the support of members of the old southern unionist establishment, which further compromised them in the eyes of their opponents. They also drew the remnants of the Redmondite tradition to themselves. They were consciously the creators and guardians of the institutions of the state, but in pursuing this obsession with institutions they neglected the sinews of ordinary politics.

None of this mattered until 1926, because there was no substantial opposition to Cumann na nGaedheal. But in that year Sinn Féin split. Éamon de Valera urged it to abandon its policy of abstention if the oath of allegiance were to be removed. By a small majority, the party refused to do so. De Valera had expected defeat and was well prepared – all too well prepared in the eyes of some contemporary observers. He immediately left Sinn Féin and established Fianna Fáil (the Soldiers of Destiny). Still abstentionist, but prepared to reverse this policy were the oath to be removed, the new party gave notice of its potential by winning 26 per cent of the poll and forty-four seats in the general election of June 1927.

The next month, the government's best intellect and most commanding personality, Kevin O'Higgins, was murdered by IRA dissidents. He had never been forgiven for being the hard man in the Civil War cabinet. His death moved the government to propose a bill obliging all Dáil candidates to swear that they would take the oath of allegiance if elected. This presented de Valera with an acute dilemma. Fianna Fáil deputies would have to take the hated oath or face the same sterile future as Sinn Féin. The whole logic of the break with Sinn Féin pointed towards the need to cut this Gordian knot. Accordingly, de Valera wrestled with his conscience and won – not for the first or last time – declaring the oath to be a mere 'empty formula', a curious conclusion in view of the fact that it had seemed worth a Civil War just five years earlier.

Cosgrave called a snap election in September. This saw the Fianna Fáil vote increase to 35 per cent and their seat count to fifty-seven. Sinn Féin was wiped out as a political force. Fianna Fáil was now clearly the standard bearer of the republican anti-treaty sentiments.

In the northern part of the partitioned island, Northern Ireland enjoyed a long sleep from the 1920s to the 1960s. The one part of Ireland that had fought most bitterly against home rule was the only part to get it. The province's devolved government was established to suit the convenience of the local Protestant unionist majority and nobody else. The IRA had done its best to strangle Northern Ireland at birth. The new state was born on the back of a military victory for the unionists in 1922. Nationalists were to be a despised enemy in the eyes of their new rulers.

Ulster unionists created a state in their own image and for

their own community. From the first, Northern Ireland was obsessed with community security. The police were augmented by the Ulster Special Constabulary (USC – the B Specials), an armed local militia, who were effectively the UVF in another guise. Many were Great War veterans. Few were squeamish about violence, a lack of scruple which was in fairness reciprocated by the IRA. The police and the USC had at their backs the Special Powers Act, originally enacted in 1922 at the height of the IRA war to give the state emergency powers. It was not repealed until 1973. In effect, it gave the minister of home affairs power to rule by decree. In its indifference to civil liberties and the normal constitutional checks and balances, it was unique in the western world.

Nor were the Unionists taking any electoral risks. Under the Local Government (Ireland) Act 1919, the British had decreed that proportional representation (PR) was needed in Ireland in order to give representation to minorities, a measure deemed unnecessary for the more enlightened 'mainland' but essential in the swampy Irish marchlands. The Free State persisted with PR but Northern Ireland did away with it, the Unionists finding the idea of representing the Catholic nationalist minority proportionate to their votes offensive to the purposes of the state. It was also feared that PR would have the effect of splitting the unionist vote and thus compromising the hegemony of the Unionist Party. As early as 1922, PR was abolished for local government elections, with the parliamentary franchise following suit in 1929. Together with a sedulous gerrymandering of constituency boundaries, this ensured the dominance of the Unionists for fifty years.

The results on the ground were impressive. Twelve local authorities which had been Nationalist under PR now produced consistent Unionist majorities under the straight vote. Two more, which had been evenly contested, became safely Unionist and yet another was merged with a neighbouring council in an amalgamation that was structured to ensure a permanent Unionist majority. The Nationalists were left in

control of a mere ten councils out of a total of seventy-three in
Northern Ireland.

Having first adopted a policy of abstention in the hope that
the Boundary Commission would make substantial territorial
adjustments in their favour, the Nationalist Party abandoned it
in 1927 and took their seats in the Northern Ireland parliament.
They declined the role of official opposition because that would
have meant formalizing their position as the 'loyal' opposition.
This was a step too far. It was all of a piece with nationalist attitudes to the statelet in general. By declining to involve itself
fully, or at all, with its institutions nationalist voices went
unheard and unionist opinions were adopted by default. On the
other hand, when they did participate in public life, as by taking
their seats in parliament, they were treated with contempt and
their concerns overborne by crude weight of numbers. Northern
Ireland made its minority feel like the enemy within and then
expressed horror and surprise when it behaved accordingly. The
minister for home affairs, Richard Dawson Bates, ensured that
no Catholics were employed in his sensitive department. He was
not alone in this policy: other ministers took a similar line. In the
fifty years under review, hardly any nationalists achieved senior
rank in the Northern Ireland civil service.

In 1932, Sir Basil Brooke, member of a long-established
marcher family in the far reaches of Co. Fermanagh and a
rising star in Unionist politics (he would end up as Lord
Brookeborough, prime minister of the province) put it succinctly,
if controversially:

There are a great number of Protestants and Orangemen who
employ Roman Catholics. I feel that I can speak freely on this
subject as I have not a Roman Catholic about my own place. I
appreciate the great difficulty experienced by some of you in
procuring suitable Protestant labour but I would point out that
Roman Catholics are endeavouring to get in everywhere. I
would appeal to loyalists, therefore, wherever possible, to
employ good Protestant lads and lassies.

Brooke later explained the context for his proscription. He had
learned of an IRA plot to kidnap his eldest son. He acted to
dismiss all his Catholic employees, or as he phrased it, 'to get
rid of every man in the place who might betray me'.

Northern Ireland was financially beholden to London and
unable to formulate any economic policy to deal with the
damage done to the local economy in the aftermath of the Wall
Street crash. Things were so bad in the early 1930s that the
unemployed briefly threw aside their sectarian animosities to
form a united front. This moment did not last and 1935 saw the
worst sectarian rioting in Belfast since 1922.

Northern Ireland was part of the United Kingdom but it
was, on most measures, by far the poorest and most disadvan-
taged part. The glory days of the late Victorian and Edwardian
eras were well gone. Poor Law relief rates were less than half
those prevailing in Glasgow and unemployment was 5 per cent
above the national average. In Belfast in 1932, the shipyards
employed fewer than 10 per cent of the workforce they had
needed in 1922.

The Second World War brought a temporary revival, as the
economy went on a war footing and unemployment was almost
eliminated. In Belfast, the shipyards built 140 warships for the
Royal Navy, including 6 aircraft carriers, as well as 123
merchant ships. Short and Harland's aircraft factory turned
out 1,200 bombers and 125 flying boats for the RAF. Munitions
factories made a notable contribution to the war effort.

There was also a generational change in unionism. James
Craig died in 1940 and was succeeded, not by one of the next
generation, but by his near contemporary John Miller Andrews.
He retained Craig's old guard but a party revolt in 1943
brought the younger and more energetic Brooke to power.
This change at the top did not signify any liberalizing of sectarian attitudes. Even the shared privations of the war – Belfast
was bombed heavily by the Luftwaffe in 1941 and hundreds
died – did nothing to lessen communal divisions or the essentially sectarian nature of the partition.

Both sides were caught in a trap with nowhere to go. Unionist gain could only mean nationalist loss and vice versa. The logic of the nationalist position was as bleak. Unable to challenge the existence of the state and incapable of recognizing its legitimacy, its politics were condemned to futility. In local government, where there might be a nationalist majority, unionists ensured their continued dominance through their shameless gerrymandering. Derry was the most notable, but not the only, example of this.

Unionist fears – there was never any shortage of these – were heightened by the defeat of the Conservatives and the arrival of the Labour government in London following their landslide victory in the 1945 election. Labour had traditionally been more friendly towards Irish nationalism than the Conservatives, who had their historical connection to the Unionist party. Dublin's declaration of a republic in 1949 and its withdrawal from the British Commonwealth was answered in London by the Ireland Act 1949 which proved unionist anxieties groundless. It gave them the reassurances they required by reaffirming Northern Ireland's place in the United Kingdom and stating that the province, or any part of it, could only withdraw from the UK by a vote of the Northern Ireland parliament. It also introduced a residence qualification for voters, thus addressing another unionist concern.

The establishment of the British welfare state after the Second World War was more troubling for unionists. The benefits of the new system – combined with those of the British educational reforms which effectively opened up secondary schooling to all regardless of income – were applied indiscriminately. Some unionist ultras resented this rewarding of treachery – as they saw it, granting full welfare and educational rights to a community that denied the legitimacy of the state – and indeed it was to have devastating consequences for unionism in the late 1960s.

From 1956 to 1962 the IRA conducted a sporadic campaign of bombings, arms raids and ambushes along the border. It was a sad coda to this whole period. It was a half-hearted effort which seemed to symbolize the enervated state of militant republicanism. There were many minor actions, but most were contained in west Ulster. There was no mass mobilization of nationalists. Belfast was almost untouched. Brookeborough introduced internment and locked up as many militants as he could find. Interestingly, de Valera did the same in the Republic: no one was going to out-republican him. In all, twelve IRA men and six policemen died in the border campaign. It was such small beer compared to what was to come.

24
DEV

De Valera (or Dev as he was popularly known) came to power in the Free State in 1932. His Fianna Fáil party was pledged to fight vigorously against partition and for the reunification of the country; for the revival of the Irish language; for the dismantling of the constitutional arrangements laid down in the treaty; for the break-up of large ranches and the creation of the greatest possible number of small family farms; and for the abandonment of Cumann na nGaedheal's free-trade policies in favour of protection and the development of native industry behind tariff barriers.

On the first two policies, Fianna Fáil failed dismally. No Irish nationalists of any kind had a clue what to do about Northern Ireland, except to hurl invective at Ulster unionists. On the language issue, it seemed that the Irish people were as utilitarian as Daniel O'Connell had been a century earlier. The whole propaganda apparatus of the state was directed to the promotion of the language. To no avail: its decline continued inexorably. Irish people voted with their tongues.

On the constitutional front, de Valera was in his element. Half Machiavelli, half sententious Jesuit, he did not hesitate. The crown's representative in the Free State, the governor-general, was effectively fired and replaced by a de Valera crony who barely appeared in public and who by his reticence made a deliberate laughing stock of the office. He abolished the oath of allegiance by legislation in 1933, to the fury of the British. He enacted a new constitution in 1937, replacing that established under the treaty. It was republican in all but name. The governor-general was replaced by a president; a formal territorial claim was made to Northern Ireland; and the 'special position' of the Catholic Church was specifically recognized.

Like Parnell before him, the old Fenian de Valera was making his accommodation with the church. In fact, he was a man of exemplary orthodoxy in religious matters. One of his principal advisers on the constitution was John Charles McQuaid, a cleric of powerful if narrow intellect, soon to be archbishop of Dublin and the dominant figure in the Catholic Church at the mid century. De Valera occupied the mainstream of Irish nationalist life in which the church was the supreme arbiter of moral value. Ireland was a country saturated in Catholicism: the unspoken assumption was that the basic integrating force in society was the shared Catholicism of its citizens. Even the GAA, with all its Fenian inheritance, was full of priests. In this context, de Valera's piety was unremarkable. It was perfectly natural that he should express the common moral values of his community.

The ease with which Fianna Fáil had taken over the state apparatus, amended it in fulfilment of its election promises and reached a *modus vivendi* with a civil service which it had previously held in suspicion indicated the extent to which a stable political consensus had been established. Fianna Fáil was the party of the nation, a populist people's party with broad cross-class appeal in the classic tradition of Irish political mobilization. Cumann na nGaedheal reacted badly to its loss of office, flirting briefly with a neo-fascist group called the Blueshirts before reinventing itself as Fine Gael (Family of the Gael). It remained pre-eminently the party of the state, emphasizing institutions rather than people; less ruthless about organization; more high-minded about policy; often wanting for the common touch and appealing disproportionately to large farmers and the upper middle class (what there was of them). Fianna Fáil leaned to the left on economic policy; Fine Gael was classically orthodox. Both parties were socially conservative, representing two versions of the post-Famine social settlement. Each asserted the superiority of rural life over urban. Neither had any coherent plan to staunch the flow of emigration. Neither had radical ideas for the reform and expansion of an education system that saw only one child in three complete the secondary school cycle – even as late as the early 1960s. As to the curriculum itself, it discounted the hard and applied sciences and treated vocational education as a poor relation. Both parties – indeed, all parties – were hugely deferential to the Catholic Church.

What both parties had was a basic commitment to democracy and the rule of law. Admittedly, there were anti-democratic elements close to both: Fianna Fáil was still indulgent towards the IRA while, as noted above, Fine Gael emerged from an entanglement with the Blueshirts, an organization of over-heated Catholic zealots in search of an Hibernian Mussolini: all they got was an ex-chief of police called Eoin O'Duffy. But the remarkable aspect of Ireland in the 1930s was the extent to which fashionable anti-democratic movements *failed* to gain ground.

On the economic front, the promise to develop Irish industry behind tariff barriers was redeemed under the direction of the energetic young minister for industry and commerce, Seán Lemass. The necessary legislation was put in place by the mid 1930s and an experiment in economic self-sufficiency began which would last for a quarter of a century. Fianna Fáil were much more energetic about establishing public enterprises such as the national airline, Aer Lingus, which was founded in 1936.

On the social side, the new government displayed considerable energy in slum clearance and the provision of new suburban public housing. But the crunch came in the countryside, because there was one more election promise to honour which caused a major crisis. De Valera had promised to with-hold the annuities due to the British Treasury in repayment of loans extended to tenants under the various land purchase acts, of which Wyndham's Land Act of 1903 was the best known. He did so. The British retaliated by slapping import duties on Irish produce, of which cattle were the most important. This so-called 'economic war' dragged on until 1938, causing much hardship in an Ireland already feeling the effects of the Depression that followed the Wall Street crash of 1929.

The economic war was finally settled under the terms of the Anglo-Irish agreement of 1938, which also tackled other irritants in Anglo-Irish relations. The annuities were converted into a single lump sum which Dublin paid to London. On the constitutional side, there was much clearing of the air, as the British reconciled themselves to de Valera's neo-republican document of 1937. De Valera also secured the return of three ports which the Royal Navy had retained under the terms of the treaty.

When the Second World War broke out, Dublin demonstrated its independence in the most emphatic way by remaining neutral. In this, it simply did what every other small nation in Europe did if it could get away with it. Public opinion was overwhelmingly for neutrality, although this did not stop significant numbers of volunteers from the south joining the British forces. Nor did it stop elements in the IRA from trying to cosy up to Nazi Germany.

It needs to be emphasized that Ireland's neutrality was entirely dependent on British benignity. George Orwell noted that it weren't for the Royal Navy, it would have been a fiction. Unlike continental neutrals such as Sweden and Finland, Ireland had no formidable army capable of resisting invasion. Any invader, especially the Germans, would have overrun the republic in short order, and the Wehrmacht would have enforced its rule with methods soon to be seen all over eastern Europe, such as would have made the Black and Tans remembered with something approaching sentimental affection. Neutrality was at once the greatest assertion of Irish independence and the greatest denier of its real substance. The republic relied on the kindness of neighbours.

Officially, de Valera maintained a policy of the most scrupulous neutrality. Unofficially, Ireland was neutral for Britain. Whether out of prudence or conviction, the government showed 'a certain consideration for Britain'. Thus, German airmen shot down over Ireland were promptly interned for the duration of the war. British (or other Allied) pilots were slipped across the border into Northern Ireland and no questions asked. Moreover, there were formal and flagrant breaches of neutrality later in the war, when Irish diplomats carried classified American documents in their diplomatic bags. Such a policy could only have been sanctioned by de Valera himself.

It was perhaps as a reaction to such secret collaboration with the Allies that de Valera felt the need to maintain the outward proprieties, even to the point of outraging world opinion. He did this in 1945 by paying a formal visit to Herr Eduard Hempel, the German minister in Dublin, to express his condolences on the death of Hitler. In part, this visit was prompted by de Valera's personal liking of Hempel, who was no Nazi and a formal diplomat of the old school. In this, he contrasted with the bombastic and bullying David Gray, the US ambassador, who was not at all to Dev's stomach.

The combination of economic isolation caused by the tariff regime, the inevitable shortages caused by the war, Ireland's geographical remoteness and its aloofness from a conflict that was convulsing the world was enervating. The reforming impulse that had made the 1930s exciting weakened and the fizz went out of the government. The war ended. Europe, boosted by Marshall Plan Aid, produced an astonishing economic recovery in the 1950s in which Ireland did not share. The country was still run for the benefit of a deeply conservative farming class. In effect, the land settlement and the absence of heavy industry had ensured that Ireland's political revolution would be socially conservative. The post-Famine consensus still held.

De Valera was a romantic reactionary. He believed in the moral superiority of the small family farm, of simple rural life over urban life, of an Ireland living as far as possible in seclusion from the world and steering her own course. The net effect of all this was that the Republic of Ireland (as it was formally declared in 1949) was the only country in the capitalist world whose economy actually contracted in the post-war years. The population of the state declined in the first forty years of independence. By the late 1950s, the game was up for social and economic self-sufficiency. This old ideal, which went back to Arthur Griffith's Sinn Féin, had brought the country to its knees.

Apart from de Valera's social vision, one reason why the Republic pursued these policies long after they had anything to offer was that they suited the country's collective self-image. Like many ethnic nationalisms across Europe, there was a distinct anti-modern side to Irish independence. The imperial master represented an oppressive modernism; freedom meant a retreat into a simpler, more moral order. De Valera's vision of domestic frugality and simplicity was reflected in popular attitudes. The rural small-holder was regarded as the ideal national type. In many European countries, this kind of sensibility produced fascist movements of one sort or another; in Ireland, at least spared that, it eventually produced a grand stasis.

De Valera was Taoiseach (as the prime minister was called under the 1937 constitution) for all but six years from 1932 to 1959. He dominated Irish life precisely because he embodied the aspirations and ideals of the population. He was tall, austere, commanding. To his political followers, he was simply 'The Chief'. To his enemies he was, in Oliver St John Gogarty's memorable phrase, 'the Spanish onion in the Irish stew'. But no one could deny his command of public opinion, his devious and serpentine intellect, his sincere passion for the Irish language and the republican ideals of the old Sinn Féin. Sadly, he overstayed his welcome by at least ten years.

One other group was entirely pleased with the introverted Ireland of the de Valera years. The Catholic Church liked the idea of Ireland as a kind of spiritual cordon sanitaire from which the excesses of secular modernity were excluded. The ultramontane church bequeathed by Cardinal Cullen in the nineteenth century was authoritarian, dogmatic and – by 1950 or so – at the height of its influence and prestige. Its moral writ ran with irresistible force.

When the coalition government of 1948–51 – the first non-de Valera administration since 1932 – tried to introduce free medical care for mothers and children under sixteen, it sparked off a church–state clash which the church won hands down. The sponsoring minister, a left-wing maverick named Noel Browne, was forced to resign. Members of the cabinet wrote to John Charles McQuaid, the archbishop of Dublin and principal opponent of the scheme, in the most fawning and obsequious terms to prove their loyalty. McQuaid's objection was that Catholic social teaching decreed that such services as Browne proposed were the province of the family rather than the state.

It was quite a thing to be a Catholic bishop in Ireland in the mid-twentieth century. It was a guarantee of immense deference and prestige. Catholic Ireland, it seemed, was the last vibrant corner of the Victorian world. Religious observance and devotion were nearly universal. Almost every Catholic went to Mass each Sunday; abstention was a social scandal. There were sodalities, public processions, devotions such as benediction and the forty hours, missions and retreats, and an overwhelming cult of the Virgin Mary. There were priests everywhere. Churches were full to overflowing. Catholic pamphlets and tracts and devotional books sold strongly. There was little or no public criticism of the Church or any tradition of anti-clericalism. It was said by some that the people were not priest-ridden rather that the priests were people-ridden, so ubiquitous was the spirit of submissive orthodoxy.

Relations with Protestants were cool to frigid. Ecumenism was for the future. For the moment, the church insisted on the primacy of its teaching and held all other Christian groups to be in varying degrees of error. This was not a church that encouraged theological speculation or internal debate.

The Irish Catholic Church also had an enormous missionary presence overseas. In every part of the English-speaking world and in most of Africa, Irish priests, nuns and brothers were to be found. By the middle of the century, there were more than 10,000 Irish missionaries scattered around the world, not counting priests of Irish birth who chose to serve overseas. It was an impressive statistic for a country so sparsely populated. The Irish church regarded its missionary outreach as a spiritual analogue to Britain's material empire and all the more honourable for that. The Irish missionaries did not simply spread the faith; they provided teachers and medical personnel in huge numbers.

At home, the entire education system was denominational – this key ambition of the church had been fulfilled promptly in the 1920s on securing independence. The schools were run by priests, nuns and brothers. The latter, in particular, educated generations of lower middle-class boys who might otherwise have received little or no schooling at all. Still, it was a utilitarian education for the most part, reminiscent of Gradgrind's unyielding method of schooling in Dickens's *Hard Times*. And behind the benign and selfless achievements of generations of clerical teachers lay the dark secret of sexual abuse of minors, in schools, orphanages and penal institutions run for the state by religious orders.

The traditional church was obsessed with sex and the sins of the flesh. These were, in a sense, the only real sins. The deep puritanism of the church was partly a further manifestation of an antique world in which Victorian values persisted long after they had been subverted elsewhere. But it was also a psychological prop in the whole post-Famine settlement. The need for marriages to be delayed until farms could be inherited; the wretched celibacy of many who had nothing to inherit and therefore nothing to offer a spouse; the extraordinary prestige in which celibate clergy were held: these were social inventions, designed to stabilize rural society in the post-Famine period. Irish society got the morality it needed. In this as in much else, church and people were one.

This unity of sentiment found many forms of expression. Few were more damaging to the country's international reputation than the ferocious literary censorship. It was put in place in 1929 and lasted until 1967. During that time nearly all contemporary Irish writers, as well as an impressive representation of modern masters, suffered at its hands. The original legislation had arisen from the report of a Committee on Evil Literature, a body whose very name suggested a begging of the question rather than an examination of it. Interestingly, the theatre was excluded from the Censorship Board's remit, so there was no institution in independent Ireland equivalent to the Lord Chamberlain in the UK. In this one particular, Ireland was formally more liberal than Britain. Even there, however, the censoring impulse was seldom absent: there were causes célèbres at regular intervals.

In 1926, in a re-run of *The Playboy of the Western World* riots of 1907, Sean O'Casey's *Plough and the Stars* caused a riot in the Abbey by offending nationalist pieties. The proximate cause of the riot was a moment in act two when the national tricolour flag is carried into a pub. This dishonouring of the flag prompted a well-rehearsed disturbance engineered by republican zealots, all of them cherishing the memory of the Easter Rising – during which the play is set – and embittered by their defeat in the Civil War, whose wounds were still fresh. The riot occurred on the fourth night of seven. The other six performances passed off without incident, and on the final night the audience gave both cast and author an ovation. On the night of the riot, however, Yeats had anticipated trouble and delivered to the *Irish Times* an advance copy of the speech with which he intended to berate the rioters. He duly gave the speech, not a word of which was heard above the tumult, but his crafty media management turned the episode into a moment of myth.

Following the rejection of his next play, *The Silver Tassie*, by the Abbey board, O'Casey left for England, never to return. He was a difficult man, but the stifling atmosphere of a country content with censorship and demanding placebos rather than challenges in the theatre was no incentive to stay. The Abbey entered a period of prolonged decline and mediocrity, despite the presence of talented individuals in its company. Its managing director from 1941 to 1967 was Ernest Blythe, who had been minister for finance in the 1920s and had famously cut the old-age pension in order to balance the new state's books. Blythe was narrow-minded and cocksure, and his period in office is generally held to have been an extended nadir in the theatre's fortunes.

It was one of the great ironies of the new state that the one artform for which Ireland had a genuinely international reputation – literature in English – should have suffered so grievously at the hands of the new establishment. Ireland had a very sparse inheritance in fine art, in architecture whether public or domestic (and much of that heritage, in the form of fine country houses, had been gleefully torched in the troubles), in public sculpture, in classical music (although rich in the folk tradition), in dance or in most of the higher arts. Its achievements in international scholarship were modest. But in literature, it had a world reputation and deserved it. At the foundation of the state, Yeats, Joyce, Shaw and O'Casey were all alive. Synge was not long dead. An Anglo-Irish tradition running back from Wilde to Farquhar and Congreve had been constantly renewed. Flann O'Brien, Patrick Kavanagh, Brendan Behan and other writers of international distinction would emerge in the bleak censorship years. Beckett was in

Paris. Louis MacNeice was in London. The astonishing productivity of Irish writers seemed endlessly self-renewing, yet their own country treated them as an enemy within. It was the ultimate revenge of the Abbey rioters on Yeats's idealism. The peasant republic was aesthetically challenged.

The securing of independence did nothing to staunch the flow of emigration. The population of Ireland had fallen in every decennial census since the Famine until the departure of the British from the twenty-six counties that became the Free State and later the Republic. The population remained almost static form 1926 to 1951, showing only a small decrease. However, that alone indicated that natural increase – in a country where large families were the norm – was insufficient to compensate for death and departure. The 1950s, however, brought a demographic collapse. It is estimated that over 400,000 Irish people emigrated between 1951 and 1961, this from a population of less than three million! This haemorrhage, combined with rates of infant mortality above the norm for the developed world and the scourge of tuberculosis among young people, offset the exceptionally high rate of marital fertility in the period. The Irish families who stayed or survived were very large by international standards, but not enough stayed or survived.

The 1950s brought the Republic firmly up against the reality that it had been pursuing an economic policy of protectionism and economic self-sufficiency that was leading it to disaster. At independence, Ireland had been modestly prosperous in comparison with most of north-west Europe and richer on any measure than many other new post-imperial nations in the old Habsburg lands, not to mention the Balkans or most of the Iberian peninsula. In one critical respect, it had an overwhelming comparative advantage: literacy levels stood at close to 100 per cent. The comparable figure in Poland was 70 per cent. Ireland was not rich, but it certainly was not poor. Yet within thirty years of independence, by the 1950s, the country was in crisis. In that decade, not only was there a terrifying rate of emigration, Ireland's economy grew at only one-fifth of the average rate for Western Europe. Between 1955 and 1957, the total volume of goods and services consumed in Ireland fell. All this happened in the middle of one of the biggest international capitalist booms in history.

Whatever case there had been for the establishment of a tariff regime in the 1930s – there had been an economic case made out, and Ireland was not the only young country then or since to try to build up its economy behind tariff barriers – there was none now. In fact, the economic case for protection had been a smoke screen. Behind it all lay an ideology, a conscious turning away from the world of vulgar modernity represented by the old imperial master: 'pagan England'. The astonishing deference shown to church leaders; the willing acceptance of censorship; the embracing of wartime neutrality; the GAA's ban on its players playing *or even attending* scheduled 'foreign games': all proceeded from a common sensibility. At its root was a determination to discover uniquely Irish answers, to insist on the autonomy of the Irish mind. It was a nice idea, but it had nothing to do with economic or sociological reality and it nearly wrecked the country.

25

LIBERALISM

It has been said of Sinn Féin and the other nationalists who had made the southern revolution of 1918–22 that they were the most conservative revolutionaries in history. It is hard to argue with this assessment. The overwhelming sense one has of the new Irish state from the 1920s to the 1950s was of an entrenched conservatism. This expressed itself in a number of ways. There was an insistent emphasis on the institutional stability of the state. The Westminster model of politics was not challenged: it simply migrated from the Thames to the Liffey. The new social and political establishment was economically sclerotic. The Irish economy was based on farming, and the farmers had had their real revolution in 1903, when Wyndham's Land Act had established them as proprietors on farms, many of which were not, and never would be, economically viable. The Irish economy was not so much un-dynamic as anti-dynamic. This induced a profound conservatism among property holders, both on the land itself and among their cousins who manned the civil service and provided the teachers, accountants and other minor professions. One historian has spoken of the triumph of the 'possessor principle' in this period: in a static economy, it pays to hold what you have. It pays to see economic and commercial activity as a zero-sum game, a form of beggar my neighbour. And so it was.

All this was compounded – indeed endorsed – by the Catholic Church in its hour of hubristic triumph. The same farmers, civil servants and teachers who were at the heart of the new nationalist consensus gave their sons and daughters to the church in extraordinary numbers. The Irish Catholic Church was still the ultramontane juggernaut that Paul Cullen had created in the nineteenth century, emphasizing obedience, deference and sexual Puritanism. Theologically, it was a non-event: the church was about control, not speculation. Nowhere was its control more marked than in education. The union of nationalism and Catholic control of education had a long history, going back to the deal struck by the bishops with Parnell in the 1880s. By the 1920s, the arrangement was formalized by the new state and the church effectively took control of the Irish education system. The schools were owned and managed by the clergy but financed, for the most part, out of taxation.

The education thus provided was overwhelmingly academic. Technical education was a discounted second best. The academic curriculum was a splendid vehicle for the preparation of priests, bureaucrats and self-reproducing pedagogues. Moreover, only primary education was free. Until 1968, secondary education had to be paid for, thus placing the working class at an enormous disadvantage. To be fair, some teaching orders – especially the Christian Brothers, as mentioned – had an honourable record of educating poorer boys. But the emphasis of the system was on social immobility. The possessor class held all the aces: its upper echelons went to relatively expensive 'private' schools and thereafter in smaller numbers to university, usually with the higher professions – medicine or law – in mind, or perhaps the management of such commercial activity as there was. The lower echelons went to less advantaged schools but nonetheless could complete the secondary cycle in the expectation of a respectable place in the lower middle class, as bank clerks and such like.

Two groups were specifically and of necessity excluded from this process of minimal mobility. First, the urban working class was effectively outside it altogether. Most were condemned to semi-skilled or unskilled work at best, unemployment or emigration at worst. Even the skilled tradesmen, the aristocracy of labour, dropped out of formal education in their teens in order to serve their time to their trade. Indeed, they often served their time to their fathers' trades, for the craft unions operated a very effective closed shop at entry: another intelligent deployment of the possessor principle. In all, the working class represented a kind of ghetto, self-sufficient in many respects but marginal in terms of the positive power it exerted. For the most part, it could wield only negative power through trades unions.

The second excluded group was the emigrants. Without emigration, the whole cosy stasis could not have succeeded for so long. Irish society never stopped deploring the evils of emigration while quietly profiting from its efficient function as a safety valve.

This petit bourgeois paradise was what ran up against the buffers in the late 1950s. In a sense, that was the last Victorian decade. Half a century after the death of the old queen, a vestige of the world she had left still subsisted – improbable as it might seem – in the poor republic to the west, once the closest part of her vast dominions. Economically and socially immobile, ostentatiously religious and mentally isolated, it was as if the first half of the twentieth century had happened somewhere else. Which, in fact, it had.

The changes that swept Ireland from the 1960s onwards need to be understood against this background. Turning the economy around was, in some ways, the easy bit. What was harder was the culture war. A new generation supplanted the ageing revolutionaries and gradually there began a movement to re-insert Ireland in to the wider world, while allowing international influences in through ever more open doors. In some ways, it was a profoundly unheroic ambition: that Ireland should aspire to be just like anywhere else.

This explains why the new 1960s middle class were much cooler nationalists than their predecessors and also why membership of what is now the European Union was probably the single project most tenaciously embraced by the 1960s elite. It also explains why so much of the change in Ireland since the 1960s has focused on cultural rather than economic issues. The old economy was a busted flush and the whole country could quickly see the product of the reforms put in place after 1958. But the culture that sustained the old consensus was more enduring and focused above all on religious issues, particularly in the areas of sexual morality.

The divorce and abortions referendums of the 1980s were a rancid low point in public discourse, with vicious rhetoric employed on both sides. Divorce was not approved by referendum until 1995 and then only by a margin of less than 1 per cent. Had the margin been so slim in support of retaining the ban on divorce, there would have been relentless pressure to put the question again. The fact that the losing side threw in the towel so tamely was a sure sign of the way the cultural wind was blowing.

By the 1990s the dam of clerical invincibility had already sprung a leak. Three years before the introduction of divorce, the bishop of Galway had been discovered to have fathered a child by an American divorcee. A few more priests – including one or two who were national media figures – were similarly discovered to be father in more senses than one. All this was faintly comic. What followed was not. Gradually, the full horror of the clerical sex abuse scandals began to emerge: the buggering and violating of minors by priests and brothers and the manner in which it was covered up by their superiors in the hierarchy. There is no doubt that these crimes were reported in some quarters with open glee: many in the media were post-1960s liberals who disliked the church (to put it no more strongly) and for them the hunt was now up. There was an unmistakeable air of 'we have the bastards now'. Yet have them they did, for there was no disguising or evading the truth.

The clerical abuse of minors had happened. It had not simply been a case of a few bad apples. It had been more widespread than anyone had imagined; it had been effectively tolerated and facilitated by a hierarchy more concerned for the integrity of the institutional church than for decency or justice. These crimes had been perpetrated by God's anointed, priests of a church that in sermons, pastorals and confessionals had always anathematized any form of sexual incontinence, even when relatively innocent. There was nothing innocent about this. It all amounted to the most complete betrayal of trust. The observant, trusting faithful were left disorientated and bemused. Mass attendance, declining since the 1960s, went into freefall. Vocations more or less ceased. The institution that had been the backbone of nationalist civil society since the 1820s, that had been at the apogee of its arrogant and self-assured power only a generation before, was subverted from within.

And as God exited left, Mammon entered right. The scandals of the 1990s coincided with the arrival of the Celtic Tiger. Ireland's baby boom had come late and a new generation born in the 1970s and early 1980s suddenly found themselves growing up in a country roaring ahead with money and expectation. This was a phenomenon without precedent in modern Ireland. In a few years, it seemed that the wholesale embrace of Anglo-American capitalism – complete with its individualist and consumerist assumptions – had effectively replaced the church as the locus of authority and longing.

We need to retrace the key steps in this generational journey.

De Valera was succeeded by Seán Lemass in 1959. He was the antithesis of de Valera. He had little charisma and projected the image of a competent technocrat. In fact, he had been the most energetic and intellectually daring of de Valera's ministers. He had put the tariff regime in place in the 1930s and had been its principal sponsor. But in the early 1950s, when it still retained iconic status, he was the first leading figure in Fianna Fáil to question its continuing utility.

As Taoiseach from 1959 to 1966, he presided over a startling reversal of policy and fortune. He adopted a plan drawn up by T. K. Whitaker, the secretary of the Department of Finance, which proposed the dismantling of tariff barriers and the introduction of inducements to draw in foreign capital in place of the obviously inadequate levels of domestic private investment. The plan developed into a government programme which mixed Keynesian economics, free trade and economic planning in a balance that was more pragmatic than intellectually coherent. However, it had two great merits. First, by pointing a way out of the mess the country was in, it lifted the sense of deep pessimism that had gripped the Republic in the 1950s. Second, it worked.

The economy grew by almost 20 per cent between 1958 and 1963. Exports grew 35 per cent by value. Although total employment did not increase in the 1960s, it changed its nature. Industrial employment increased to the point where it could absorb the rural surplus. Emigration practically stopped, for the first time since the Famine. The population, which had fallen at every census since the foundation of the state (except for one tiny and insignificant upward blip in 1951), increased successively in 1966 and 1971. By the latter date, it had recovered to the 1926 figure, thus reversing the haemorrhage of a generation.

The point about Irish economic growth in the 1960s is that it was no big deal by international standards. Ireland belatedly hitched a ride on the capitalist post-war boom. Success came from the intelligent application of conventional international wisdom to local circumstances. This habit of borrowing from abroad became increasingly commonplace in the 1960s: television, ecumenism, supermarkets – all made their entry in that decade. The one achievement that had the greatest effect on the future was the introduction of universal, free secondary schooling throughout the state in 1967.

There was a generational change, as the old revolutionaries retired and died. The new men were characterized by an energetic rejection of pessimism. Some in Fianna Fáil embraced a freebooting form of capitalism that had more than a whiff of third-world new money about it. These were the so-called 'men in the mohair suits'. Others were more deferential towards inherited pieties and correspondingly suspicious of rising stars like Charles Haughey, the most obviously able of the mohaired young Turks. A small but important liberal middle class formed which was influential in the media and the universities. Some of them, looking for a political home and failing to find it in the ripsnorting populism of the new Fianna Fáil, preferred the more genteel embrace of a Fine Gael that now found itself pulled between an international liberal wing and its old domestic reactionaries. A similar form of colonization gripped the Labour party, traditionally a trade union vehicle, which now found that it had some radical chic bourgeoisie aboard.

Institutional developments in the Republic reflected the continued influence of British precedents. This was unsurprising given the common language, the common currency and the penetration of British media, in books, newspapers, magazines, radio and television. It was no surprise, therefore, that when the Republic decided to establish its own television service, it looked instinctively to the British model. In 1959, when the Broadcasting Act that enabled the new service was passed, that meant an attempt to clone the BBC. In Britain itself, independent television was a recent novelty whereas the BBC had been in situ since the 1920s and had long since become part of the national mental furniture.

However, the means of financing the BBC was uniquely British, in that a flat tax was levied on all owners of television sets in the form of a licence fee. This meant that the corporation was not dependent on advertising, unlike most other stations around the world, and was thus insulated to a degree from the insistent vulgarities of commerce. The BBC became a model of liberal high-mindedness. In a brilliant phrase, the writer Michael Frayn identified such people as tended to rise to the top of the BBC as 'herbivores', slightly guilty at their own eminence but determined to bring high culture to the masses. Thus they were distinguished from the carnivores, hard-headed, flinty realists more inclined to give the market what it wanted than what was good for it.

Telefís Éireann, the Irish television service (now Raidió Telefís Éireann, RTE) started broadcasting in 1961. It was the creation of Irish herbivores, most especially of Leon Ó Broin, the secretary of the Department of Posts and Telegraphs (the department sponsoring the enabling legislation). He was a man of wide cultural formation, a historian of distinction, a sponsor of the arts – especially music – and an early ecumen-ist. He was one who found the BBC model admirable in its top-down impetus. This ensured that the new Irish station would also be based on a licence fee although in a poor coun-try – as the Republic still was in the early 1960s – it was unrealistic to expect the licence fee to bear the full financial burden, so RTE took advertising from the start. It was there-fore something of a hybrid.

The element of top-down control was a comfort to the political elite as well. The Lemass government made no bones about its view that RTE should be an arm of the state, although the Taoiseach himself was almost blasé in his easy acceptance of the new medium. He saw its potential for the importation of new ideas and new fashions from abroad and was generally unconcerned about this. In contrast, the spokesmen of the older Ireland were much more apprehensive. On opening night, de Valera, now president of the Republic, inaugurated the new station with these words: 'I must admit that sometimes when I think of television and radio and their immense power, I feel somewhat afraid.' His concerns were echoed by the primate of All Ireland, Cardinal John D'Alton.

The arrival of television had the inevitable effect of increas-ing the country's openness to outside influences. While this caused an understandable angst among nationalist intellectuals who deplored the dilution of those aspects of Irish culture that were unique, it also inculcated the habit of looking abroad for comparative analyses of Irish performance. Nowhere did this have a more beneficial effect than in education. A Council of Education (comprising thirty-one members, most of them from within the existing system and only two of whom had science degrees) reported on the secondary system in 1962. They solemnly intoned that 'the principal objective of education . . . was the religious, moral and cultural development of the child'. However, another body had also been enabled to examine the Irish education system, established under the joint auspices of the government and the Organization for Economic Co-operation and Development, another example of the reflexive glance to overseas comparisons. It comprised a mere three people and its 1965 report, *Investment in Education*, is arguably one of the most important documents in the history of the southern state.

Investment in Education regarded the education system as the key driver of economic cohesion and growth, something that might be thought of as commonplace now but which was revolutionary in its day. It advocated the extension of secondary education to all regardless of means. It analysed a system that was both unequal and dysfunctional. In the primary schools in 1962–3, only 28 per cent had passed the state certificate examination that completed the primary cycle. In the secondary system, fewer than 10 per cent of pupils took any science subject. More than 25 per cent of pupils in the secondary system completed fewer than three of the six-year cycle.

Reforms were already in train in the system from the mid 1960s, but the capstone was the introduction of so-called 'free education' by the maverick minister, Donogh O'Malley, in 1967. This meant a state-funded universal system of secondary education, together with a school transport infrastructure in support of it. Surprisingly the church, traditionally suspicious to the point of hysteria of state control of education, raised few objections. This was an interesting straw in the wind: times were changing. Free education has been correctly thought of as one of the Republic's great leaps forward, a measure beyond the wildest hopes of reformers until it was announced. There is every reason to believe that Lemass put O'Malley up to it while leaving the Department of Finance in the dark. Of course, once the announcement had been made, there was no abandoning the course of action.

Other outside influences made themselves felt. Tourism boomed, bringing with it the need for better restaurants (or *any* restaurants in some places) and a growing sophistication in matters of food and wine. Air travel increased, although modestly by the standards of later decades. The country's application to join the European Economic Community (now the EU) made people aware of the wider continent beyond Britain. The application was not successful until 1972, but joining Europe was a seminal moment and one that was a high-water mark for the new bourgeois elite.

There were great set pieces: John F. Kennedy visited in 1963, just months before his assassination, to embody the material achievements of the post-Famine diaspora. The golden anniversary of the 1916 rising was celebrated with due ceremony. But that anniversary also reintroduced the serpent in the Irish garden: sectarian murder in the north. It was also the fiftieth anniversary of the battle of the Somme, at which the UVF (otherwise the 36th Ulster Division) had suffered appalling casualties. This conjunction of anniversaries across the communal divide resulted in the re-formation of the UVF and the murder of two Catholic men and an elderly Protestant woman (burned to death in her own home in error).

Yet, at the time, this seemed to contemporaries a tragic renewal of the past rather than a pointer to the future. When Brookeborough had stood down in 1963, he had been succeeded by Captain Terence O'Neill, a big-house old Etonian. His more talented rival Brian Faulkner had the misfortune to be middle class rather than landed. Such distinctions still mattered in the antique world of Ulster unionism. O'Neill set a new tone, not quite of liberalism, but at least of cautious accommodation.

The most dramatic initiative of O'Neill's premiership came in 1965, when he invited Lemass to visit Belfast. Lemass had been markedly more conciliatory than de Valera on the partition issue: in keeping with his character, he regarded it as a problem to be resolved rather than a fundamental moral issue. He accepted O'Neill's invitation. The two men met in Belfast in January 1965, with O'Neill reciprocating the following month. Other ministers followed. A north-south tourism committee was established and other cautious forms of cross-border cooperation were explored.

O'Neill was never fully in control of his party or of his people. In the Unionist party, Faulkner resented the manner in which the leadership had been denied him; others on the right objected to any softening of rhetoric towards Catholics and north-south contacts generally. Outside the party, the unionist ultras found a voice in the Revd Ian Paisley, a dissident Presbyterian ranter. O'Neill sounded pretty pallid compared to the ultra-charismatic Paisley.

Still, the explosion in Northern Ireland, when it came, took nearly everyone, north and south, by surprise. It brought a grim close to a decade of hope.

26

TROUBLES

In January 1967, the Northern Ireland Civil Rights Association (NICRA) was formed. Its purpose was to fight discrimination on the grounds of equal citizenship. Implicitly, it accepted the position of Northern Ireland within the United Kingdom. The bogey of partition was thrust aside for the moment. The demand was for equal citizenship for all in the UK. This is not to deny that there were many republicans in the NICRA, happy to use it as a front: any lever would do to challenge unionist hegemony.

On 5 October 1968, the NICRA called a protest march in Derry. The Belfast administration, in the person of the minister of home affairs, banned it. NICRA defied the ban. The RUC batoned the marchers off the streets. But unlike the old days, there were television cameras present. The pictures went round the world. This fetid little corner of the United Kingdom was about to become world news.

Terence O'Neill called an election to get a new mandate but won only a pyrrhic victory and resigned in April 1969. His successor was another plummy big-house gent, Major James Chichester-Clark, a nonentity. By the summer, Northern Ireland was ablaze. Months of civil disturbance followed the NICRA march, culminating in wholesale sectarian battles in Derry and Belfast in August. The residents of the Catholic

Bogside ghetto in Derry fought the RUC to a standstill over three days. In Belfast, thousands of Catholics and some Protestants were burned out of their homes. Lemass's successor as Taoiseach, Jack Lynch, made a famously ambiguous television speech which might or might not have been a threat to intervene. In the end, it was the British army that intervened, sent in by a bemused and unwilling London government to keep the sides apart.

When the civil disturbances of 1969 reduced Northern Ireland to anarchy, the words 'IRA: I Ran Away' appeared on gable walls. The IRA had swung to the left in the 1960s, following the failure of the 1956–62 campaign and had come under the influence of a Dublin-based socialist leadership. There was a consequent emphasis on social action and lack of emphasis on traditional republican concerns. This proved costly when working-class Catholic ghettos came under attack from loyalist mobs, often aided and abetted by the police and B Specials. The movement split. The left-wingers formed the Official IRA and the more traditional – and it must be said more practical – elements became the Provisional IRA. The Provos concentrated on community defence in the first instance – to purge the 'I Ran Away' smear – and then moved on to a resumption of the 1920–22 civil war and an attempt to shoot and bomb the British out of Ireland altogether. The Fenian tradition had shrunk to the working-class ghettos of nationalist Northern Ireland, but was still alive and kicking.

Following 1969, and only under direct pressure from London, the RUC began a rolling series of reforms that, no matter what they did, would never convince nationalists that they were anything other than a sectarian arm of the state. The B Specials were abolished. The local government franchise was reformed to end the sort of gerrymandering that obtained in Derry. It was too little too late. The Provos were set on their unwinnable war with the British, which they pursued for the best part of thirty years. They did enough, however, to ensure that the British could not defeat *them*.

On the Protestant side, any pretence of political unity had evaporated under the pressures of the early troubles. The old Unionist party had been an umbrella group, sheltering Protestants in a nervous coalition against the common sectarian enemy. But it had always been fragile. It was open to attack from the left in the form of the Northern Ireland Labour Party and from the right by loyalist ultras. The former had rattled the Unionist cage occasionally in times of peace but ceased to be of any account in times of crisis. The loyalists were quite another matter.

Working-class Protestants had always harboured a sense of resentment against the so-called 'fur-coat brigade', the aristocratic elite who dominated the upper reaches of the Unionist party. O'Neill and Chichester-Clark were models of the type: English-accented, educated at Eton and generally children of privilege. In English terms, they would have been traditional patrician Tories. But a great number of their party supporters would, in English terms, be Labour. The working-class loyalists found their voice in the Revd Ian Paisley, moderator of the Free Presbyterian Church (which he had established in 1951, finding the mainstream Presbyterians insufficiently hostile to Rome). In addition to the urban working class, Paisley's other principal appeal was to rural Protestant religious fundamentalists.

Paisley was an orator of spellbinding power, beside whom most of the other dramatis personae in Northern Ireland – most obviously O'Neill and Chichester-Clark – seemed and were distinctly uninspiring. He shattered Unionist Party unity, first challenging and nearly defeating Terence O'Neill in his own constituency and then taking the seat when O'Neill stood down from active politics. He founded and led the Democratic Unionist Party (DUP) in 1971. For most of the troubles, it was a minority within unionism (but a significant one) although it was to emerge on top of the heap when peace was eventually restored. In this, its fortunes mirrored those of Sinn Féin on the nationalist side. Paisley set his face against any and all concessions to nationalism, preached an incendiary sectarianism as lurid as anything in Ulster history and was the focal point for the unionist right. He was never respectable and he was never ignored.

He always denied any involvement with illegal loyalist paramilitary groups such as the Ulster Defence Association (UDA) and Ulster Volunteer Force (UVF), which were between them responsible for some of the most disgusting acts of violence in an age of violence. Nonetheless, suspicions persisted: Paisley's rhetoric was not of a kind to suggest restraint in confronting the enemy. Unlike the IRA, which could claim political cover for its murders, the loyalist paramilitaries were nakedly sectarian at times. Rogue groups like the notorious 'Shankill Butchers' displayed a psychopathic enjoyment of violence for its own sake, provided it was visited on innocent members of the other community.

The early troubles were enough to secure the resignation of Chichester-Clark and the elevation of Brian Faulkner. He was decidedly not of the fur-coat brigade. A middle-class businessman, he had had a long career in the Unionist party, displaying a mixture of ability and opportunism that impressed students of public life. He was a cut above the prevailing mediocrity in the party, and not always loved for that. Nor was he any kind of liberal. Faulkner had been minister of home affairs during the 1956–62 campaign and reckoned he knew how to deal with the IRA. In August 1971, he introduced internment – imprisonment without trial. It was a botched job, based in part on faulty and out-of-date security information. But even if it had been a perfect operation, it would have remained a disastrous error of judgement. Northern Ireland had moved on a lot in fifteen years and the nationalist community was no longer in a mood meekly to accept extra-legal bullying. Internment massively increased nationalist alienation from the state. Correspondingly, support for the Provos increased dramatically and their operational capacity remained undiminished.

The following year, 1972, was the most violent of the troubles, with 470 deaths, over 10,000 shooting incidents and almost 2,000 bomb explosions. In the same year, London closed the Belfast parliament and imposed direct rule. This followed what was perhaps the single most shocking event of the entire thirty-odd years (although there would be much dismal competition for that award): Bloody Sunday.

On 30 January, a civil rights march in Derry was attended by 10,000 people. The Parachute Regiment of the British Army, a force specifically trained to be deployed in situations where shooting first and asking questions later was the order of the day, was acting in support of the police. Of all the regiments in the army, they were probably the least appropriate to deploy in a tense law-and-order situation. In the almost inevitable confrontation between some demonstrators and the law, the last thing needed was the employment of lethal force. Yet that was exactly what the Paras delivered on Bloody Sunday. They shot dead thirteen unarmed men. A fourteenth died later.

The British government set up an inquiry under Lord Widgery, a high court judge, who produced a report that was recognized from the very start as a mendacious whitewash. It took years, and another enormously costly and time-consuming report from Lord Saville, to finally exonerate those dead marchers who had been accused by Widgery of carrying arms. Only with the publication of the Saville Report in 2009 did the deceased get posthumous justice. The Paras had killed fourteen unarmed civilians in what was nominally a British city.

Bloody Sunday represented a point of no return. It was a recruiting call for the Provisional IRA. The Irish ambassador was recalled from London and the British embassy in Dublin was burned to the ground. It was the symbolic moment when the demand for civil rights mutated into a radical quickening of nationalist aspirations.

The IRA's response to Bloody Sunday in Derry was Bloody Friday in Belfast. On 21 July 1972, it exploded twenty-six bombs at various locations in the city centre, killing 11 people and injuring 130. In retaliation, the Shankill Butchers made their first appearance later that day, abducting a wholly innocent Catholic whom they beat and stabbed to a pulp before dumping his body on open ground. Ten days later, three car bombs in Claudy, Co. Derry, killed eight people: the perpetrators were never identified, but were almost certainly a rogue republican unit. Two weeks after that, an IRA bomb at a border customs post killed the three men who planted it and six others. The British army mounted its biggest operation since Suez, codenamed Motorman, to break up no-go areas in nationalist parts of Belfast and Derry, causing havoc and destruction as they did so. So the province sank into barbarism, with one side answering the other in kind.

The Provisional IRA represented the nationalist extreme. The mainstream was represented by the Social Democratic and Labour Party (SDLP) whose principal theoretician was John Hume from Derry. He preached a reconciliation of the two traditions through negotiation and movement towards an agreed future for both parts of Ireland. The SDLP was totally opposed to the violence of the IRA, not to mention the reciprocated assaults from loyalist paramilitaries.

In 1974, the British and Irish governments and the main Northern Ireland parties – but not Sinn Féin or the DUP – reached a deal at Sunningdale, near London, for a power-sharing, devolved government in Belfast. It also proposed a Council of Ireland, which was included at Dublin's insistence and over Faulkner's objections. He feared, quite correctly, that it would be viewed by unionists as a vehicle to begin the journey towards Irish unity. Unionists might just have taken power-sharing – although even that is doubtful in the circumstances of the mid-1970s – but they were never going to swallow this.

The Executive was duly set up and lasted a mere five months. A British general election showed Faulkner's party to be badly split on power-sharing, with anti-Faulkner candidates doing best. Any legitimacy the Executive had in unionist eyes now evaporated. It was finally brought down by a loyalist general strike a few months later. This was the point at which the unionist establishment looked the other way while loyalist vigilante thugs took control of the streets. Nor was Harold Wilson's government in London any better: it shrugged its shoulders impotently in a manner unthinkable had a similar insurrection occurred on the mainland. London's writ ran but imperfectly in this part of the United Kingdom. With the success of the loyalist strike, the last hope of a political solution to the troubles receded for a generation.

Thereafter, the troubles rumbled on from one atrocity and ambush to another, with dirty tricks on both sides. The deaths of ten republican hunger strikers in 1981 probably represented a psychological low point, although it also alerted the more intelligent people in the IRA and Sinn Féin that while the war could not be lost it could not be won either. Hunger strike candidates won by-elections and demonstrated the potential for political action. It took the best part of twenty years for this potential to transmute into practical politics. The republican movement was steeped in a culture of violence and would require much subtle persuasion to wean it off the gun. There were practical problems, of which the question of paramilitary prisoners was the most pressing (this consideration also affected loyalist groups). In the meantime, the troubles consumed 3,000 lives. The Provos' war – it was theirs, no one else's: they started it and when they stopped, the troubles stopped – grew out of the intolerable sectarian discrimination of the old unionist regime. But it soon acquired an ideological life of its own that went way beyond communal defence.

The most important political development of those years was the Anglo-Irish Agreement of 1985, signed by Margaret Thatcher for the UK and Garret FitzGerald for the Republic. It marked the beginning of a genuine rapprochement between Dublin and London and increased cooperation between the two governments. Crucially, it set up a joint ministerial conference supported by a permanent secretariat in Belfast. It stopped short of joint authority but gave Dublin a voice in the governance of Northern Ireland for the first time. Although it led to predictable unionist rage at a deal done over their heads, it created the conditions that made the peace process of the late 1990s possible. It also recognized the simple reality that more than one-third of the population of Northern Ireland had no loyalty to the state and had no reason to have any such loyalty.

As early as 1988, John Hume, the leader of the SDLP, and Gerry Adams, president of Sinn Féin, began a series of exploratory talks to see if a pan-nationalist consensus could be reached in Northern Ireland. The SDLP was the dominant group electorally: they out-polled Sinn Féin roughly two to one among nationalist voters. They were famously well-connected in Dublin, Washington and Brussels. It is worth recalling that, all through the troubles, a large majority of nationalists consistently denied electoral support to the polit-ical arm of the IRA. The talks were inconclusive at first but were resumed in 1993. They resulted in a document that Hume presented to the Dublin government of Albert Reynolds – Haughey's successor – who thought it sufficiently interesting to begin an initiative jointly with the British prime minister, John Major. This led to the Downing Street declara-tion of December 1993. A document of great subtlety, its essential importance lay in a British acknowledgement that the Irish people were entitled to a self-determination of their own future, thus diluting the claim to absolute sovereignty. The Irish government, for its part, conceded that any steps towards Irish unity could only be taken with the support of a majority in Northern Ireland, thus compromising the territo-rial claim in the 1937 constitution.

The declaration could not have happened without the Hume-Adams talks or, even more importantly, without the regular Dublin–London contacts now long established by the Anglo-Irish Agreement of 1985. It led to the IRA ceasefire of August 1994 which lasted until February 1996. The republican drift from violence to politics was painful: Adams demonstrated political skill of the highest order in facilitating the change without splitting the movement.

The drift towards peace eventually produced the Belfast Agreement of 1998, in which all parties – except the Paisleyite DUP but including representatives of Sinn Féin and the two principal loyalist paramilitary groups – reached a nervous accommodation. The bones of the deal were as follows: the union with the UK would remain as long as a majority in Northern Ireland desired it; in return, there would be a devolved power-sharing executive and cross-border institutions to cooperate on matters of mutual concern; paramilitary violence of all sorts was to end; early release of paramilitary prisoners would be a priority.

Seamus Mallon, deputy leader of the SDLP, famously called it 'Sunningdale for slow learners'. Like Sunningdale, it was overwhelmingly endorsed by nationalists while dividing unionist opinion. It required the endorsement of both communities in Northern Ireland and of the electorate in the Republic. Nationalists on either side of the border did so readily. Ulster unionists showed no such certainty, many of them dismayed by what they regarded as rewarding IRA terrorism. Only a frantic campaign, involving British Prime Minister Tony Blair, American President Bill Clinton and even Nelson Mandela, produced a wafer-thin unionist consent.

In a formal sense, the troubles are over. But the intercommunal hatred that divides Protestant and Catholic in Northern Ireland persists. The province is as much a voluntary apartheid society as ever: different housing areas, different schools, different sports, different loyalties. Low-level sectarianism continues unabated, occasionally erupting virulently. Ceasefires or no, paramilitaries still control the ghettos and engage in beatings and knee-cappings of those who incur their displeasure. The distinction between political paramilitarism and gangsterism is not always clear: much of Northern Ireland's black economy and drugs trade flourishes on the ambiguity.

As late as December 2004, the IRA were able to pull off the biggest bank robbery in post-war Europe while ostensibly engaged in negotiations – via their Sinn Féin surrogates – towards a new political rapprochement with the unionists!

The Belfast Agreement remained the formal political anchor point, but in reality it was a dead letter less than a decade after it was signed. It worked in a hesitant manner for a few years: a power-sharing executive was formed with David Trimble of the Ulster Unionist Party (UUP) as first minister and Seamus Mallon of the SDLP as his deputy. It contained two Sinn Féin ministers. Paisley's DUP was not represented, since they rejected the entire process. It was bedevilled with tensions and distrust from the beginning, mainly focusing on the reluctance of the IRA to decommission their weapons, as they were obliged to do under the terms of the Belfast Agreement. Sinn Féin answered Unionist charges of bad faith on decommissioning by calling loudly for police reform.

The whole rickety arrangement collapsed finally in 2005. The British general election of that year saw Paisley's DUP sweep the boards on the unionist side, while Sinn Féin outpaced the SDLP on the nationalist side. Thus the extremes in both communities were now in command. More seriously, Paisley's triumph – and the virtual annihilation of the mainstream UUP – marked the effective withdrawal of Protestant consent to the Belfast Agreement. That consent had been hesitant and feeble in any case. The perception among Protestants that all the concessions had been made to the other side, with little received in return, was enough to elevate Paisley to the leadership of unionism for the first time ever. At least the decommissioning issue was more or less laid to rest in 2005, when the IRA finally – if belatedly – destroyed enough of their arsenal to satisfy international observers.

And then, in the most astonishing development of all, came the St Andrew's Agreement of 2006 which resulted in Paisley and Sinn Féin agreeing to share power in a new devolved system of government. The moderate parties on both sides were bypassed and the implacable enemies joined hands. The system has worked thus far after a fashion. There is still internal opposition to the deal on both sides of the divide and dissident republicans maintain a constant paramilitary threat. Northern Ireland has been trumpeted as a lesson to the world in conflict resolution. It is not: every conflict is different. But it is sufficient to know that after all the turmoil and hatred in the history of modern Ulster, it is not the moderates who have redeemed the province but the extremists coming in from the cold. There is hope for the future.

27

ASPIRATION

The Republic joined the European Economic Community (now the EU) in 1972. It was the culmination of a decade of effort and preparation. The European project appealed principally to three groups: those who supported the new free-trade economics that had lifted the Republic's economy; the liberal intelligentsia; and, crucially, the farmers. This group was unconcerned about European idealism or Ireland emerging from behind the British shadow; they were, however, hugely attracted by the Common Agricultural Policy, which contrasted with Britain's cheap food policy and guaranteed high prices to producers.

Europe appealed to cool nationalists like Garret FitzGerald, soon to be foreign minister. Hot nationalists – such as Charles Haughey and hardline Donegal republican Neil Blaney, who Jack Lynch had sidelined in 1970 because of their apparent collusion in supplying arms to northern Nationalists – were generally opposed, hankering for the old simplicities of Sinn Féin's policy of self-sufficiency. The new generation of self-styled socialists in the Labour Party affected to oppose Europe on the grounds that it was a vast capitalist conspiracy. On examination, such people turned out over time to be bourgeois liberals all along: most revealed their genuine enthusiasm for the EU in due course. Real socialists and ultra nationalists

– each out on the far margins of Irish political life – continued to be the mainstay of anti-European feeling in Ireland until the development of the Green movement in the 1990s.

Membership of the EU has hugely enriched the Republic of Ireland. Farmers, most obviously, have profited from the grotesquely wasteful Common Agricultural Policy. EU social funds have been generously disbursed to bring the country's social infrastructure up towards continental standards and to aid hitherto neglected regions. Industrial exports found new markets. Inward investment, especially from the United States, expanded, as Ireland provided an anglophone access to European markets. The country's traditional dependence on Britain lessened to the point that Ireland entered the European Monetary System in 1979 although Britain stayed out. It meant breaking the link with sterling that had existed since 1826 (the currency union had survived independence) and reinstating an independent Irish currency. It lasted until the launch of the euro in 2002.

Entry into Europe was, in one sense, an admission of failure. The full aspiration of nationalism – for self-sufficiency and economic autonomy – had faltered. The nationalist adventure that began with O'Connell had either run out of steam or succeeded all too well, depending on how you read it. Going into Europe was abandoning the full nationalist impulse for a kind of benign imperialism. It certainly meant compromising sovereignty, although how much meaning that term has for a small, free-trading, open economy in a globalized world is open to question. It also reconnected Ireland to continental Europe in a manner not seen since the eighteenth century.

The Republic mismanaged the economic legacy of the 1960s in the following decades. It was unlucky in that the world economy turned down following the oil crises of 1973 and 1979, but successive governments compounded their ill-luck by gross economic mismanagement. Charles Haughey staged a spectacular comeback to seize the leadership of Fianna Fáil and the office of Taoiseach in 1979, promising to clean things up.

He only made them worse. Garret FitzGerald, by now leader of Fine Gael, produced his party's best-ever election performance in 1982 which allowed him to form a secure coalition with Labour. They began the job of rescuing the economy but were ideological opposites: as a result, their efforts were well-meaning but incoherent. The process had to await Haughey's return in 1987. Alan Dukes, the new Fine Gael leader in succession to the now retired FitzGerald, adopted the so-called 'Tallaght Strategy' – named after the Dublin suburb where the speech announcing it was made – in which he pledged opposition support for the corrective government measures. It was courageous and patriotic: neither Dukes nor his party got any thanks from the government or electorate.

Gradually, the recovery policies worked, helped by the need to prepare the Irish economy for entry into the single European currency. Strict EU conditions had to be met. By the mid-1990s, Ireland had taken advantage of its geographical and linguistic position to become an offshore powerhouse of the American technology boom. It was this, more than anything, that underwrote the stunning economic success story of the Celtic Tiger in the years 1995 to 2001. More dubiously, government policy also established the country as a tax haven, with a rate of corporation tax well below that of other EU states or of the United States itself. This enabled overseas companies, the least desirable of them little more than 'brass plate' operations, to avoid domestic taxes by declaring their profits in Ireland. This understandably caused resentment abroad, although no voice could be found to criticize it in Ireland.

By the turn of the new century, a series of public enquiries had revealed a systematic maze of planning corruption and tax evasion among many prominent citizens from the 1960s generation. Haughey himself was the most notable malefactor to be outed: he had lived for years like a prince on money donated by wealthy friends. And as we saw the Catholic Church fell spectacularly from grace, hoist with its own petard: sex.

* * *

As the two sides within Northern Ireland continue their historic stand-off, the two parts of the island are moving farther apart than ever. The southern economy finally roared into life in the 1990s, with the Republic achieving spectacular rates of economic growth. From 1991 to 2003, the average annual growth rate was almost 7 per cent, peaking at a vertiginous 11 per cent in 1999. After a brief hiccup in 2002 and 2003, the boom appeared to return from 2004.

What caused this transformation in a country previously known for economic under-achievement? In one sense, this way of posing the question suggests part of the answer. The Republic was coming from farther back than it should have been: there was simply more ground to be made up and therefore more scope for growth. The eventual rectification of the national finances after the profligate 1970s and 1980s was an essential precondition. The low level of corporation tax gave the country a key competitive advantage for the attraction of inward investment, which was most visible in the IT sector. A well-educated young anglophone population also helped. So did a policy of social partnership, in which government, employers and trades unions negotiated centralized multi-annual agreements, thus making Ireland one of the most stable labour environments in the world. Until the early years of the new century the cost of employing labour was significantly lower than in most other EU countries, although such costs began to run out of control from about 2002 and were not checked by the sleepy, complacent Fianna Fáil governments of Taoiseach Bertie Ahern. A policy of low personal taxation moved the country decisively towards the American model of capitalism.

As with the United States, the price paid for all this was increasing inequality: those left behind in the boom are farther back than ever, and this has contributed to an underlying sense of unease. And certain areas are still chronically problematic, notably the health and transport systems.

Nonetheless, it is hard to argue for long with a process that reduced unemployment from 18 per cent when Charles Haughey was Taoiseach in the 1980s to 4 per cent in Bertie Ahern's Ireland of the new century. The consequences were spectacular. The country was visibly richer. Car ownership – a key indicator of consumer buoyancy – doubled from 1980 to 2005. There was a spectacular boom in house prices, which grew to ten times their early 1990s values at a time when inflation was low. This made millions of Irish people asset rich in a manner beyond their dreams. Interest rates stayed low, facilitating easy credit – too easy, some said. Entry to the European single currency, the euro, in 2002, opened a treasure chest of credit.

A country that half a century before was haemorrhaging emigrants became a magnet for immigrants. These were not just the Irish abroad coming home to a better country, as was the case with the net immigration of the late 1960s and early 1970s. People flocked into Ireland to work in the course of the boom. Immigrants voted with their feet: their presence was the greatest vote of confidence a country could have. There were over 100,000 Poles in Ireland in 2006, for example, and their numbers were being augmented by a regular bus service from Warsaw to Dublin. The capital's evening newspaper, the *Evening Herald*, had a weekly thirty-two page section in Polish. It became commonplace, no longer worth remarking on, to be served by an immigrant in a pub, restaurant or hotel. No one turned a hair at the sound of a foreign language. The building boom that gripped twenty-first century Ireland would not have been possible without skilled and semi-skilled immigrant labour.

One company more than any other symbolized the sheer swagger of Celtic Tiger Ireland. In 1990, Ryanair was five years old and had accumulated losses of £20 million. As early as 2005, it was already established as the biggest low-fares airline in Europe, where it has completely revolutionized air travel. In 1991, it crept into profit and carried 650,000 passengers. In 2009, it carried 66.5 million passengers on 940 routes and posted a profit of €318 million. At €5.3 billion, it had the largest market capitalization of any airline in Europe. It is one of the most recognized online brands in the world. It has done this in the teeth of official discouragement – neither governments nor national flag-carrying airlines were exactly supportive – and by copying a business model first developed in the United States. Once again, the Celtic Tiger drew its influence from across the Atlantic at a time when tensions between Europe and the United States had seldom been stronger. Indeed, weakening support for the EU in Ireland – a 1998 referendum on an EU treaty was actually lost in Ireland, something hitherto unthinkable – almost certainly reflects the headlong embrace of American cultural and economic values.

Ryanair, not always loved for its noise and aggression, but hugely successful, was at least the real deal. The building mania, and the property bubble that developed from 2002 onwards, was not. It was real only in the sense of being a classic bubble and, like all such bubbles in history, its bursting caused immense hardship. It had been a case of unrestrained irrational exuberance. Banks competed with each other in a race to the bottom, providing vast amounts of credit for speculative construction projects. It was fine until the markets crashed in the autumn of 2008, whereupon the banks discovered that they were insolvent. It took them forever to admit it and they repeatedly lied – whether out of badness or denial – to the government, which bailed them out by guaranteeing all bank Irish deposits. The state thus exposed itself to potential liabilities which, if all were called in, would provoke a sovereign default.

It was a sorry end to an era of genuine hope, one of the few that a traditionally poor country had ever been able to enjoy for long. Economists reassured the public that while the property boom would not last forever there would be a 'soft landing'. There were legions of economists in the country, many of them compromised by their employment in lending institutions (not that that ever stopped them from repeating the party line) and not enough economic historians. The few Cassandras among the latter, who had actually studied property booms in other countries and analysed the pattern of the subsequent busts, predicted disaster. No one wanted to hear. Young people were urged to 'get on the property ladder', as if that were the only proof of personal virtue, and those that bought in late soon discovered that their 'asset' was now worth less than they had borrowed to purchase it in the first place.

The governments of Bertie Ahern, himself an adept at playing the regular guy next door, was asleep on the job and let all this madness rip. The ideology of light regulation carried all before it. Any suggestion that the Financial Regulator should apply himself in a muscular manner to restrain the excesses of the banks was regarded as heresy. Indeed, the most reckless of the bankers, Sean Fitzpatrick, the chief executive of Anglo-Irish Bank (which turned out to be utterly toxic when the crash came and collapsed in the biggest corporate failure in Irish history), made a particularly brazen speech in 2005 deploring the manner in which poor entrepreneurs like him were put upon by a culture of oppressive regulation, thus stifling the spirit of enterprise. This was not just untrue: it was the polar opposite of the truth.

Ahern and Fianna Fáil were extremely close to the bankers and the developers. Indeed, Fianna Fáil had enjoyed a symbiotic relationship with the construction industry since the 1960s. They were not going to do anything to stop the party. For this dereliction of duty, they were rewarded by a grateful electorate which returned them to power in three successive general elections. Happily for Ahern, he was extruded from office just before the roof fell in and he went off to enjoy a lucrative retirement. So at least it all worked well for him. But his party reaped the whirlwind in the 2011 General Election. Fianna Fáil, which had utterly dominated Irish politics since 1932, was reduced to a rump, falling from 78 TDs to a mere 20.

In 2011, Ireland is a richer country than it was in 1990. Not everything has been lost but much of the gross gain has been squandered. For young people, the immediate future is bleak and emigration has resumed. Any recovery will take some years. Economic sovereignty has, for the moment, been devolved to the European Commission and the International Monetary Fund without whom the country would have been unable to meet its obligations to its bondholders on the international money markets. Ireland's woes thus became part of a bigger game: the need to protect the integrity of the euro and to ensure that no country in membership should suffer a sovereign default.

On Saturday 26 February 2007, Ireland played England in a rugby international. The normal Dublin venue for rugby, Lansdowne Road, was under reconstruction and so the game was played on the other side of the city at Croke Park, the headquarters of the Gaelic Athletic Association. The GAA had conducted an impassioned internal debate before allowing its ground to be used for what for many years it had anathematized as one of the foreign games which its members were forbidden to play. That proscription had been removed in 1971, but there was another, more potent, historical reason for them to hesitate. In allowing rugby to come to Croke Park during the reconstruction of Lansdowne Road, they knew that the ordinary rhythm of the international programme would bring the English team to their stadium.

In that same stadium on a Sunday afternoon in 1920, British troops had burst in during a football match between Dublin and Tipperary. They were bent on vengeance for the murders of British agents that morning at various locations in the city at the hands of Michael Collins's 'squad'. Twelve people died when they opened fire, including the Tipperary goalkeeper Michael Hogan. The principal stand on the west side of the ground was subsequently named for him.

So Croke Park was not just sacred soil for the GAA, it was a place where a particularly vicious British atrocity was perpetrated on innocent Irish people. The GAA was nothing if not nationalist and even after the passage of the years, the thought of an English team in the stadium offended many. But the further thought that, in the normal way of these international matches, 'God Save the Queen' would be sung there at the start of proceedings was what really galvanized opposition. Nonetheless, the event went ahead.

The British national anthem is mercifully short. It was listened to with the utmost respect and without a note of protest. It was a moment of release. Everyone who was there or who watched it on television knew the symbolism of the thing. It made most Irish people immensely proud that what had happened was so *normal*, just the ordinary courtesy that one would show to a guest. After all the ups and downs of the Anglo-Irish story, that seemed good enough for the moment. (And in the game itself, Ireland stuffed them!)

It also was a reminder for Irish people of what they can accomplish at their best. The immediate future is unpromising. The country is awash with pessimism and a sense of opportunity squandered. That in itself can be debilitating. But the memory of that Saturday afternoon should linger. People who can put that much bad history behind them can do anything to which they aspire.

BIBLIOGRAPHICAL ESSAY

General Surveys

Thomas Bartlett's *Ireland: A History* (Cambridge 2010) is the most recent complete overview. Unlike the present work, it ignores the prehistoric past, beginning with the first written documents in the fifth century CE. It is, therefore, a history in the truest sense of the term, eschewing speculative exploration of the vast span of time from the end of the Ice Age to the coming of Christianity. It is a robust and authoritative survey in which the author shrinks neither from interpretation nor opinion.

Jonathan Bardon's *A History of Ireland in 250 Episodes* (Dublin 2008) is based on a BBC Northern Ireland radio series which the author – the most distinguished modern historian of Ulster – wrote. Its span is prehistory to the 1960s, with an epilogue in the form of an essay summarizing developments since then.

James Lydon's *The Making of Ireland: From Ancient Times to the Present* (London 1998) has the great merit of being written by one of the country's leading medieval historians, so that his perspective is informed by insights developed in his studies of that period. Indeed, he devotes about 40 per cent of his text to the period up to the end of the sixteenth century. The equivalent in Bardon is 30 per cent. He is also close to Bartlett in dispatching pre-Christian Ireland in a couple of pages.

Another medievalist, Sean Duffy, has written a useful popular illustrated book entitled *The Concise History of Ireland* (Dublin 2000), the definite article in the title being perhaps a little brash. Nonetheless, for those less inclined to tackle the more demanding academic surveys already mentioned, this is an excellent popular point of departure. The same author is general editor of *Atlas of Irish History* (2nd edition, Dublin 2002).

An Illustrated History of the Irish People by Kenneth Neill (Dublin 1979) is another general survey. While the text is unremarkable, the selection of images is excellent. The author, an American, sourced many of his illustrations in US archives and collections. A. T. Q. Stewart's *The Shape of Irish History* (Belfast 2001) is a lucid short account of fewer than 200 pages written from a unionist perspective. Hugh Kearney's *The British Isles: A History of Four Nations* (Cambridge 1989) is the work of an Irish historian that places the Irish story in its archipelagic context.

Of the various short and brief histories of the island – and there have been many – it is perhaps worth mentioning *A Short History of Ireland* by John O'Beirne Ranelagh (2nd edition, Cambridge 1994). The author is a distinguished British journalist of mixed Irish and American parentage and the book is written with a journalist's felicity.

Despite the popular perception of the Irish past as a conflict-strewn saga, the island has witnessed very few catastrophic and destructive wars compared with continental Europe. Indeed, it is more like Scotland in that regard. The two standard military histories are Thomas Bartlett and Keith Jeffrey (eds), *A Military History of Ireland* (Cambridge 1996) and G. A. Hayes-McCoy, *Irish Battles: A Military History of Ireland* (London 1969).

One work worthy of mention is Patrick Corish, *The Irish Catholic Experience: A Historical Survey* (Dublin 1985), a succinct attempt to do what the author freely admits is an impossible task: to produce an overview of his subject in fewer than 300 pages. Written before the calamities that have engulfed the church in scandal, its conclusions might not be asserted with such confidence today. Nonetheless, it is the work of a very substantial historian, himself a priest, and it addresses what has been the key institution in nationalist Ireland until recent times.

L. M. Cullen's *Life in Ireland* (London 1968) is an early work by the leading economic historian of his generation. Its focus is on social and economic concerns ranging from prehistory to the late nineteenth century. It remains a valuable survey, not least because it concerns itself with aspects of the past often crowded out by political and military events.

An important book comprising thematic essays which addresses what might be called the Irish historical personality is *Inventing the Nation: Ireland* by R. V. Comerford (London 2003). The author is, like Cullen, given to emphasis on non-political issues like language, literature, music and sport (there is a question being begged in that summary, but let it go). The influence of Benedict Anderson's seminal *Imagined Communities* (London 1981) is clear in this rich, subtle work.

A number of multi-volume surveys have been attempted and not completed. One that has is the six-volume 'New Gill History of Ireland' (NGHI, Dublin 2005–9), itself based on a series first part-published in the 1990s and which in its turn replaced a previous eleven-volume series in the 1970s. The individual volumes will be mentioned at the appropriate places in this essay.

Finally, it is impossible not to note two of the great warhorses of Irish historical writing. Edmund Curtis's *A History of Ireland* (London 1991) is the latest edition of a work first published in 1936. It is very much a book of its time and place – Curtis was Lecky Professor of Modern History at Trinity College Dublin – and it reflects an essentially Anglo-Irish reading of the past. Having taken over 350 pages to get to 1800, it disposes of the period 1800 to 1922, where it ends, in a mere 58 pages. However, he does not devote disproportionate space to the eighteenth century, as one might have expected. More than half the book is concerned with the period to 1600, which leaves even Lydon far behind. Although now superseded by more modern works, it remains a robustly written and enjoyable introduction. *The Course of Irish History* (Cork 2001) by T. W. Moody and F. X. Martin was first published in 1966 to mark the fiftieth anniversary of the 1916 rising and has been continuously in print ever since, a remarkable achievement.

Other Surveys

There have been a number of very distinguished surveys which basically cover the early modern and modern periods. First among them is J. C. Beckett's classic *The Making of Modern Ireland 1603–1923* (London 1966). Like Curtis, it is now showing its age but it was the foundation text for the generation of scholars who re-interrogated Irish history from the 1960s onwards. Written with exceptional elegance and clarity, it gives roughly equal space to the seventeenth, eighteenth and nineteenth centuries, although its conclusion on partition – that it ushered in a period of greater tranquillity than Ireland had known since the 1700s – was to be tragically mocked by events in Northern Ireland within two years of its publication.

Its generational successor was Roy Foster's *Modern Ireland 1600–1972* (London 1988), probably the high-water mark of the so-called revisionist school of Irish history, that is those who challenged the pieties of nationalist historiography under pressure of contemporary events in Northern Ireland. A major work that covers the full span of its subject from the eighteenth century to the present but which is crucial to the period of the union is Richard English's *Irish Freedom: The History of Nationalism in Ireland* (London 2006).

F. S. L. Lyons's *Ireland since the Famine* (London 1971) has held its place as the best overview of the period 1850 to 1970. Alvin Jackson's *Ireland 1798–1998* (Oxford 1999) and Paul Bew's *Ireland: The Politics of Enmity 1789–2006* are both compelling overviews, with Bew's work informed by the scepticism of a liberal unionist. A more specialist work, but an exceptionally fine one, is Cormac Ó Grada's *Ireland: A New Economic History 1780–1939* (Oxford 1994).

Ancient and Medieval

There have been a number of books surveying Irish prehistory. Among the more successful have been John Waddell's *The Prehistoric Archaeology of Ireland* (Bray 2000) and Laurence Flanagan's *Ancient Ireland: Life before the Celts* (Dublin 1998), which speculated on patterns of social and economic life based on the author's career as a distinguished archaeologist.

The two principal overviews of the Middle Ages are Michael Richter's *Medieval Ireland* (NGHI 1, Dublin 2005) and Dáibhí Ó Cróinín's *Early Medieval Ireland 400–1200* (London 1995), the first volume in a projected series. J. F. Lydon's *The Lordship of Ireland in the Middle Ages* (Dublin 1972) remains one of the key works on this period. Richard Roche's *The Norman Invasion of Ireland* (2nd edition, Tralee 1995) is a traditional nationalist account of the event, fluently rendered. A more specialist work, Marie-Therese Flanagan's *Irish Society, Anglo-Norman Settlers, Angevin Kingship: Interactions in Ireland in the Late Twelfth Century* (Oxford 1989) has been influential among scholars. Kathleen Hughes's *The Church in Early Irish Society* (London 1966) remains an important work, as do each of the first six slim volumes in the original Gill History of Ireland: Gearóid Mac Niocaill, *Ireland Before the Vikings* (Dublin 1972); Donncha Ó Corráin, *Ireland Before the Normans* (1972); Michael Dolley, *Anglo-Norman Ireland* (1972); Kenneth Nicholls, *Gaelic and Gaelicised Ireland in the Middle Ages* (1972); John Watt, *The Church in Medieval Ireland* (1972) and James Lydon, *Ireland in the Later Middle Ages* (1973). These six small-format paperbacks, now long out of print, aggregate to an impressive 1,000 pages plus; whereas Richter's one-volume replacement is less than 200 (admittedly impressive) pages covering roughly the same span of time. Ó Cróinín, whose period is somewhat shorter, nonetheless accommodates it in fewer than 300 pages of text.

Early Modern

The standard survey histories of the sixteenth century are Steven Ellis, *Ireland in the Age of the Tudors 1447–1663: English Expansion and the End of Gaelic Rule* (London 1998) and Colm Lennon, *Sixteenth-Century Ireland: The Incomplete Conquest* (NGHI 2, Dublin 1994). For the seventeenth century, Raymond Gillespie, *Seventeenth-Century Ireland: Making Ireland Modern* (NGHI 3, Dublin 2006) is an interpretative survey from the collapse of Gaelic Ireland to the final triumph of the Protestant interest after the battles of Aughrim and the Boyne.

While much of the debate about revisionism in Irish history focused on the modern period, one could argue that Tudor and Stuart Ireland has been the focus of the most outstanding revising scholarship of the past generation. The following is a brief selection of the most important contributions. Nicholas Canny, *Making Ireland British 1580–1650* (Oxford 2001) locates the English plantations in Ireland in a broader Atlantic context. S. J. Connolly's *Contested Island: Ireland 1460–1630* is one of a number of works listed in this essay by a consistently excellent interpretative historian. Hiram Morgan's *Tyrone's Rebellion* (Dublin 1993) is the best history of the Nine Years War. Similarly, John McCavitt's *The Flight of the Earls* (Dublin 2002) is the outstanding book on the subject. An interesting if challenging interpretative work is Samantha A. Meigs, *The Reformations in Ireland: Tradition and Confessionalism 1400–1690* (Dublin 1997), one of the more persuasive attempts to explain the failure of the Protestant cause in most of Ireland. Ciaran Brady, *The Chief Governors: The Rise and Fall of Reform Government in Tudor Ireland 1536–1588* (Cambridge 1994) examines the several expedients employed by the English government to establish their rule in Ireland.

One of the great classics of Irish historical literature is Edward MacLysaght, *Irish Life in the Seventeenth Century* (revised edition, 1979) which, although first published in 1939, has stood the test of time in fine style. Michael Perceval-Maxwell has written two important books: *The Scottish Migration to Ulster in the Reign of James I* (London 1973) and *The Outbreak of the Irish Rebellion of 1641* (Dublin 1994). Philip Robinson's *The Plantation of Ulster* (Dublin 1984) is the work of a historical geographer and remains the most complete account of the plantation to date. Michelle O'Riordan's *The Gaelic Mind and the Collapse of the Gaelic World* (Cork 1990) traces its subject through the work of the bardic poets.

For the Cromwellian period, Micheál Ó Siochrú's *God's Executioner: Oliver Cromwell and the Conquest of Ireland* (London 2008) has superseded all previous literature on the subject.

There is no general history of the Williamite Wars, a surprising lacuna in the literature, but Piers Wauchope's biography entitled *Patrick Sarsfield and the Williamite War* (Dublin 1992) is a more than useful substitute, focusing on the tragic hero of that conflict. Although projecting its analysis well into the following century, Eamonn Ó Ciardha's *Ireland and the Jacobite Cause 1685–1766* (Dublin 2002) has its roots in that conflict and is a work of the first importance.

The Georgian Era

One of the great absences in Irish historical writing was a compelling overview of the eighteenth century. That gap has at last been made good by the publication of Ian McBride's magisterial *Eighteenth-Century Ireland: The Isle of Slaves* (NGHI4, Dublin 2009). This is one of the very finest works published in the last generation, in a field where the competition is impressively strong.

Toby Barnard, *A New Anatomy of Ireland: the Irish Protestants 1649–1770* (London 2003) is a major study from a major historian. A useful short survey from the same author is his *The Kingdom of Ireland 1641–1760* (Basingstoke 2004). Equal to Barnard in accomplishment is S. J. Connolly's *Religion, Law and Power: The Making of Protestant Ireland 1660–1760* (Oxford 1992) from the leading proponent of the *ancien régime* view of the eighteenth century, as distinct from the colonial perspective.

Charles Chenevix Trench's *Grace's Card: Irish Catholic Landlords 1690–1800* (Cork 1977) is a useful survey of an occluded subject. Likewise, C. D. A. Leighton's *Catholicism in a Protestant Kingdom: A Study of the Irish Ancien Régime* (Dublin 1994).

Although a regional study, David Dickson's *Old World Colony: Cork and South Munster 1630–1830* deals with a key area of the island, wealthy and settled, which was central to the later development of nationalism. Gerard O'Brien, *Anglo-Irish Politics in the Age of Grattan and Pitt* (Dublin 1987) is a short but excellent survey of political life in the brief heyday of the Ascendancy. Two other useful works in this area is James Kelly's *Prelude to Union: Anglo-Irish Politics in the 1780s* (Cork 1992) and A. P. W. Malcolmson, *John Foster: The Politics of the Anglo-Irish Ascendancy* (Oxford 1978) which refracts its subject matter through the personality of the last speaker of the old Irish parliament. Finally, Thomas Bartlett's *The Fall and Rise of the Irish Nation: The Catholic Question 1760–1830* is indispensable. Another influential work in this area is Kevin Whelan's *The Tree of Liberty: Radicalism, Catholicism and the Construction of Irish Identity 1760–1830* (Cork 1996).

No mention of the eighteenth century can overlook another classic, Maurice Craig's *Dublin 1660–1860* (Dublin 1980) which, although it overspills the century fore and aft, is firmly anchored in it. It is the best account we have or are likely to have of the capital in its golden age, all the better for being written with a Mozartian lightness and zest.

The 1790s is the most violent decade in modern Irish history and has prompted an impressive library of published works. Marianne Elliott, *Partners in Revolution: The United Irishmen and France* (London 1982) is a standard background work, as is the same author's *Theobald Wolfe Tone: Prophet of Irish Independence* (London 1989). Also valuable is Dáire Keogh's *The French Disease: The Catholic Church and Radicalism in*

Ireland 1790–1800 (Dublin 1993). The same author is co-editor, with David Dickson and Kevin Whelan, of a distinguished collection of essays entitled *The United Irishmen: Republicanism, Radicalism and Rebellion* (Dublin 1993).

For the climactic year of 1798, the only attempt at a synoptic work covering the Leinster, Ulster and Connacht uprisings remains Thomas Pakenham's *The Year of Liberty* (London 1969). That said, its substantial emphasis is on Wexford. Its conclusions and methodology have been challenged by a later generation of scholars and Daniel Gahan's *The People's Rising: Wexford 1798* (Dublin 1995) is now regarded as the most complete account to date of that revolutionary moment. A collection of essays edited by Dáire Keogh and Nicholas Furlong, *The Mighty Wave: The 1798 Rebellion in Wexford* (Dublin 1996) broadly endorses Gahan's secular nationalist reading of events. This view is challenged in one of the most intriguing books to emerge from the bi-centenary of 1798, Thomas Dunne's *Rebellions: Memoir, Memory and 1798* (Dublin 2004), a minor masterpiece. The rebellion in Ulster is the subject of two books by A. T. Q. Stewart, *A Deeper Silence: The Hidden Roots of the United Irish Movement* (London 1993) and *The Summer Soldiers: The 1798 Rebellion in Antrim and Down* (Belfast 1995) which reflect an Ulster particularist view of these events.

The risings of 1798 were followed by the Act of Union, the standard modern account of which is Patrick Geoghegan's *The Irish Act of Union: A Study in High Politics 1798–1801* (Dublin 1999). The same author has written a fine biography of Robert Emmet.

Ireland under the Union

The nineteenth century was one of social upheaval and reconstruction, so it is best to begin with three works of social history. T. W. Freeman, *Pre-Famine Ireland: A Study in Historical Geography* (Manchester 1957) has remained influential, as has the even more venerable K. H. Connell, *The*

Population of Ireland 1750–1845 (Oxford 1950) while Samuel Clark and James S. Donnelly Jr (eds), *Irish Peasants: Violence and Political Unrest 1780–1914* (Manchester 1983) is unusually coherent in its editorial discipline for a collection of essays: it reads like an authoritative monograph.

D. George Boyce, *Nineteenth-Century Ireland: The Search for Stability* (NGHI 5, Dublin 2005) surveys the period from the union to the early 1920s. The same author's *Nationalism in Ireland* (Dublin 1982) is a useful overview. Likewise K. Theodore Hoppen, *Ireland Since 1800: Conflict and Conformity* (London 1999). The same author's more specialized *Elections, Politics and Society in Ireland 1832–1885* (Oxford 1984) is a treasure trove of information not to be found elsewhere. Robert Kee's three-volumes that constitute *The Green Flag* have been consolidated in a one-volume paperback edition under the same title (London 2000). It is a highly accessible survey of nationalism by a distinguished journalist and historian.

The political scientist cum historian Tom Garvin has two substantial contributions to the period: *The Evolution of Irish Nationalist Politics* (Dublin 1981) and *Nationalist Revolutionaries in Ireland 1858–1928* (Oxford 1987). S. J. Connolly's *Priests and People in Pre-Famine Ireland* (Dublin 1982) and his *Religion and Society in Nineteenth-Century Ireland* (Dundalk 1985) are both illuminating. Fergus O'Ferrall, *Catholic Emancipation: Daniel O'Connell and the Birth of Irish Democracy 1820–1830* remains the standard work on that decisive event. There are fine biographies of O'Connell by Oliver MacDonagh and Patrick Geoghegan. Richard Davis, *The Young Ireland Movement* (Dublin 1987) gives the best account of the internal opponents of the later O'Connell within the nationalist tradition. Donal Kerr, *Peel, Priests and Politics: Sir Robert Peel's Administration and the Roman Catholic Church in Ireland 1841–6* (Oxford 1982) is a subtle account of a key political issue on the eve of the Famine.

The Famine itself dominates the mid century and much thereafter. The best synoptic modern account is Christine Kinealy,

This Great Calamity: The Irish Famine 1845–52 (Dublin 1994). A more compact book of scholarly essays is Cathal Póirtéir (ed.), *The Great Irish Famine* (Cork 1995). The Famine quickened the nationalist demand: Nicholas Mansergh's *The Irish Question 1840–1921* (revised edition, London 1965) remains a useful work, particularly valuable for its comparative European perspective. A more controversial thesis is that advanced in Stephen Howe's *Ireland and Empire: Colonial Legacies in Irish History and Culture* (Oxford 2000). The most lasting effect of the Famine was the massive emigration that it triggered, and among the many fine works that emerged from that tragedy few have as powerful a resonance as David Fitzpatrick's *Oceans of Consolation: Personal Accounts of Irish Migration to Australia* (Cork 1994), a book of raw emotional force based on the personal letters of Irish emigrants to the Antipodes.

A book of thematic essays that are genuinely illuminating is Oliver MacDonagh, *States of Mind: A Study of the Anglo-Irish Conflict 1780–1980* (London 1983). An important political-military survey is Charles Townshend's *Political Violence in Ireland: Government and Resistance since 1848* (Oxford 1983).

Studies of the nineteenth-century Catholic Church are dominated by the work of the Irish-American scholar Emmet Larkin, whose series of seven detailed scholarly studies covering the second half of the century have set the benchmark for all who research and write in this area. Not all of these titles, regrettably, are available outside the United States. An important aspect of church life was its effective control of Catholic education. The book to read in this regard is Barry M. Coldrey's *Faith and Fatherland: The Christian Brothers and the Development of Irish Nationalism 1838–1921* (Dublin 1988).

Urban and rural contrasts may be found in Mary E. Daly, *Dublin, the Deposed Capital: A Social and Economic History 1860–1914* (Cork 1985) and James S. Donnelly Jr, *The Land and People of Nineteenth-Century Cork* (London 1976), another regional study that transcends its geographical confines.

The era of Parnell, from the 1870s to his death 1891, was

dominated by the twin questions of land and nation. Paul Bew, *Land and the National Question 1858–82* (Dublin 1978) makes this connection explicitly. Alvin Jackson's synoptic *Home Rule: An Irish History 1800–2000* (London 2003) is useful, as is Philip Bull, *Land Politics and Nationalism: A Study of the Irish Land Question* (Dublin 1996). That key group, the Fenians, have at last got the scholarly notice they deserve thanks to Owen McGee, *The IRB: The Irish Republican Brotherhood from the Land League to Sinn Féin* (Dublin 2005).

In the welter of books about the revolutionary period, there is only room to mention a few. Conor Cruise O'Brien, *States of Ireland* (London 1972) is, like just about everything O'Brien wrote, a compound of disguised autobiography, history and polemic, but its interpretation of Irish public life from the fall of Parnell to the outbreak of the Northern Ireland influenced a generation as few books have done. The standard work on the greatest labour dispute in Irish history is Padraig Yeates, *Lockout: Dublin 1913* (Dublin 2000). The two best books on the 1916 rising are Charles Townshend, *Easter 1916: The Irish Rebellion* (London 2005), the most complete modern account, and Max Caulfield, *The Easter Rebellion* (Dublin 1995), a re-issue of a work first published in 1964. It had the great advantage that the author was able to interview survivors of the rising: their testimony gives the book an immediacy that is its hallmark.

By far the best account of the social realities of the period is another one of those regional studies that transcends its geography. David Fitzpatrick's *Politics and Irish Life 1913–21: Provincial Experience of War and Revolution* (Dublin 1977) is a dense but deeply rewarding study. Arthur Mitchell, *Revolutionary Government in Ireland: Dáil Éireann 1919–22* (Dublin 1995) tells of the remarkable parallel civil and legal administration that Sinn Féin put in place as British power declined in nationalist Ireland.

The best account of the Anglo-Irish treaty negotiations remains Frank Pakenham's *Peace by Ordeal* (London 1935).

Michael Hopkinson has produced the two standard works on the 1919–23 period: *The Irish War of Independence* (Dublin 2002) and *Green Against Green: The Irish Civil War* (Dublin 1988). More controversially, two books by the late Peter Hart have challenged nationalist pieties by raising the spectre of sectarianism: *The IRA and its Enemies: Violence and Community in Cork 1916–23* (Oxford 1998) and *The IRA at War 1916–23* (Oxford 2003).

Ulster

One of the very finest books to emerge from the troubles was the travel writer Dervla Murphy's *A Place Apart* (London 1978). Taking the hint from her title, I have concentrated the books relating to Ulster and Northern Ireland in this section.

The standard history of the province, and one of the very best books published in Ireland in a generation, is Jonathan Bardon, *A History of Ulster* (Belfast 1992), a marvellous *tour d'horizon* that runs from the Mezolithic Age to the 1990s, just before the apparent permafrost of the conflict began to thaw. It also contains the best account of the Industrial Revolution in the province, the only part of Ireland to experience this historical phenomenon.

Thomas Hennessey, *A History of Northern Ireland 1920–1996* (Dublin 1997) explains itself. The distinguished journalist Susan McKay's *Northern Protestants: An Unsettled People* (Belfast 2000) is an 'insider's' account of the community that formed her, although she has long since settled in the Republic. Counterpointing her are Marianne Elliott, *The Catholics of Ulster: A History* (London 2000) and Oliver P. Rafferty, *Catholicism in Ulster 1603–1983: An Interpretative History* (Dublin 1994). An important work, often overlooked, is Peter Brooke's *Ulster Presbyterianism: The Historical Perspective 1610–1970* (Dublin 1987).

A. T. Q. Stewart, *The Ulster Crisis* (London 1967) is a compelling and sympathetic account of unionist opposition to home rule in the years before the Great War. The same author's

The Narrow Ground: Aspects of Ulster 1609–1969 (revised edition, London 1986) is a deeply influential book originally published at the outset of the troubles. Its interpretation of Ulster particularism was troubling for nationalists.

There are many accounts of the troubles themselves and of the IRA but the best, as it seems to me, is Richard English, *Armed Struggle: The History of the IRA* (London 2004). David McKittrick and David McVea, *Making Sense of the Troubles* (London 2001) is a lucid account. The British journalist Peter Taylor has written two insightful books, one each about the 'two sides': *Loyalists* (London 2000) and *Provos: The IRA and Sinn Féin* (London 1998). Finally, Paul Bew and Gordon Gillespie, *Northern Ireland: A Chronology of the Troubles 1968–1999* (Dublin 1999) is part reference work, part extended essay and in any event essential.

The Republic

Dermot Keogh's *Twentieth-Century Ireland: Nation and State* (NGHI 6, Dublin 2005) belies its title by virtually ignoring the North, for which the reader must look to Hennessey (above). But as an account of how the newly independent state, soon to be the Republic of Ireland, established and consolidated itself, it is excellent. By contrast with Keogh, Henry Patterson, *Ireland Since 1939: The Persistence of Conflict* (Dublin 2006) does straddle the border although – perhaps inevitably given the long shadow of the troubles – it gives more space to the North than to the Republic.

J. J. Lee's crackling *Ireland 1912–1985* (Cambridge 1990) is the work of a frustrated nationalist, a torrentially eloquent lament for missed opportunities and foolishness that never departs from a basic endorsement of the nationalist project. More recently, Diarmaid Ferriter's *The Transformation of Ireland 1900–2000* (London 2004) is an astonishing work of synthesis by the finest Irish historian of his generation. Not yet forty, Ferriter has read everything (or seems to have) and has an impressively wide range of intellectual interests. Terence

Brown, *Ireland: A Social and Cultural History 1922–2001* (revised edition, London 2010) is an update of a classic survey first published in the 1980s. The author is one of Ireland's leading literary critics and a biographer of Yeats, but unlike many literary critics interrogating history he carries little ideological and political baggage masquerading as postcolonial theory.

Irish neutrality during the Second World War has produced a rich literature that does much to explain the political culture of the new state. Robert Fisk, *In Time of War: Ireland, Ulster and the Price of Neutrality* (London 1983) was instantly hailed as a classic. The author is one of the world's very finest journalists. Three more recent books are worth noting. Brian Girvin, *The Emergency: Neutral Ireland 1939–45* (London 2006) argues that neutrality was against the national interest and scuppered the chance of attaining a united Ireland, not a reading that everyone will agree with. Claire Wills, *That Neutral Island: A Cultural History of Ireland during the Second World War* (London 2007) is, like Brown, the work of a literary critic who brings her skills to bear on the Irish cultural elite and on neglected sources such as provincial newspapers to produce an analysis of neutrality that combines high culture and demotic social history: a genuinely original approach. T. Ryle Dwyer, the standard authority on the American dimension of neutrality, has written a startling book entitled *Behind the Green Curtain: Ireland's Phoney Neutrality during World War II* (Dublin 2009), in which he establishes that far from simply 'showing a certain consideration for Britain', de Valera permitted Irish diplomats to carry Allied secrets (actually American: British would have been a step too far for Dev) in their diplomatic bags, thus compromising any claim to real neutrality.

The post-war period is well covered in the general surveys noted earlier but two books deserve special mention here. John H. Whyte's *Church and State in Modern Ireland 1923–79* (Dublin 1980) was the second edition of a work that had first appeared ten years earlier. It remains the best and most level-headed account of twentieth-century Ireland's key institution, the Catholic Church, and its relationship to the new state. Tom Garvin, *Preventing the Future: Why was Ireland so Poor for so Long?* (Dublin 2004) answers the question posed in the subtitle with characteristic brio.

The literature covering the second half of the twentieth century in the Republic is not especially rich, inevitably over-shadowed by the northern troubles. But the Celtic Tiger boom, followed tragically by the property bubble, produced first a crackerjack celebration of the good times. David McWilliams, *The Pope's Children: Ireland's New Elite* (Dublin 2005) was the exuberant work of an economist turned journalist with an enviable talent for analysing and explaining arcane economics in a lucid and compelling manner. Nor was he a mere cheer-leader: at a time when few wanted to listen, he was one of a tiny band who warned of trouble ahead. When the crash did come in 2008, it produced a torrent of books on how the country had got itself into this mess. Most were focused on economic analy-sis or narrative of one kind or another: there was no shortage of material. Fintan O'Toole, *Ship of Fools: How Stupidity and Corruption Sank the Celtic Tiger* (London 2009) is a social and cultural analysis. O'Toole, the finest journalist in Ireland, is a left-wing elitist who rages at the populist idiocies and easy options that characterized the crowd-pleasing Ahern years, the corrupt cronyism and the public complicity in a culture of moral evasion.

INDEX